"We are rough men used to rough ways"

—*Bob Younger, 1876*

For Tim

Designed by Gibson Parsons Design.
Edited by Diane Furtney.
Text © 1997 by Marley Brant. All rights reserved.
© 1997 by Elliott & Clark Publishing, an imprint of Black Belt
Publishing, LLC. All rights reserved.
No part of the contents of this book may be reproduced without the
written permission of the publisher.
Any inquiries should be directed to:
Elliott & Clark Publishing
P. O. Box 551
Montgomery, Alabama 36101
Telephone (334) 265-6753

8 7 6 5 4 3 2 1   2003 2002 2001 2000 1999 1998 1997

Library of Congress Cataloging-in-Publication Data
Brant, Marley.
    Outlaws : the illustrated history of the James-Younger gang / by
Marley Brant.
        p.   cm.
    Includes bibliographical references and index.
    ISBN 1-880216-36-1
    1. Outlaws—West (U. S.)—History—19th century.
2. Younger, Cole, 1844–1916. 3. Younger, James, 1848–1902.
4. James, Frank, 1844–1915. 5. James, Jesse, 1847–1882.
6. West (U. S.)—History—1860–1890—Biography. I. Title.
F594.B73 1996
978' .02—dc20   95-46715
                            CIP

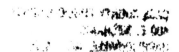

OUTLAWS

THE
ILLUSTRATED
HISTORY
OF THE
JAMES-
YOUNGER
GANG

BY MARLEY BRANT

ELLIOTT & CLARK PUBLISHING
Montgomery, Alabama

CONTENTS

ACKNOWLEDGMENTS

   I am grateful for the friendship of a group of special people who have traveled with me down the confusing, exciting, and often frustrating paths of research into the James-Younger Gang. Milt Perry was someone with whom I could always share the excitement of new information and speculations. My conversations with Milt often resulted in animated and wonderful discussions of theory. His absence from the world of outlaws is something many of us often feel. Dr. Bill Settle's gentle approach to a volatile subject set the standard whereby the study of the James-Younger Gang was elevated from folklore to historical examination. I am grateful for his interest in my work and his friendship. I remain indebted to Wilbur Zink, "Keeper of the Younger Flame," for taking me to Younger bluff and introducing me to the tranquility it offers and the secrets it has hidden. Seekers of the truth can always count on Wilbur to open his door and offer his special knowledge. Ted Yeatman is one of the foremost current authorities on the James family, and I thank him for sharing his information and insights.

   I'd like to acknowledge and thank descendants of the members of the James-Younger Gang, the families of those involved with the Gang, and certain James and Younger family historians for their unique contributions: Betty Barr, Thelma Barr, Lawrence Barr, Patrick Brophy, Naohm Hoffman Coop, Mary Withrow Davidson, Nancy Ehrlich, Ruth Coder Fitzgerald, Carolyn Hall, Donald R. Hale, John Mills, C. E. Miller, John Nicholson, Chuck Parsons, James R. Ross, N. David Smith, Lee Smith, June Spicer, Nancy Samuelson, Phillip W. Steele, George Warfel, Ruth Whipple, Florence Wiley, Jack Wymore, Dreat Younger, and Ethelrose James Owens, a charming lady and a lovely friend.

   I am indebted as well to all of those who shared their photographs and materials. I would particularly like to acknowledge the Blue Earth County Historical Society, Brookings Library, Buffalo Bill Historical Center, JoAnn Byland, Cass County Historical Society, California Historical Society, California State Library, Gary Chilcote, Naohm Hoffman Coop, James Chase, Dallas Historical Society, Mary Withrow Davidson, Armand De Gregoris, Fred Egloff, Sue Garwood, Goodhue County Historical Society, Frank H. Graves, Grayson County Historical Society, Donald R. Hale, Carolyn Hall, Jack Hall, Historic New Orleans Collection, Historical Society of Southern California, Margarette Hutchins, Jay Jackson, Jackson County Historical

Society, James Farm, Jesse James Museum at Adair, Dave Johnson, Kansas State Historical Society, Othor MacLean, Robert G. McCubbin, C. E. Miller, Minnesota Historical Society, Missouri State Archives, Nashville *Banner*, Northfield Historical Society, Ethelrose James Owens, Patee House Museum, F. M. Rawlins, E. Lisle Reedstrom, Rice County Historical Society, James R. Ross, Marjorie Settle, Nora Lee Smith, Fae Sotham, State Historic Society of Missouri at Columbia, Phillip W. Steele, University of Oklahoma Library, George Warfel, Washington County Historical Society, Watawon County Historical Society, Wayne County Historical Society, Ruth Whipple, Harriet Baird Wickstrom, Jack Wymore, Ted Yeatman, Dreat Younger, Gene Younger, and Wilbur Zink.

I am always thankful for the blessing of my family. My husband, Dave Bruegger, has helped not only through his support of my career but by his appreciation of the controversies involved with the study of the James-Younger Gang. My mother, Gladys Olmstead, has always encouraged me to persevere, whatever my goal or dream. She and my dad, Red Olmstead, advocated that I avoid comparison and be happy with my own accomplishments, a lesson I have tried to review regularly as a writer. My son Tim has been understanding of his mother's need to stare at a computer screen and is, plain and simple, a great kid. Kathie Montgomery assisted my research and allowed me to take advantage of her computer expertise. Her love of the subject has been an inspiration.

I would like to add my thanks to my agent, David H. Smith, for his professional assistance and support, Carolyn Clark for giving me the opportunity to do this book, Paige Meginley for helping me keep my sanity, Mary Parsons for her wonderful design, all the folks at Elliott & Clark for their enthusiasm and commitment to historical accuracy, and finally, to the friends and family members who encouraged my research and writing, especially Jean and Harry Avery, Willie and Carol Olmstead, John and Nanette Olmstead, Frances O'Neil, Bob Wall, and Bill and Jeanette Wall.

INTRODUCTION

Cole Younger and Frank James granted a combined interview to a reporter from the Nashville *American* while they were touring with The Great Cole Younger and Frank James Historical Wild West Show in 1903. Asked again to name his accomplices during the Northfield, Minnesota, bank robbery a quarter of a century before, Cole repeated his long-standing denial of ever having been affiliated with what had come to be known as the James-Younger Gang. The old ex-outlaw even went so far as to deny the existence of such a gang: "The James boys were not with me in this raid, and we never were together in any other." Frank James also refused, as he had for years, to discuss any illegal activities. Preferring to play the role of the old war hero, Frank announced, "I am going this season with our show, and then I am going to retire." He added, "I saw a chance by doing this to feather my nest in my old age. I am going to buy a farm when this season ends, and then settle down there to pass the rest of my days in peace and quiet."

That the two men were alive to grant such an interview was remarkable in itself. These two ex-Confederates, aged fifty-nine and sixty in 1903, had weathered turbulent and terrible times. Frank and Cole, together with their brothers, survived fierce guerrilla warfare, history-making bank and train robberies, life spent either in seclusion or on the run, and, in the case of the Youngers, long decades behind bars. They had suffered gunshot wounds and had seen their brothers—Jesse James and John, Bob, and Jim Younger—die as a result of violence: from a deliberate and government-orchestrated assassination, from murderous gunplay, from illness brought on by gunshot wounds, and from suicide. As young men they had seen the northern establishment brutalize their families and demolish their prosperous farms and businesses. They fought the battle of their lives at a time when life as they knew it ceased to exist and the privileged world in which they played an integral role fell victim to the worst internal confusion and strife the United States of America has ever known.

The determined political activism and retaliation of the James-Younger Gang was viewed by many, including themselves, as a wreaking of vengeance that was well deserved. They pushed beyond the limits of the acceptable confines of society in an attempt to redeem a dignity only they could define. There was no limit to their tenacity, and they reaped the rewards of adventure, entertainment, terror, and grief as a result of their ruthlessness.

Had Cole Younger and Frank James earned the right to retire? Many people at the time thought not, though many did feel that the fact that Cole and Frank had survived the Border War, the bloodier Civil War, and the continuing devastation of Reconstruction qualified the two for a measure of respect. The two old Rebels who stood before the reporter in Nashville undoubtedly had regrets. Yet Frank and Cole were well on their way to becoming international legends; that they had survived the exceptional lifestyles they had chosen and had been rewarded with the notoriety they sought is a testament to their perseverance.

The members of the James-Younger Gang would be remembered in popular song, television programs, and dozens of feature films even some 120 years after their glory days. Jesse James would become America's foremost folk hero, ranking first above Mickey Mouse and Mark Twain in an international survey of famous Americans. As evidence of the public's continuing fascination with both his story and the controversies surrounding him, in 1995, more than a century after Jesse's body was first laid to rest, a privately funded forensic study was conducted by Professor James E. Starrs of George Washington University after exhumation of Jesse's body from its grave at Mt. Olivet Cemetery in Kearney, Missouri. DNA samples of living relatives of the family of Zerelda and Robert James were compared to DNA in the bones taken from Jesse's grave, in an effort to put to rest the folklore that Jesse James had not been assassinated in 1882 but rather had paid an imposter to take his place. At least three different men have claimed to be the 100-year-old and older "surviving" Jesse James. It came as no surprise to Jesse's real family that these claims were proved fraudulent. Professor Starrs has provided convincing proof that the body buried in 1882 was indeed that of Jesse Woodson James. Folklore relating to other aspects of the life and times of Jesse James will now have to suffice.

Vengeance, justification, devotion, malice, fidelity, and treachery are all words that are used often in the telling of the James-Younger Gang story. The Gang originated out of three men's urgent need to take action during the oppressive Reconstruction. It was terminated when that urgency gave way to instability, greed, and misplaced family allegiance. Hollywood has failed in its efforts to date to create a tale more captivating than the real lives these men led. The genesis, the exodus, and all the points between make the exploits of the James-Younger Gang a fascinating story unlike any other in history. Frank and Jesse James, Cole, Jim, John, and Bob Younger are permanent American legends.

FAMILY BEGINNINGS: ROBERT JAMES AND ZERELDA COLE

Robert Sallee James, the father of Frank and Jesse James, managed to do well for himself even though his childhood had been far from easy. Born in Logan County, Kentucky, on July 17, 1818, Robert was the fifth of eight children. His father, John William James, was a highly respected Baptist minister and farmer from Goochland County, Virginia, while the father of his mother, Mary "Polly" Poor, rode in "Light-

Rev. Robert Sallee James.

horse Harry" Lee's Partisan Legion. His parents died within months of each other when Robert James was nine years old. His older sister Mary had only recently married John W. Mimms, but the young couple took on the responsibility of raising Mary's five minor siblings, including Robert. They even eventually raised another six children of their own, one of whom, born in 1845, was a lovely daughter, Zerelda Amanda Mimms. (Zerelda's generation would link the family even more tightly when she later married her first cousin, Robert's son Jesse James.)

The earlier years of Robert James's life contained the hardships of an extended and struggling family. Robert managed to obtain a secondary education and in 1839 was ordained as a Baptist minister, like his own father. He then pursued a college education at Georgetown College in Kentucky, where he was accepted as a ministerial student. It was while attending Georgetown that the quiet, bright, and bookish Robert James met a magnetic young woman, Zerelda Elizabeth Cole.

Zerelda came from a family that included American poet Vachel Lindsay and future Kentucky State Senator David Herndon Lindsay. Yet like Robert James, Zerelda had also known adversity in her childhood. Born in Woodward County, Kentucky, to James Cole and Sallie Lindsay on January 29, 1825, Zerelda's upbringing was not as family-oriented as Robert James's. Like Robert, however, Zerelda had lost a parent early in life; she was two years old when her father died from injuries after falling from a horse. Sallie Cole took her toddler daughter and her infant son Richard Jesse to live with their grandfather, Richard Cole, owner of the Black Horse Tavern near Lexington. Cole's establishment had by this time become well-known as a popular place for lively discussions. Many local and national politicians, including Henry Clay, visited the tavern while campaigning in the area. Some of the disapproving local citizens referred to the Black Horse as "Sodom" because of the raw whiskey served there and the tavern's raucous atmosphere.

Sallie married Robert Thomason, a widower with several small children, after the death of her father-in-law. When the new family decided to relocate to Missouri, young Zerelda stubbornly insisted on remaining in Kentucky and so was sent to live with her uncle James Lindsay in Stamping Ground. Although not a Catholic, Zerelda was enrolled in St. Catherine's Academy in nearby Lexington. She had just turned fifteen when she met Robert James at a dance.

The introspective and easygoing Robert James found his opposite in Zerelda, known for her opinionated spirit, vitality, and wonderful sense of humor. They married on December 28, 1841, at the home of Zerelda's uncle in Stamping Ground. The couple traveled to Missouri the following summer to visit Zerelda's mother and brother Jesse. Robert returned to Georgetown before fall to complete his education. Zerelda stayed on and wrote to him during her long visit. Zerelda's letters described opportunities open in the new frontier and asked her husband to consider relocating permanently in the west. Zerelda had another reason for not wanting to travel from Missouri: she was expecting their first child.

(Top) *The Lindsay home in Kentucky, where Zerelda Cole married Robert James.* (Bottom) *The James farm in Clay County, Missouri.*

Robert James agreed to join his wife at her mother's as soon as his work at Georgetown was complete. He asked Zerelda to look for suitable farmland in Clay County for them to make a home. Because education was so important to Robert, he returned to Georgetown for short periods as part of his work toward a master's degree after finally moving to Missouri. During one of those absences, on January 10, 1843, his son Alexander Franklin James was born. Robert James was not able to reunite with his wife and meet his new son "Frank" until later that year.

The young family purchased a 275-acre farm in 1845 near Centerville (later renamed Kearney), a spot northeast of Kansas City. There Robert worked his farm with the help of seven slaves. On Sundays, he preached. A second son, named Robert, was born in July 1845 but survived only five days. The family was elated when a third son, Jesse Woodson James, was born on September 5, 1847.

The characters of both James brothers would include some of the stalwart dedication to principles exhibited on their father's side as well as the fervor and defiance of their mother. Zerelda doted on her eldest son and referred to him frequently as "Mister Frank." Frank read the classics and was fond of quoting Shakespeare. More than one of his acquaintances noted that Frank seemed to prefer his books to interacting with other people. Less impulsive than his younger brother, Frank nevertheless had his own boldness. Where Jesse was flamboyant, Frank could be downright dangerous. Frank found scant amusement in tomfoolery and his approach to life was straightforward and serious, sometimes deadly serious.

Jesse James, four years younger, preferred socializing to book reading. He did read one book often, though. Emulating his father, he peppered his speech with verses memorized from the Bible. The serious, dignified quotations made a startling contrast to Jesse's impetuous nature, and it caught people's interest. He was a hotheaded teenager and a daring, changeable man, impulsive and quick-witted. Jesse indulged a sly sense of humor and enjoyed practical jokes. Later his theatrical flair would lead him, while hiding out in Kentucky, to pose for an entire year as a nervous coward and weakling too afraid to defend himself on the street. In Kansas City he would choose to play an ill-tempered misanthrope and loner. Many a train passenger and bank official would also find himself part of an improvised performance by Jesse James.

(Top) *Henry Washington Younger.* (Bottom) *Richard Marshall Fristoe, maternal grandfather of the Younger brothers.*

FAMILY BEGINNINGS: HENRY YOUNGER AND BURSHEBA FRISTOE

Another Kentucky family saga was unfolding to the south of Georgetown. Like Robert James, Henry Washington Younger was born to Virginia aristocracy. His grandfather, Joshua Logan Younger, served with George Washington's army at Valley Forge, while his mother was a relative of "Lighthorse Harry" Lee. His father, Charles Lee "Charlie" Younger, acquired a reputation

Bursheba Leighton Fristoe.

throughout the South as an adventurer and entrepreneur. Before Henry's birth on February 22, 1810, Charlie joined a volunteer group formed to fight Indians in eastern Missouri, a group that, according to the Younger family history, included Daniel Boone. After the death of his first wife, Charlie Younger relocated to Crab Orchard,

Jackson County Courthouse. Richard Fristoe served as a Jackson County judge.

Kentucky, to breed and race horses. He later made a large profit traveling to Colorado with a mule-driving expedition. He then decided to settle in Clay County, Missouri, where he purchased several hundred acres of prime farmland. There his astute business sense made him one of the wealthiest landowners in western Missouri.

Not much is known about the early life of Charlie Younger's son Henry other than the fact that Henry was the fifth of Charlie's nineteen children. By 1830 Henry had married Bursheba Leighton Fristoe of Tennessee. Born on June 6, 1816, Bursheba was also descended from wealth and social position. Her father, Richard Marshall Fristoe, was a grandnephew of United States Chief Justice John Marshall. He fought alongside Andrew Jackson at the Battle of New Orleans as a lieutenant in Captain Daniel Price's Company of Mounted Volunteer Infantry from East Tennessee. Bursheba's mother, Mary "Polly" Sullivan, was a grandniece of United States President Zachary Taylor.

Bursheba's father became a highly respected landowner, businessman, and county judge in Jackson County, and the Fristoe family was extremely popular and influential within the Independence social set. After their marriage, Henry and Bursheba moved quietly within that milieu, establishing themselves as the second generation of Jackson County society.

They welcomed their eldest son, Charles Richard "Dick" Younger, in 1838. Their next son, Thomas Coleman Younger, known as "Cole," was born on January 15, 1844. James Hardin "Jim" Younger was born on Cole's birthday in 1848, John Harrison Younger in 1851, and Robert Ewing "Bob" Younger arrived on October 29, 1853. Another son, Alphae, was born in 1850 but died at the age of eighteen months.

Seeking opportunities as his father had done, Henry Younger purchased land in Jackson and Cass Counties and became comfortably wealthy from his landholdings. By 1859, after fourteen children, Henry Younger was a popular and successful merchant and was serving as the second mayor of the town of Harrisonville. He owned and operated a livery and a general store. He also held the United States mail contracts for the Midwestern District of Missouri. His eight daughters by Bursheba included Laura, Isabelle "Belle," Martha Anne "Anne," Josephine "Josie," Caroline, Sarah "Sally," Emilly "Emma," and Henrietta "Retta." All would eventually play some role in events that would overtake their tightly knit family during the 1850s and later.

Though they experienced many of the same life-altering events, Cole, Jim, John, and Bob Younger were extremely different men. Cole Younger would become a dashing and aggressive man whose exploits during the war were remarkably brave. Like other men who are unwilling to be threatened or intimidated, he sometimes threw his weight around. Cole bossed his brothers. On the other hand, he was gallant and courteous to almost everyone else, and he in-

The Younger farm in Harrisonville, Missouri.

spired loyalty to the death from both family and friends. For good reasons, he would become Frank James's closest friend: Cole shared Frank's taste for adventure, had a similarly fierce pride, and, like Frank, believed in revenge at all cost. Cole was a bit of an exhibitionist, with a sense of irony and of drama. Later, with twelve bullets in him, Cole Younger would stand up in a wagon and tip his hat to a cheering crowd.

Jim Younger was the peacemaker in the family and the one the brothers were especially fond of. Left to his own devices he almost certainly would have lived a quiet life as a rancher in Texas or California. Jim possessed a fervent family loyalty; this highly intelligent and gentle man would constantly alter his life to suit the needs of his family. He became a reluctant outlaw, out of dedication to his brothers. Eventually, he had decades in prison to pursue his reading preferences for theology, metaphysics, and literature.

John Younger was the hot-blooded one, sensitive to what he perceived as slights against his honor. He was considered a good fellow, but he was fond of rowdy entertainment and seemed always in pursuit of his next escapade. John was the one likely to escalate an argument into violence and then take some impulsive action. He was especially close to Bob, two years younger, but John also relied on Jim for support and advice.

Bob was the youngest, nine years younger than Cole. He was also the tallest, a handsome man with chiseled features and a strong jaw. He was usually quiet, but direct and candid when he spoke. Bob Younger was so polite, even when in pain and in jail, that one reporter would dub him "The Knight of the Bush." Bob's actions seem to indicate that he longed to be his own man but was unable to separate his life from the lives of his brothers.

Like the James boys, the Youngers were adventurous and restless, unable to settle into a single occupation or locale for more than a few months or at most a few years at a time. Also like the Jameses, the Youngers' only genuine home would be the maternal homestead in Missouri. All six men were excellent horsemen. They were comfortable in the saddle and were able to ride long distances as a matter of course. They were farmers and ranchers and cowboys. It would serve them well that they were all skilled with firearms, having learned to shoot early in their turbulent youths.

ROBERT JAMES ON THE CIRCUIT

Life went well for both the James and the Younger families in western Missouri during the 1840s. In Clay County, Robert James was kept busy with his family and his work. He reorganized and became Pastor in Residence of New Hope Baptist Church, which went on to become the largest Baptist church in northwest Missouri. Soon Reverend James was riding the circuit and preaching in other churches in the area as well. He established two new churches in the county, the Providence Baptist Church and the Pisgah Baptist Church of Excelsior Springs. He became one of the founders of William Jewell College at nearby Liberty, Missouri. He was well-liked and respected as an educated and caring man of the cloth.

In 1848 Robert James was awarded a Master of Arts degree from Georgetown College. On November 25, 1849, Zerelda gave birth to their one daughter, Susan Lavenia James. The growing family seemed content on their Centerville farm. Then in the early spring of 1850, Robert James suddenly announced to his wife that he intended to follow his brother, Drury James, west to the California gold fields, where he would preach to the miners around the Hangtown area. Members of his family would later claim that Robert was taking a short leave from his family to escape the constant nagging of his wife. Zerelda often complained about the circuit preacher's many absences from home.

This next absence would be for good. Zerelda later related that little Jesse pleaded with his father not to go, so much so that Robert told his wife that he would cancel his plans if he had not already spent so much outfitting for the trip and had not promised he would go. On April 12, 1850, Robert James left Zerelda and his young children and journeyed west with his close friend, William Stigers. He wrote to his wife from the trail: "Give my love to all inquiring friends and take a portion of it

Birthplace of Jesse James.

to yourself and kiss Jesse for me and tell Franklin to be a good boy and learn fast."

Reverend James arrived in Hangtown (later renamed Placerville) on July 14, 1850. A few weeks later, at the age of thirty-two, he was dead from one of the dysentery-type illnesses that struck down so many of those struggling to strike it rich in the gold fields. He was buried in an unmarked grave.

ZERELDA REMARRIES, BURSHEBA LOSES A SON

With three children and a farm to look after, Zerelda James would likely benefit by finding a new husband. She became serious with a wealthy widower two years after Robert James's death. On September 30, 1852, she married Benjamin A. Simms, who was twenty-five years older than herself. Simms's father had served at Valley Forge, and his family was well respected. Simms owned an enormous farm in Clay County and another near Clinton, Missouri.

(It has not been documented that the James and Younger families were friendly prior to 1862. Both families lived in the same county for many years, however, and it is likely that they were at least acquainted. The families became distantly related when Benjamin Simms's niece Augusta married Henry Younger's older brother Coleman.)

There were problems within Zerelda's new marriage from the beginning. Their relatives claimed that Frank and Jesse were not pleased to have another man try to replace their cherished father. They did not get along with Simms. Zerelda's world revolved around her children, but she agreed to send Frank, Jesse, and Susie to her relatives while she and Simms tried to adjust to their marriage. The couple moved to Simms's home in northern Clinton County.

Zerelda was miserable there. The records of Dr. Absolam Kerns indicate that she suffered a miscarriage in early 1853. After a few months Zerelda returned to her home in Clay County and retrieved her children. Benjamin Simms stayed behind. About a year later, on January 2, 1854, Simms was killed in a horse accident.

Not wanting to raise her children alone in the wilds of western Missouri, the twice-widowed Zerelda James Simms married again on September 12, 1855. Her new husband, Dr. Reuben Samuel, had come to Clay County from Kentucky in 1840, although he left for a while to attend Ohio Medical College in Cincinnati. Samuel first practiced medicine in Liberty, Missouri, then set up an office above the general store of William James, one of Robert's brothers, in Greenville, a village three miles east of the James farm. Zerelda would see Reuben Samuel whenever she visited William James's store. Before long they were a couple.

Charles Richard "Dick" Younger, the eldest of the Younger brothers, born in 1838 in Jackson County, Missouri.

The personalities of Zerelda and Reuben Samuel were extremely different, but their marriage turned out to be successful. The kind and loving Dr. Samuel was quite taken with Zerelda's children. Slowly, the bond between Samuel and the boys grew into a strong, affectionate, and loyal one, though Frank and Jesse still retained their esteem for their lost father. Zerelda and Reuben Samuel eventually had four children together: Sallie, John, Fannie, and Archie.

Down in Jackson County, the family of Henry and Bursheba Younger also suffered a loss that reshaped the lives of their children. Dick Younger, their oldest boy, was a charming, educated, and handsome young man on whom his parents and others of the community placed great expectations and who was almost worshiped by his siblings. At the age of twenty-two Dick was already a partner in an up-and-coming construction business, and he was extremely popular in Jackson and Cass County social circles. Cole Younger, the second son, had some mixed feelings about Dick and felt the difficulty of standing in his older brother's shadow. Although not as polished nor as respected as Dick, the teenaged Cole was good-looking and popular with the young people of his community. Looking for ways to win his father's favor and demonstrate his own abilities, he offered opinions on current events and learned to handle his father's stock.

Dick Younger suddenly took ill on August 16, 1860. He died the next morning, presumably from appendicitis. The Younger family was devastated. Cole, at age sixteen, was now the oldest son. Looking for ways to demonstrate his competence and independence, it seemed to his brothers that Cole tried even harder to gain his father's approval. Conditions along the Missouri-Kansas border soon provided him with opportunities to do so.

THE BORDER WAR

By the late 1850s events were developing along the western Missouri border with Kansas that would eventually alter the prosperous lives of the James and Younger families. Missouri farmers and businessmen close to the border became increasingly drawn into animosities between the state of Missouri and the territory of Kansas, which had been established since 1854. The Missouri Compromise of 1820, which admitted Missouri as a slaveholding state but prohibited slavery in other western territories, had been overturned in 1845 when the Kansas legislature left it to Kansas settlers to determine this issue for themselves through an election. Missourians grew increasingly uncomfortable when Kansas began to be settled by a large number of families from the northeastern, slave-free states. Although the percentage of slaves in Missouri's population was less than ten percent, nearly eighty percent of Missouri settlers came from slave-state backgrounds. Missourians feared their property would be overrun by the antislavery contingents of both Kansas and Missouri if the Kansas vote called for a slave-free state. The local press encouraged Missourians to relocate to Kansas in order to influence the pending election and to force the Northeasterners to settle farther north or west. Many Missourians did take up Kansas residence, but most border-county residents remained in Missouri and did what they could to protect their interests.

One of these men was Henry Younger, a conservative Unionist and owner of a large number of slaves. Henry served in the 1855 Kansas legislature while living in the Missouri-Kansas border district of Shawnee Mission. It is not clear how Henry accomplished this, as no evidence of his ever having residency in Kansas has surfaced. His name does, however, appear on the legislature's official rolls for that year. His recorded public sentiments extolled the virtues of "order and liberty."

Kansans were not happy with the interference of their neighbors to the east, and a great deal of resentment began to grow on both sides of the border. Meanwhile, the northeastern, antislavery contingents, along with the newly formed Republican Party, escalated tensions by promoting their position in the local and national press. The controversy was presented as a single-issue dispute: abolition. Occasional border skirmishes and altercations were exaggerated by the press as full-scale warfare.

Abolitionist John Brown.

Missourians and Kansans soon reached the point of actual violence worse than any press reports. Northern abolitionist John Brown practiced his rhetoric in Kansas and assembled his "Free-Soil" crusaders there. Shortly after becoming captain of a local militia company, Brown and six of his followers massacred five Kansas men known to hold proslavery views. An assembly of outraged Missourians retaliated with their own violence. Although Brown and his group were eventually run out of Kansas, altercations became increasingly common along the border.

Conflict over land claims and political patronage added to the distrust and mounting resentments. Individuals and small groups who reacted with force were not in the majority in Missouri, but the results of their actions affected everyone in the border counties. Reprisals and counterreprisals escalated throughout the late 1850s and continued into the 1860s when Kansas was admitted as a free state in 1861. Meanwhile, through all the eastern regions of the country, differences and dissension between North and South were hardening into a call for war.

Both the James and the Younger families were made up of Southerners who sympathized with those willing to fight for Missouri independence and for the preservation of their customary ways of life. Henry Younger, though, tried to maintain neutrality after his attempt to calm the dissension through service in the Kansas legislature. He befriended and did business with sympathizers from both camps. He and Bursheba tried to isolate their children from the violence taking place only a few miles away, but

Cole, aged seventeen in 1861, felt certain things would get worse. He argued often with his father that the situation could not simply be ignored. He urged his father to support those who enacted rough "justice" on anyone who threatened families like the Youngers.

To the north, in Clay County, the outspoken Zerelda James Samuel was making her own pro-Southern convictions well-known. She was, after all, a Southerner through and through. The James-Samuel family did own slaves, although their slaves were treated as family. The issue to Zerelda, however, was not so much one of slavery but rather the right of an individual to make a living without government interference. Most slaves in Missouri were viewed much the same as hired help; they were provided food and lodging and treated fairly. It was not the same situation as that of large enterprises on plantations in the Deep South. For the most part, farmers who owned slaves in Missouri operated family farms and often worked as hard as their slaves. Henry Younger held more of a managerial position with his slaves, but the black people associated with the Younger farms enjoyed a warm relationship with their owner-employer.

Zerelda encouraged both her boys to express disapproval of Kansans and Northerners. The quiet and unassuming young Frank James came to believe that the integrity of the farmers of western Missouri should be defended at all costs. The James family noticed that young Jesse listened attentively to his mother's outbursts and was heard to repeat her words in public.

By 1861, the legislature of Missouri was made up mostly of Southern sympathizers. When the secession issue reached the western states, the Missouri legislature decided to put the matter to a vote by the citizens. To the surprise of those who had formerly controlled the state, pro-Union delegates, for the most part representing counties in eastern Missouri, became a new majority as a result of the winter election. It was decided that Missouri should remain neutral for the time being and monitor developments taking place in the eastern states.

After the firing on Fort Sumter, Missouri Governor Claiborne F. Jackson, a champion of the people of western Missouri and a vocal supporter of the Confederacy, began to assemble and arm a state guard. Opposing the governor and representing the interests of eastern Missouri, John C. Fremont, Frank P. Blair, and others argued that Missouri should enter the war in support of the Union. Soon an armed confrontation took place near St. Louis between Jackson's state guard and a group organized by Fremont, a skirmish that was won by the men under Fremont and Blair. An

(Top) *Kansas Sen. James H. Lane.* (Middle) *Union Col. Charles R. Jennison, leader of the Kansas "Jayhawkers."* (Bottom) *Young "Buffalo" Bill Cody served with the Seventh Kansas Volunteer Cavalry.*

outraged Governor Jackson called for fifty thousand men to fight against invasion by Northern soldiers. In response, Frank Blair requested Union troops.

THE JAYHAWKERS

James H. Lane was elected United States Senator from the new free state of Kansas in January 1861. Throughout the Border War, Lane had been an outspoken anti-Missourian. After the war widened, Lane gained the favor of Abraham Lincoln by successfully organizing protection for the capitol. Lincoln readily extended the authority requested by Lane to raise troops in Kansas to respond to anticipated problems from the pro-Confederate Missourians. Lane assembled a group that became known as "Jayhawkers," men who had represented Kansas interests during the Border War. The Third, Fourth, and Fifth Kansas regiments were formed.

Another group of Kansas Jayhawkers was led by an eastern abolitionist, Charles R. Jennison. Jennison had recently been commissioned a colonel in the Union Army. He now set out to place his marauding group of volunteer troops under military discipline. Young "Buffalo" Bill Cody was a member of Jennison's Seventh Kansas Volunteer Cavalry. The soldiers from these regiments would soon become known as "Redlegs" from the blood-colored leggings they wore.

The conflict that became known as the Civil War now surpassed the earlier anxieties and concerns of the people along the Kansas-Missouri border. Missouri citizens remained as divided as their infighting legislature. Several Missouri communities felt the need to form local militia units for self-protection. Eighteen-year-old Frank James joined one of these, the Home Guard unit of Centerville. On May 4, 1861, he took an oath pledging his support of the Confederacy. His mother, Zerelda, was no doubt proud to see her oldest boy march off in defense of the Southern principles she had tried to teach all her children.

Thirteen-year-old Jesse watched his brother's departure with envy. Young as he was, he vowed to protect the family's interests at home and to join Frank in a fighting unit as soon as possible. As for Cole Younger, aged seventeen, he was waiting and watching from Harrisonville during the early summer of 1861.

In July the Missouri state convention met to remove pro-Confederate leaders and to appoint a governor whose sympathies were clearly with the Union. By August, Frank James had participated in his first major battle when the troops of Confederate General Sterling Price defeated their Union counterparts at Wilson's Creek, Missouri. The victorious Price then marched north, to the delight of farmers in western Missouri.

Infuriated, James Lane sent fifteen hundred of his Jayhawkers across the Missouri line. They annihilated farms and settlements. The town of Osceola was ransacked, looted, and burned. More than a dozen civilians were murdered as they attempted to rescue their belongings.

Teenaged Frank James.

Henry Younger's livery in Harrisonville offered a large target for Jayhawker raids. The successful businessman who had tried for so long to remain neutral found himself robbed of fine horses, carriages, and wagons worth more than four thousand dollars. Again and again in the following months Younger's Livery was relieved of horses and equipment by Jayhawkers and Redlegs.

QUANTRILL'S GUERRILLAS

With factions growing larger and more violent in the borderland, it was not long before someone organized the loose associations of Southern sympathizers. The motivation behind one such organizer, William Clarke Quantrill, continues to be debated. Quantrill, twenty-four years old, originally from Ohio, had spent time in Kansas during the Border War, aiding and abetting the Jayhawker movement. What opportunism or change of perspective drew him to the Confederate side and across the

Missouri border is not clear. In the small western-Missouri towns, Quantrill soon established himself as a leader of disenchanted young men eager to assert themselves against a government representing what their hard-working families and ancestors opposed.

Quantrill provided the loosely knit groups with well-organized opportunities to fight back against the Kansas and Union supporters. Many young insurgents, hearing about his disciplined organization, traveled to join Quantrill's guerrillas, who were soon recognized by their adversaries as a deadly force with which to be reckoned. The Rebel group's reputation grew with each merciless foray.

THE MOCKBEE DANCE

Cuthbert Mockbee was a close Harrisonville friend of Henry Younger's. As part of his attempt to live as normally as possible in spite of the rising conflict, Mockbee sponsored a dance in the fall of 1861 for his daughter Martha and the other young people of Cass County. Sally and Caroline Younger attended the party, held at Mockbee's large home. They were accompanied by their brothers Cole and Jim. During the evening one of the Younger women was approached by Irvin Walley, a pro-Union militiaman stationed at Harrisonville. Walley asked the young woman to dance, but she did not wish to keep company with a militiaman and rejected his offer. Walley persisted. Cole Younger stepped in, advising the soldier to leave his sister alone. Walley tried to embarrass the teenager by flaunting his military position and demanding that Cole tell him the whereabouts of William Quantrill. A fistfight ensued when Cole answered that he had no idea and Walley called him a liar. Cole's friends saw to it that no physical harm came to the soldier, and Cole was quickly ushered from the party. Jim escorted his sisters home.

When the young people told their father about the evening, Henry Younger became alarmed. With emotions running so high, the Harrisonville militia would welcome an excuse to threaten or imprison any of the area's pro-Confederate young men. Cole's impassioned debates in support of the South had already made him conspicuous, so Henry felt it was in his son's best interests to leave the area. He suggested Cole stay in Jackson County for a few days.

Cole was in the barn preparing to leave when Colonel Neugent, in charge of the militia, rode up to the Younger farm with a small group of soldiers. He informed Henry Younger that his son was a spy for Quantrill; he demanded Cole's surrender. Henry denied his son's involvement with the guerrilla leader and told the band that Cole was not at home. Neugent turned to leave, but not before swearing that he would find Cole Younger.

Cole heard this exchange and made a decision. Violating John Fremont's order that no Missourian was to bear arms unless affiliated with a recognized militia group, Cole took one of the family's shotguns and a revolver. Illegally armed, Cole Younger was now officially an outlaw, at age seventeen.

Cole quickly rode the few miles to the home of his brother-in-law, John Jarrette. Jarrette was one of Quantrill's staunchest

Cuthbert Mockbee house, site of the Mockbee dance.

supporters. He had married Josie Younger not long before and had made up his mind to eventually join Quantrill's group. Cole decided to join with him. The two located the guerrilla band, presented themselves, and were welcomed.

FRANK AND COLE JOIN THE GUERRILLAS

Over the next few months Cole and Jarrette took part in a number of guerrilla skirmishes, several near Independence. Cole would also fight the following summer at Lone Jack, a small town in Jackson County, in one of the most fiercely contested and bloody battles fought on Missouri ground. The determined but compassionate young recruit would be hailed as a hero for his efforts for his Confederate comrades at Lone Jack. At the same time he would attract favorable attention from the opposition for his intervention on behalf of a wounded Union officer when he asked his commanding officer that Col. Henry Foster not be put to death. Colonel Foster was then spared. Cole Younger's reputation as a fair, honest, and reliable soldier grew throughout the war; the esteem in which he was held would be remembered and cited until the end of his life.

Frank James's war experience was not so illustrious. In February 1862 he had the humiliating experience of falling ill with measles and being left in the field hospital near Springfield to be captured by Union troops. Officers in charge allowed the eighteen-year-old boy to return home on parole on April 26, but not before he signed the Oath of Allegiance in which he had to swear that his days as a Rebel were behind him. A story in the Liberty *Tribune* in May 1862 listed Frank James among those who had posted bond and taken the oath before Col. William Penick. Privately, the young man, fondly called "Buck" by his family, told his parents and his brother Jesse that in no way had he turned his back on the Confederacy.

In April 1862 the Congress of the Confederate States of America passed the Partisan Ranger Act, authorizing President Jefferson Davis to commission officers and raise troops. Under that Act, Col. Gideon W. Thompson swore Quantrill and his men into Confederate service on August 14, although the status of the guerrillas would remain that of "irregulars."

Confederate forces could not hold Missouri even with the addition of guerrillas to their ranks. Strife along the western border increased as dominant Union forces took ruthless action against Confederate sympathizers. Farms were destroyed and businesses disrupted. The lives of those who had so enthusiastically opposed the North were threatened to the point that many farmers felt they had to retreat from their convictions to focus on the survival of their families. Many young men eager at first to represent the Confederate cause returned home. Union leaders tried to encourage the disenchantment by offering amnesty to all those whose participation had not included serious war crimes. Two conditions for amnesty were that the Rebel must swear his allegiance to the United States government and provide a bond with good security representing his future conduct. Many young Missouri men grudgingly accepted these conditions.

The provisional Missouri government passed legislation on July 22, 1862, requiring every man of military age to enroll in the state militia and be subject to pro-Union service if called. The people of western Missouri were outraged, convinced they had been duped by amnesty agreements into being forced now to serve the cause of the opposition. A large number of young men who had returned home under terms of amnesty took to the bush again and joined Quantrill.

Quantrill led his men on successful skirmishes up and down the state of Missouri and eastern Kansas. A large number of his troops were eventually assigned to Joseph O. "JO" Shelby's Confederate Army brigade in Arkansas. By the end of 1862, guerrillas had taken part in battles at Cane Hill and Prairie Grove, Arkansas. Cole Younger may have been in both battles, but because the guerrillas were such a loosely connected group it is difficult to document the irregulars who participated in each engagement.

Affectionately known as "Bud" to his family and now also to his new guerrilla friends, Cole Younger rapidly gained favor with William Quantrill. Cole was recognized for his loyalty to the cause and his dependability as a soldier. He was frequently called upon to perform extra duties and to accompany superior officers on supply raids and scouting missions. On one such raid in May 1862, Cole, Quantrill, and Quantrill's second lieutenant George Todd traveled to Hannibal, Missouri, to obtain ammunition. Their mission was successful, and they were back in Kansas City in June. Cole was proud of his part in the mission; it would become one of his favorite war stories. He did not know that he was about to receive a devastating personal blow.

(Top) *Confederate Gen. Joseph O. "JO" Shelby.* (Bottom) *George Todd.*

THE MURDER OF HENRY YOUNGER

Cole's father Henry continued to try to live as if the war and its losses would soon end and his family would return to the lives they had enjoyed before. In the spring of 1862 he made a journey to New York to buy seasonal goods to sell in his dry goods store. Cole later wrote that besides purchasing sundries Henry conducted business in Washington, D.C., relating to his mail commission. Back home, Henry began advertising his new eastern wares, and as part of reorganizing his livery business he and several employees traveled to Kansas City to sell some horses. There was a great demand for horses and Henry planned to buy superior mounts in mid-July. Although he had a good deal of capital invested and had suffered repeated raids on his business,

1862 flyer from Henry Younger's dry goods store.

Henry Younger had been able to realize a healthy profit from his livery business. As for Cole's association with Quantrill, which was well-known by this time, his father did not discuss it. He simply repeated his desire to stay neutral on the matter.

His horse sale completed, Henry let his employees stay in Kansas City for a day or two as a reward for their assistance. He began his trip home alone in his buckboard on the morning of June 20, 1862. He was carrying more than fifteen hundred dollars in currency in his money belt around his waist and under his coat. South along the Westport Road, he encountered two of his wife's teenaged nieces, traveling to Kansas City to buy provisions for their family. He stopped to chat with the young women, then resumed his journey alone. Later accounts by acquaintances of Henry claimed that when he stopped at the house of a friend he mentioned that he was being followed by a militia group. Whether out of stubbornness or an ingrained optimism, Henry resumed his trip soon after.

Shots suddenly rang out behind him. Henry Younger was struck in the back by three bullets and died instantly. Falling from the buckboard, his body lay in the dirt until Mrs. Washington Wells and her farm hand, a young man named Charles Pitts who was using the name of "Samuel Wells," came upon him. Mrs. Wells guarded the corpse while the teenager rode north to report the murder to the commanding militia officer at Kansas City. A grateful Cole Younger befriended the young man who tried to help his father, and Charlie Pitts remained a friend of the Younger family for the rest of his life.

The motive for the cold-blooded murder of Henry Younger was obviously not robbery: Henry's money belt remained untouched. Following an investigation, Irvin Walley, the Union militiaman whom Cole Younger had defended his sister against at the Mockbee dance, was charged with the murder of Henry Younger. Missouri State Militia Brig. Gen. Benjamin Loan later wrote that he arrested Walley for the murder of Henry Younger and that the motive was robbery: "The evidence of his guilt was so clear and conclusive that he confessed it." Loan ordered the convening of a court to try Irvin Walley. Soldiers of the Fifth Regiment Missouri State Militia who were expected to testify against Walley, however, were bushwhacked and murdered on their way to the trial.

Henry Washington Younger shortly before his death.

(Top) Henry Younger and his eldest son Dick may have been buried beneath this tree in Cass County. (Bottom) The Walley Hotel, owned and operated after the war by Irvin Walley.

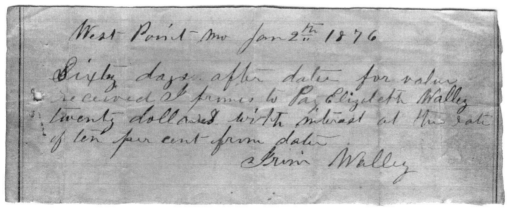

Signed by Irvin Walley in 1876, this receipt indicates that Walley survived the war and was not murdered in retribution for the assassination of Henry Younger.

Loan claimed that the bushwhacker was the son of the murdered man—implying Cole Younger. It is a likely charge. It is possible that Cole was unaware that the soldiers intended to testify against Walley. Perhaps Cole mistakenly believed Walley was among the group. In any event, the trial could not be held and Walley was released. Cole later wrote, "During the war I did everything within my power to get hold of him, but failed." Why none of the Youngers avenged their father's death by taking Walley's life remains unclear. It is possible they were asked by their mother not to seek revenge and honored her wishes.

COLE AS AN OLD WOMAN

After burying his father, Cole returned to Quantrill and to intense guerrilla warfare. In August 1862, after the protracted and deadly battle of Lone Jack, Cole went on a lone spy mission into the midst of Union troops encamped outside Independence. To gain information to help Quantrill plan his attack, Cole dressed up as an old woman selling apples and penetrated well within the enemy camp. His disguise was believed until, on the way out, "the old woman" ignored a picket's command to halt. Cole shot the picket and successfully brought his information back to his commander. After a fierce battle two days later, Union troops surrendered and the guerrillas found themselves possessed of wagonloads of food and ammunition.

Among the jubilant Confederates, Cole Younger was the man of the hour. Within two days, Cole was sworn into the Army of the Confederacy by Col. Gideon W. Thomas, along with the others of Quantrill's men. Cole later wrote that he "was sworn in as first lieutenant in Captain Jarrette's company in Colonel Upton B. Hays's regiment, which was a part of the brigade of General Joseph O. Shelby."

In the winter of 1862 General Shelby came close to being captured by Union forces. On the night preceding the battle of Prairie Grove there was a dramatic eleventh-hour rescue of the leader that was later said to have been led by Capt. John Jarrette. The account of at least one of the guerrillas there that day mentioned Frank James among those present at Shelby's rescue, although this has not been verified and probably is not true. Shelby came to have great respect for the efforts of Quantrill's guerrillas. A lasting bond was formed during the war between Frank James, Cole Younger, General Shelby, and Shelby's adjutant John Newman Edwards, a bond strong enough to bring Shelby to the witness stand on Frank's behalf two decades later and

Edwards to the defense in print of Frank, Cole, and their brothers on numerous occasions. Possibly that unwavering loyalty resulted from Frank James's and John Jarrette's involvement in the rescue of Shelby, but it may have grown simply out of Shelby's respect and affection for his irregular troops.

After fighting diligently through the fall of 1862, the guerrillas traveled to the area of Mt. Pleasant, Texas, to rest and regroup over the winter. They would return to Missouri ready to resume the fight in the spring.

HARASSMENTS AT HOME

Meanwhile, the James and Younger families continued to suffer indignities and bullying at the hands of the Union. Militia and Union soldiers repeatedly visited the area farms to demand the whereabouts of those they suspected might be with Quantrill. Jesse James by this time was even more eager to fight with the guerrillas. One story has it that Jesse asked to join the group around this time but that Quantrill refused since the boy had only recently turned fifteen. Jim Younger, aged fourteen in 1862, was also too young to join. For the time being he and Jesse would fight the battle on the home front.

Problems on the home front continued. During this time, eighteen-year-old Sally Younger was molested by a Union captain. Cole wrote in his autobiography that he had to coax his distraught sister into telling him what happened and was so infuriated that he pledged that the captain would never bother her again. Cole claimed that he and his

Sally Younger Duncan with great-granddaughter Harriet Baird. Sally was born September 2, 1846. She married farmer Jephthah Duncan. Their children were Jeanette, Harriet, Minnie, Charles, Elizabeth, and Robert. Sally died May 1, 1925.

friends ambushed the captain and thirteen of his men. As he wrote, "I walked out and stood beside the [body of the] Captain. I said out loud, 'Sister, I have kept my word.'"

Whenever federal soldiers appeared at the Younger home in Cass County to try to extract information about the whereabouts of Cole, Jim Younger would hide in the backwoods while his mother Bursheba and his younger brothers were questioned. Jim was the oldest boy on the farm and his family was sure the troops suspected he was involved with Quantrill as well. Militia appeared again at the Younger farm to interrogate Bursheba in February 1863. She asked that her family be left in peace, but the militia informed her they would be back.

The James-Samuel family was experiencing much the same harassment up in Clay County. One of the James family stories claims that Frank James was arrested at home on one occasion after he reaffiliated himself with the Confederate Army, after which he was jailed for three days in Liberty. If true, Frank James was back in action by late May of 1863 with one of Quantrill's unit leaders, Fernando Scott.

The militia was aware of Frank's association with the guerrillas and would frequently ride in groups onto his mother's farm to look for him. Zerelda would berate the intruders while others of her family stood stoically beside her, revealing nothing. Young Jesse, though, would sometimes respond to the insults and talk back to the soldiers. On more than one occasion, he was roughly pushed or struck or kicked.

Dr. Reuben Samuel sits under the coffee tree from which he was hanged.

One such militia visit turned particularly brutal. Certain that Zerelda and Jesse were providing information to Quantrill's men, Union soldiers tried to force Dr. Reuben Samuel to reveal what they thought he knew. The soldiers threw a rope around the doctor's neck and hoisted him four times from the branch of a coffee tree in the yard. When this failed to bring forth new information, the soldiers repeatedly shoved the pregnant Zerelda Samuel and shouted obscenities at her while accusing her of being a Confederate spy. Young Jesse was chased through the cornfields. The soldiers eventually caught the boy and whipped his back until he was bloody. Finally the soldiers left, but with a promise that they would return soon.

The consequences of that visit from Union soldiers were far-reaching for the James-Samuel family. The repeated hangings restricted the oxygen supply to Dr. Samuel's brain for such a long time that his mental capacities were never again as keen as they had been before. Zerelda suffered a miscarriage. Her hatred for her Northern enemy intensified and Jesse, too, was enraged. He became more determined than ever to find someone in Quantrill's organization who would let him join the ranks and avenge the brutalities he and his family had experienced.

CONFEDERATE WOMEN IN JAIL

Cole moved around Missouri with various members of Quantrill's group and participated in several engagements during 1863. The guerrillas had split into several units by this time, led primarily by George Todd, John Jarrette, Bill Anderson, and Quantrill. Two sons of a prominent Cass County man, Reason Judy, were killed by guerrillas some time after the battle of Lone Jack. Cole claimed that Judy's first son was killed by guerrillas Dick Maddox and Joe Hall at Paola while Cole was in Austin, Missouri; he further denied involvement in the death of the second son. Judy never-

theless felt so convinced of Cole's guilt that he swore out a warrant for his arrest—this according to Cole, who also claimed that Judy's warrant was the instrument by which he first became a "wanted man" and which restricted his life in terms of being able to move about openly in his home neighborhood. A search of circuit court records fails to turn up any record of such a warrant.

Nannie Harris and Charity Kerr. These two sisters-in-law, cousins of the Youngers, were among those arrested and imprisoned in Kansas City by order of General Ewing. Charity was killed when the jail building collapsed. Nannie, the daughter of Reuben and Laura Fristoe Harris, was married to guerrilla Jabez McCorkle. Charity was the sister of Jabez and John McCorkle.

Now Quantrill's men were striking against their enemy at every opportunity. Their unorthodox methods, such as traveling in small bands and hiding deep in the brush to spring out suddenly at their unsuspecting enemies, were increasingly effective. The frustrated federal leadership authorized Union Brig. Gen. Thomas Ewing to curtail guerrilla aggression by whatever means necessary. Ewing's plan, intended to undermine the morale of the irregulars, involved the arrest and imprisonment of a representative sampling of the wives, sisters, and mothers of identified guerrillas. The women would then be unable to aid the guerrillas with information, food, and hideouts. In addition, the women would serve as hostages, a tactic which would certainly have an effect on Quantrill's movements.

Zerelda James Samuel was arrested shortly after the disastrous visit by Union soldiers to the James-Samuel farm. She and her two small daughters were forced into a makeshift jail in St. Joseph. It was later said by the family that they remained there twenty-five days; probably, though, they were not there that long. Josie Younger Jarrette, Caroline Younger Clayton, Sally Younger, and several of the Younger cousins were among those taken into custody at a temporary jail in Kansas City. More than a hundred frightened young women were jailed there.

The guerrillas were not intimidated but further enraged by Ewing's actions. They gathered together to lay plans to liberate the women, but on August 14, 1863, the three-story building in Kansas City where the women were being held mysteriously collapsed. Several young women were killed and many were seriously hurt. The Younger sisters escaped harm, but their cousin Charity Kerr was killed. One of Bill Anderson's sisters died and another was badly injured. Anderson became inflamed with a hatred that intimidated even the most hardened of the guerrillas under his command. With a fury that would earn him the nickname "Bloody Bill," Anderson called for immediate and costly retribution.

THE LAWRENCE, KANSAS, MASSACRE

General Order 10 was approved by Union Gen. John Schofield and issued by Thomas Ewing about the time of the imprisonment of the Confederate women. This order made it legal to force all families of guerrillas, and anyone who assisted the guerrillas in any way, to leave Missouri. Guerrillas were further incensed by this latest scheme against their families. Earlier in the war, Kansas leaders Charles Jennison and James Lane had orchestrated the devastating raid on Osceola, Missouri. Townspeople had been robbed of their possessions, buildings had been burned, and a number of people had been killed. It was a travesty still fresh in the minds of the guerrillas, who held James Lane as responsible for Osceola, just as they blamed Thomas Ewing for the attacks on their women. Quantrill's group now decided to even the score against those who would so callously harm women, children, and noncombatants. The target: Lawrence, Kansas, the hometown of James Lane.

(Top) William "Bloody Bill" Anderson. (Bottom) Union Gen. John M. Schofield.

More than 450 of Quantrill's irregulars assembled in Johnson County, Missouri, on August 19, 1863—five days after the collapse of the women's prison building— and made preparations for the two-day ride to the mid-size Kansas town. The length of the journey gave the men time to work themselves into a frenzy. It was decided that Lawrence would pay for everything that had transpired at the hands of Lane, Ewing, and all their soldiers. Four large groups had mounted, led by Quantrill, Bill Anderson, John Jarrette, and George Todd. Cole Younger and his new friend Frank James followed close behind their respective leaders.

Events in Lawrence, Kansas, can only be described as butchery. The guerrillas entered the town at seven o'clock on the morning of August 21. Bloodcurdling Rebel yells woke the sleepy inhabitants to confusion and fear. The guerrillas had decided that all the men in the town were to die, regardless of age or status. Death came as a kindness to some of the young men, old men, and men unable to defend themselves who were rousted from their hiding places, chased, and pulled into the streets to be slaughtered before the eyes of their mothers, wives, and daughters. Homes and businesses were looted, the guerrillas stuffing whatever they could

Massachusetts Street, Lawrence, Kansas, ca. 1860.

carry into their saddlebags and tossing additional booty over the backs of their horses. Men assigned to set the town on fire followed their orders with glee, torching occupied stores, public buildings, hotels, and houses. The air hung putrid with the smells of dust and burning wood and death. At least 150 men lay dead by the time it was over.

One of the men given the assignment to capture James Lane was Cole Younger. Lane fled from his home and hid in a cornfield when he heard the first Rebel yell, and neither Cole nor any of the others was able to locate him. By the time the Confederates left the scene of the massacre, Lane still had not been found.

Cole Younger had refused to take part in the slaughter or looting and later said he was happy to have been assigned to look for Lane. It is not known exactly what role the teenaged Frank James played in the events at Lawrence. He never publicly addressed his activities that day.

Approaching Union troops put an end to the bloodbath, but the guerrillas safely returned to Missouri to celebrate their revenge. Only one guerrilla life was lost in the foray. There has been considerable controversy as to whether the men who ravaged

Lawrence that day rode away under a "black flag." Cole stated years later that the only black flag he was aware of that day was one belonging to James Lane. It had been given to Lane by the "Ladies of Leavenworth" and was carried off by the guerrillas as a souvenir.

RETALIATION FOR THE LAWRENCE RAID

Union Brig. Gen. Thomas Ewing.

Union leaders were as outraged by events at Lawrence as the Confederates had been at the wanton destruction of Osceola. President Lincoln demanded that something be done to stop the devastating guerrilla warfare. Senator Lane formulated General Order 11, to be carried out by General Ewing, which would force the mass evacuation of all Confederate sympathizers within the border counties of Missouri. Those who could prove their loyalty to the Union would be allowed to move to the nearest military post. Those who could not prove their loyalty would have to leave the area within fifteen days. Most were forced out of their homes long before the deadline. New refugees watched in melancholy and horror and anger as their homes and farms were torched to the ground.

Union militia returned to the Younger farm to teach the family another lesson. The soldiers informed Bursheba that since she was aiding and abetting the enemy, they had brought an order from the commanding officer to burn the Younger farm. Bursheba pleaded to no avail. She, her young sons John and Bob (ages twelve and ten), her small daughters Emma and Retta, her loyal slave Suze, and a small black boy were all ordered to leave the premises at once. Bursheba was ill at the time, and her children begged the soldiers to give their mother additional time to prepare to leave. The response from the militia sounded like a compromise: they would allow the family to take a few possessions from the house before they burned it. The children placed their ailing mother in a wagon, then watched in shock as their home was immediately set on fire and all traces of their father's accomplishments destroyed. It was a scene none of the children, certainly not John and Bob, would ever forget. Cole in his later years told his friend Harry Hoffman, "Seven persons were in that wagon; not one among them had ever done anyone a wrong in their lives."

The James-Samuel family's farm was not located in a border area affected by the evacuation order. Their harassment by Union troops continued nonetheless. It was not unusual for Union soldiers and agents to appear suddenly at the James-Samuel farm to question the family about Frank's activities or simply to make their presence known. It was common knowledge in Clay County that Zerelda James Samuel and her teenage son Jesse were adamant and outspoken Southern sympathizers. Everyone in the area was aware that Frank James was with Quantrill and that his mother wholeheartedly supported his guerrilla activities. Jesse continued to lament openly that he was not yet allowed to join the group. The boy told his family and neighbors he would jump at the opportunity as soon as he was old enough.

By October 1863 Quantrill and most of his men had returned to Texas for the winter. The irregulars found themselves not so warmly welcomed by those in the regular army. News about the repulsive slaughter in Lawrence had circulated, and many in the Confederate Army now regarded the guerrillas as barbarians. Many in Quantrill's group were overwhelmed with guilt at what they had participated in; many abandoned the group altogether.

The disintegration of Quantrill's cohesive outfit continued for months. Quantrill himself was extremely weary and decided to step down from his position of foremost leadership. A number of guerrillas elected to join or rejoin the regular Confederate Army. Others threw in their lot with George Todd or Bill Anderson. In the spring of 1864 Todd and Anderson returned with their separate units to Missouri, where combat continued with much the same ruthlessness.

Suze Younger. Suze came to live with the Youngers in 1850, when she was fourteen. She assisted at the births of Alphae, John, Emma, Bob, and Retta. She remained loyal to the Youngers after Emancipation and was regarded as one of the family. After Bursheba Younger's death, Suze married John Handy. The couple eventually took positions with the Jackson County Poor Farm, run by Emma Younger and her husband Kitt Rose. Suze died there many years later.

COLE ON ASSIGNMENT, AND "DINGUS" JOINS UP

In 1864 Cole Younger was handpicked for a scouting mission to Arkansas by Adj. Gen. John Newman Edwards, on assignment from General Shelby. The mission was successful, and Cole was rewarded with another mission, this time to Colorado with Col. George S. Jackson, to disrupt the transcontinental telegraph line. Cole had even been awarded the temporary rank of captain when John Jarrette, his superior officer, was sent to assist Shelby. Upon Jarrette's return, however, Cole's rank was reduced to lieutenant. Cole wrote in his autobiography that he was then sent with Jarrette to escort an officer to British Columbia to deliver papers for the purchase of two "vessels" to be used by the Confederacy. From Canada Cole traveled to California to await further orders.

In the meantime, Cole's brother Jim, aged sixteen, had become dispirited by the incessant harassment of the family. Jim had to stand by helplessly as his mother and younger siblings were forced to move from town to town to escape constant bullying by the militia. Jim later wrote that he eventually came to feel that only by joining the waning forces of Quantrill could he play an active role in bringing about the end of the war. When Quantrill returned from Texas that year with a much smaller band of loyal men, Jim Younger took a place in the group.

Jesse James, Confederate guerrilla, at age seventeen. This painting was made from the photograph taken in Platte City, Missouri, on July 10, 1864, after guerrillas captured the town. It was probably Jesse's first foray.

"Bloody Bill" Anderson had separated his outfit from the official Quantrill group, but he continued to fight for the same cause and with the same methods. Upon his return to Missouri in 1864, Anderson was approached by a young would-be recruit in the company of Fletch Taylor, one of Anderson's devoted men. Once "Bloody Bill" saw the fierceness and hatred in young Jesse James's eyes, the ruthless guerrilla agreed to let him join and took the boy under his wing. Shortly after Jesse joined the group he was seriously wounded on the right side of his chest. Taken to the home of the Mimms family in Harlem, near Kansas City, Jesse recovered quickly and apparently was back in action by September.

The privately conducted wars of Bill Anderson and George Todd were combined on September 25, 1864. A consolidated group of about 225 guerrillas descended on the small Missouri town of Centralia. The group terrorized the people of the town with boorish bullying, then Anderson ordered his men to stop a train approaching the Centralia station. Before the engineer could notice what was going on and roll the train through, Anderson's men climbed aboard. Among the passengers were twenty-five unarmed Union soldiers on furlough. The soldiers were forced to leave the train and strip off their uniforms. The guerrillas were glad to exchange their tattered jackets and pants for Union garb, especially since it would disguise them in the field.

"Bloody Bill" then ordered the Union soldiers executed where they stood, one by one. The vicious slaughter that followed would remind many of the guerrillas' work at Lawrence. Under Anderson's orders, his group then withdrew from Centralia to their encampment outside town. Accounts indicate that both Jesse and Frank James were with Anderson and Todd in Centralia, but it is not known what roles they played.

Union Maj. A. V. E. Johnston, arriving with troops shortly after Anderson's men left town, immediately set out to find the perpetrators of the carnage. A battle resulted that turned out to be another disaster for the Union troops. More than 100 Union soldiers died. Jesse and Frank James not only participated in the Centralia battle; writers have often claimed that Jesse scored his first big victory as a recruit by firing the fatal round that ended the life of Major Johnston.

Around this time Jesse acquired the nickname of "Dingus." During a handgun accident, the tip of the middle finger of his left hand was pinched off. The teenager's response was simply to remark that it was the "goll-dingus" thing he had ever seen. After that example of stoicism and panache, the seventeen-year-old recruit was on his way to acquiring a legendary reputation.

Union Maj. A. V. E. Johnston.

The battle of Centralia was to be Anderson and Todd's last victory in the field. George Todd died in October 1864 during a skirmish near Independence. A week later, Anderson and his men, Jesse included, were ambushed by Union Maj. S. P. Cox. Anderson was killed, but Jesse and others of the band escaped. "Bloody Bill" Anderson was so despised by Union troops that his corpse was beheaded and his head put on display.

QUANTRILL'S DEATH AND THE END OF THE WAR

Guerrilla forces were now rapidly diminishing. In a last effort, Quantrill resumed leadership of Todd's and Anderson's men and tried to move his base of operations from Missouri to the east. Quantrill probably realized time was running out for the Confederates, and he wanted his men away from the fate sure to befall them if they were caught inside Missouri at the close of the war.

As for Cole Younger at this time, he heard limited reports about events in Missouri while he waited on the west coast. Cole was staying in San Jose at the home

(Top) *San Jose, California, ca. 1860.* (Middle) *Coleman Purcell Younger.* (Bottom) *John Ringo. Cole Younger enjoyed visiting his father's family in California during the war. One relative he may have met there was John Ringo, his Uncle Coleman's nephew by marriage. Ringo would later become a notorious desperado who played a role in the life of Wyatt Earp.*

of his father's brother, Coleman Younger, a successful cattleman who was socially prominent among the pioneers of the city. Cole anxiously awaited new orders; he did not realize for some time that he had completed his last wartime assignment.

Anderson's guerrillas left for the south in the winter of 1864. Frank and Jesse arrived together in northeast Arkansas in November. There the James boys split up, Jesse going on to Texas with George Shepard and his group of guerrillas while Frank crossed over into Tennessee with Quantrill. Frank James and Jim Younger stayed with the guerrilla leader as he made his way into Kentucky.

In early May 1865 a band of guerrillas led by Dave Poole and Arch Clements returned from Texas, arrived in the area around Warrensburg, Missouri, and raided the town of Holden. It is known that Jesse James was part of a group that sacked the railroad town of Kingsville, Missouri, soon after, and so it is possible that he also may have been involved in the raid on Holden.

Meanwhile, Quantrill and his group continued eastward through Kentucky, engaging in several confrontations along the way. On the night of May 10, 1865, they halted near Louisville at the farm of a Confederate sympathizer, Jeremiah Wakefield. Some of the men boarded in Wakefield's barn while others camped nearby. Quantrill and his men inside the barn were so exhausted and disheartened they failed to hear the approach of Union Capt. Edwin Terrill and his men until the first shot was fired. Many of the guerrillas lay dead or wounded after the attack, including William Quantrill. Surviving irregulars were arrested, and other small groups of guerrillas in the area were captured as well. Some of the guerrillas were jailed in Lexington before being imprisoned at the federal penitentiary at Alton. The seriously wounded Quantrill was transported to the military prison hospital at Louisville, where he died several days later.

Guerrilla John McCorkle later wrote that Jim Younger was captured during a skirmish near Harrodsburg, Kentucky, on January 29, 1865, but John Newman Edwards wrote that Jim was taken prisoner west of that town on February 9. Cole Younger, however, claimed that Jim was taken with Quantrill at Wakefield's barn. Jim himself never made it clear where or when his short stint as a guerrilla came to an end.

Frank James had been with one of the groups that did not bed down in Wakefield's barn. Scattered in the field, his group of leaderless irregulars soon realized that continuing to fight on their own was futile. Frank and his comrades surrendered to the Union Army at Samuel's Depot, Kentucky, on June 26. They were paroled shortly thereafter.

A few days after Poole's and Clements's men, with Jesse James among them, made their assaults on Holden and Kingsville in May, the guerrillas were stunned to hear that Robert E. Lee had surrendered at Appomattox on April 9, more than a month before. However, they refused to give up. Clement even demanded the surrender of Lexington, Missouri, although nothing came of his demand. Eventually, word reached Union Col. Chester Harding, Commander of the District of Central Missouri, that approximately 100 guerrillas wished to surrender but feared they would be killed if they did so. Before negotiations could be completed, there was a small skirmish south of Lexington.

(Top) *Confederate guerrillas (l to r): Fletcher Taylor, Frank James, and Jesse James.* (Bottom) *Guerrillas John McCorkle and T. B. Harris.*

There have been several accounts of what happened to Jesse James at this time. He later told Judge Thomas Shouse, a boyhood friend of his from Clay County, that around May 15, 1865, he had been on his way to Lexington to surrender when he and his group were fired on by drunken Union soldiers. Jesse was shot in the chest, the bullet perforating his lung, but he was able to shoot the horse of one of the men pursuing him and escape. His horse gone, he crawled to a nearby creek where he passed the night. In the morning he crawled up a bank. A farmer saw him and helped him get medical attention. Delirious from loss of blood, Jesse claimed he took the required Oath of Loyalty while lying in his bed at the nearby Virginia Hotel. "J. W. James" from Lafayette County is listed in official military records as having taken the oath along with forty others at Lexington.

With the death of William Quantrill the war was officially over for Missourians, including the James and Younger brothers. The deep resentments promoted before and during the course of the war continued, however, as did the harassment against Southern sympathizers. Taking the Oath of Loyalty was one thing, but living in the postwar South would prove to be another. In a way, the Missouri guerrilla warfare would not come to an end for decades, not until the imprisonment of the Youngers and the death of Jesse James.

ENTER THE CARPETBAGGERS

Random raids, daily conflicts, open warfare, and the struggle to maintain food and shelter had left the people of Missouri exhausted. Their land had been ravaged, their farms and businesses wrecked and burned, and a long-familiar way of life had come to an end. Confusion and fear did not lessen after 1865, but in fact escalated for many citizens of the borderland who were trying to plan their future. Those who had been evicted from their farms and homes by the enactment of General Order 11 returned now to wastelands where there had once been thriving fields and sturdy farm buildings. Unable to earn much income while in exile, these Missouri families encountered a new economic situation that forced them into more poverty and suffering.

Those Missourians who had sided with the Union were affected by the new economic reality as well. There was little money in circulation, and loans were needed to finance the purchase of basic equipment and seed. Bankers and investors from the north and east, a familiar sight with their carpet-clad luggage, arrived to offer loans for rebuilding projects. Their interest rates, however, were so exorbitant that restoration of Southern communities would be slow for many years.

Additional political restrictions were placed on Confederate sympathizers by the Drake Constitution, enacted in 1865. In an effort to control the former Rebels or force them from the state, the Missouri legislature decreed that Confederate sympathizers could not vote, could not hold public office at any level, and could not be employed in any professional position. There would be no amnesty for those who had taken up arms against the United States government. On the border farms the possibility of arrest and imprisonment at the whim of the militia remained a daily threat.

These drastic measures impeded economic progress and frustrated and embittered people in the border counties. Other Missourians, ones who had served the Union, expressed the view that Southern sympathizers were being treated far better than they had the right to be. It was said that it would have been easier and within bounds for Union officers to have executed anyone who served with the Rebel forces. Missouri Southerners slowly rebuilt their lives, but most of them did not respect or forgive the new sanctions. Some of them, such as the James and Younger brothers, would eventually seize their opportunities to rebel in a different way against the unfairness of the Reconstruction.

HOME FOR CHRISTMAS: THE SCATTERED YOUNGERS

When word of Lee's surrender reached the West Coast, Cole Younger was still with his uncle in San Jose. He had not taken the Oath of Loyalty and had no intention of doing so. If he returned to Missouri, then, his family would be in jeopardy, and as a wanted man he would be subject to immediate arrest or hanging. His mother Bursheba wrote to him from Jackson County to suggest he stay in northern Missouri with her uncle Thomas Fristoe in Howard County. That way Cole would not be far from the family should they need him. His enemies would think he was not in the area and would leave the family alone.

Jim Younger later wrote that he served a few months as a prisoner of war at Alton Prison in Kentucky at the end of the war. He agreed to take the loyalty oath so that he would be allowed to go home. Jim then began looking for his family in Missouri. He was not sure where they were, but felt certain they were somewhere in the state, probably with relatives.

John and Bob Younger, now ages thirteen and twelve, were still with Bursheba. It is likely that all three were staying with Bursheba's sister Frances Twyman in Independence. Both boys wanted the family to return to Harrisonville, where their house in town was still standing. However, life would be difficult in Harrisonville and particularly painful for Bursheba. The Younger family fortune had been decimated, both because of the war and because Henry Younger had neglected to leave a will. Henry's brother Frank had tried to keep the family businesses afloat but had been forced to

(Top) *The Younger house in Strother, Missouri. The house was built around 1856 by Henry Younger and his family, but the Youngers did not reside in the house until after the war. Slated for demolition in the early 1980s, the house was purchased by the author and dismantled. Following restoration by the citizens of Lee's Summit, the house will serve as The Younger Family Home and Study Center. (Bottom) Caroline Younger, born in 1842, known affectionately by her family as "Duck." She married guerrilla George M. Clayton and had two children, Leola and Gustavus. She died in 1865 of unknown causes.*

sell what remained in order to provide Bursheba and her children with funds to make a new start.

Another tragedy befell Bursheba's family that year when Caroline Younger Clayton fell ill and died at the age of twenty-three. Caroline left two small children and her husband, former guerrilla George Clayton.

Bursheba Younger wanted her eldest sons, wherever they were, to return to a somewhat familiar location. The house that Henry and his family had built in 1857 in Strother, Missouri, had been rented to tenant farmers before the war, but was now unoccupied. Bursheba moved in and tried to ready the house for Cole's and Jim's return.

The Younger family was reunited at Christmas 1865. It was the first holiday they had shared since their father's murder. Jim later claimed that Cole was pleased to see that his three youngest brothers had grown to be competent young men, but was surprised and troubled to find they resented his paternal attitude toward them. John and Bob argued constantly with their oldest brother while Jim tried to serve as peacemaker. All were relieved when Cole decided to go back to their Uncle Thomas at the end of December.

JESSE CLOSE TO DEATH

In late 1865 or early 1866, after Frank James had been paroled, he traveled west from Kentucky to rejoin his family. He did not know if he would find them in Rulo, Nebraska, where they had fled to wait out the war, or back on the farm in Clay County.

On June 13, 1865, Jesse James, aided by his friends, was sent by steamboat to stay once again at the boarding house of his uncle John Mimms near Kansas City. At that time his mother, Zerelda, was still with family members in Rulo. On July 15, Jesse joined them there to continue his recuperation.

It had been touch and go with Jesse. The chest wound he received near Lexington had been so severe it was not certain he would survive. Jesse stayed with his mother for six weeks and grew despondent at his continued weak condition. He pleaded with his mother to help him return to Missouri before he died. Zerelda finally agreed that the journey would probably make no difference to her son's condition.

Jesse was transported by boat down the Missouri River to John Mimms's boarding house by August 26, where he was nursed by his cousin, Zerelda Mimms. Named for his mother, Zerelda was a lovely young woman two years older than Jesse. She rarely left his side during the weeks when he was struggling to live. Because her name was the same as his mother's, Jesse fondly called her "Zee." Jesse stayed from August until late October while he gradually regained his strength. The couple fell in love, and Jesse swore to Zee that some day when things were better he would make her his wife.

Eventually, Jesse recovered sufficiently to return to the James-Samuel farm in Clay County. There he was reunited with his brother Frank and others in his closely knit family, all of whom had finally returned to Missouri. Frank was helping their stepfather, Reuben Samuel, to rebuild the farm, and Jesse joined them when he was able. Frank and Jesse exchanged war stories, and things were peaceful on the farm for the first time in years. Jesse was even baptized in the Baptist Church in Kearney.

(Top) *Zerelda Amanda "Zee" Mimms, born July 21, 1845, to Mary James and John Mimms. Her mother was the eldest sister of Rev. Robert Sallee James, the father of Zee's future husband.* (Bottom) *The James-Samuel farm near Kearney, Clay County, Missouri. The log cabin section of the farmhouse was constructed in 1822. The farm remained home to the James-Samuel family from the time it was purchased by Robert Sallee James in 1845 until his heirs donated the property to the Clay County Parks Department in 1977.*

There was little outward animosity within the Kearney community in 1866. Only occasional harassments from outsiders disrupted the lives of the residents. Whenever such a posse appeared, Frank and Jesse busied themselves elsewhere while Zerelda, still defiant and proud, berated the soldiers for hounding her boys. Frank and Jesse plowed the fields and planted crops, but privately discussed ways to avenge the suffering their families and friends had endured.

JOHN YOUNGER SHOOTS GILLCREAS

In January 1866 Bursheba, John, and Bob Younger made a trip to Independence to stock up on items to make their Strother home comfortable. With the shopping almost completed, John went to retrieve a gun that Cole had left with a merchant to be repaired. While loading the family's wagon outside the sheriff's office, John and his mother were taunted by a former Union soldier named Gillcreas, who recognized the Youngers and made some disparaging remarks to Bursheba about her son Cole. John was not pleased at having his mother subjected to this and told the man to be quiet. Annoyed at being reprimanded by a fourteen-year-old boy, Gillcreas stepped up with a parcel in his hand and slapped John across the face with a frozen mackerel wrapped in paper. John was enraged as he fell to the ground. Thirteen-year-old Bob then yelled to John from his place in the wagon, "Why don't you shoot him?"

John picked himself up from the dirt and began to move toward the back of the wagon where he had stashed Cole's gun. Seeing this, Gillcreas reached for his sling-shot, which was considered a deadly weapon at the time, and aimed it at the boy. Without hesitation John grabbed the gun and fired in Gillcreas's direction. The bullet hit Gillcreas squarely between the eyes and killed him instantly. Witnesses to

Independence Square in the late 1800s.

the event moved John quickly into the sheriff's office for his own protection. He was held overnight but released the next morning after it was determined that he had fired in self-defense.

Bursheba Younger decided that the border counties were still too dangerous for her younger children and sent John and Bob farther south, to St. Clair County, to stay with her deceased husband's brothers. Her youngest girls were sent to Pleasant Hill to stay with their sister Anne. Jim accompanied his mother to Harrisonville, where they attempted to get the family's monetary affairs in order.

THE LIBERTY BANK HOLDUP

Cole Younger remained for a while in northern Missouri and often visited his Confederate comrades. He watched his movements carefully, however. He could not freely walk the streets of any Missouri town until he surrendered and stood trial. Cole believed, probably with good reason, that the chances of his not being lynched or of coming out of a trial with less than a death sentence were not good in view of the fact that he had been one of Quantrill's most trusted men.

"Wayside Rest," the Cass County home of the Robert Brown family. Cole often spent evenings there listening to Lizzie Brown play the piano. Her brothers served as Confederates with Cole, and the family remained his lifelong friends.

Sometimes Cole would make a quiet journey south to visit friends such as the Brown family in Harrisonville. Probably he got in touch with Frank James around this time. During the war, Frank and Cole had often shared stories of their families. Cole had not met Jesse but felt as if he knew the fiery young man from Frank's proud descriptions of his little brother's wartime escapades. Frank, of course, had later become acquainted with Cole's brother Jim when the two joined Quantrill's trek to Kentucky.

There is no firm evidence that Frank, Jesse, and Cole planned the robbery of the Clay County Savings Bank in Liberty, Missouri. Stories by their contemporaries ascribe the initial idea to Frank and Jesse. Jesse was still in a weakened condition in February 1866, but he could easily have come up with a plan to make the Yankee carpetbagging bank investors feel some discomfort. The James brothers certainly would have found a ready ally in Cole Younger. He, too, harbored a great deal of

This photograph is said by its owner to be of Jim Younger (l, standing) with his brother Cole (l, seated) and Frank James (r, seated). The photo was probably taken shortly after the war. The identity of the young man standing on the right is not known.

resentment and was eager for revenge. The most likely scenario has Jesse planning the robbery, then Frank sharing the idea with Cole. As for finding accomplices, that would not have been difficult. Throughout Missouri were young guerrillas who had lived with danger every day for three or four years and who had not experienced anything like the thrill of battle since.

The town of Liberty was a familiar and unpleasant name to Missouri Confederates: a band of forty guerrillas led by Col. Ben Parker had held the town for several hours in March 1862. At a public meeting in Liberty in July 1864, some Clay County citizens had condemned the guerrilla movement and labeled its participants "monsters of society." However, Liberty was also home to William Jewell College, the school that boasted Reverend Robert James as one of its founders and benefactors.

At two o'clock on the gray afternoon of February 13, 1866, a bedraggled group of young men numbering between ten and fourteen and wearing bits of Union Army clothing rode into Liberty. A few others waited outside town. Such a large group did not draw as much attention as it might have, due to the fact that court was in session and many townspeople were watching a trial. Besides that, a snowstorm looked imminent and people were off the streets. The riders dismounted and tried to look nonchalant. Two of them, later described as tall, entered the Clay County Savings Bank. Probably these were Frank James and Cole Younger.

(Top) *Clay County Savings Bank, Liberty, Missouri.* (Bottom) *The vault and cashier's table in the Liberty bank.*

No one was in the bank except Greenup Bird and his son William, at work at their desks. One of the two strangers warmed himself in front of the stove while the other, approaching the counter, said he wanted to change a bill. William Bird left his desk to help the customer. By the time he arrived at the counter he was looking down the barrel of a gun. The man holding the weapon demanded all the money in the bank or else both men would be shot. William Bird was forced inside the vault and ordered to place all coin in the sack. His father was being held at gunpoint by the other bandit. The elder Bird later reported, "He hoisted the lid of the box, took out Greenbacks 7/30 and UM Bonds and told the robber in the vault to put them in the sack and to be in a hurry." After all the money was collected, the two Birds were shoved into the vault and the vault door closed behind them. Then the robbers quickly joined their comrades in the street.

The Birds opened the unsecured door of the vault and ran to the window even as the men outside were mounting their horses. They yelled out to anyone who might hear that the bank had been robbed. Two college students strolling down the sidewalk in front of the Green House, opposite the bank, heard the cries. Before either could act, one of the bandits spotted them. The robber ordered the boys to stay where they were and fired what was evidently meant as a warning shot. One of the students, George "Jolly" Wymore, was struck and killed. More shots were then fired at another observer, who found his coat ripped through with a bullet. Seconds afterward, the group was fully mounted. They galloped out of the town square whooping the Rebel yell as they headed east down Franklin Street.

This first daylight, peacetime bank robbery in the history of the United States netted a fortune: approximately sixty thousand dollars in currency and bonds. Various accounts have named Oliver Shepard, Bud and Donny Pence, Frank Gregg, James Wilkerson, Joab Perry, Bill Wilkenson, Ben Cooper, and Red Monkers as participants. Another likely suspect was William Quantrill's trusted captain, John Jarrette. All these had served under Quantrill and most were residents of Clay or Jackson counties. Many years later, the names of Cole Younger and Frank and Jesse James were added to the list of probable suspects. Another likely candidate was Allen Parmer, who would later marry the James brothers' sister Susie.

It is questionable whether Jesse James was well enough to ride in the group. Evidently he was still weak several months after the event. As Cole later wrote, "when I saw him (Jesse) early in the summer of 1866 he was still suffering from the shot through the lung he had received in the last battle in Johnson County in May, 1865." It has been often suggested that Jim Younger was present in Liberty that day, but this is unlikely since Jim was averse to the idea of outlawry and was living in Cass County with his mother at the time.

It was reported that several of the bandits crossed the Missouri River by boat after the robbery. A posse of about thirty men led by a Captain Garth was immediately formed in Liberty. The posse doubled in number as others joined up. The robbers had been able to cross the Missouri well ahead of the posse, and the robber group seemed to know how to leave a scene quickly and efficiently. Soon the snowstorm made tracking their escape almost impossible. Newspaper accounts indicated that the bandits recrossed the river near Sibley, Missouri, and gathered at the Mount Gilead Church to divide the stolen money. The bonds were apparently awarded to Cole Younger and Frank James.

Mt. Gilead Church, 1981.

The Clay County Savings Association immediately offered a five-thousand-dollar reward for apprehension of the robbers. The Liberty Savings Association and Clay County Sheriff James M. Jones offered another two thousand dollars. Warrants were issued within the next few days for three men who probably were not involved: Aaron Book, William Easter, and James Couch. These men were singled out although the bank employees recognized no one and even though R. L. Raymond would later state that no one in the posse knew the identities of the men they chased. Captain Minter of Liberty and David Duncan of Cedarville both claimed they recognized Frank James and Bud Pence, but later admitted they were uncertain. No charges were ever filed against Book, Easter, or Couch. Couch was arrested but soon released due to insufficient evidence. Meanwhile, Joab Perry escaped from jail in Independence, where he was being held on another charge. Several of the other possible suspects, including Wilkerson, Gregg, and Monkers, gave sworn statements about their activities elsewhere on the day of the robbery. When suspicion fell on members of the former guerrilla movement, the list of suspects was extended to include Anderson Tate, Jim White, Bill Chiles, J. F. Edmundson, Arch Clement, George Shepard, Dick Burns, William Clay, Arnold Foster, Bill Ryan, Andy Maguire, Jim Anderson, L. S. Smith, and Payne Jones. However, the actual murderer of young Jolly Wymore was never named or caught. The guerrillas remained true to their code of silence.

ILL-GOTTEN GAINS

Over the next few years, Cole Younger cashed bonds throughout the United States. He later wrote, "At one point I was happy to cash bonds given to me by friends who had not had the opportunity to cash them. I never knew where the bonds came from as I never asked it of the friends who had given them to me to cash." Cole consistently denied any knowledge of or participation in the Liberty robbery. He claimed he did not even meet Jesse James until the following summer, when a group of former guerrillas from Jackson County met to discuss the amnesty movement initiated by a group of attorneys in Independence regarding the raid on Lawrence. However, Jesse James had not participated in that raid; there was no reason for him to have attended such a meeting. As to their connection to the Liberty holdup, Frank and Jesse remained silent.

Jim, John, and Bob Younger almost certainly knew that the Clay County bank had been robbed; the topic was big news at the time. It is not known whether any of the three were aware of Cole's involvement. Jim was still with Bursheba and her friends in Harrisonville. John and Bob were staying on their uncle's farm in St. Clair County and beginning to experience the carefree youth that the war had denied them. During their explorations of the area they discovered a secluded cave along the banks of the Osage River. They often climbed to the top of the bluff above the cave where they could see for miles in all directions. Only their most trusted friends were allowed to join them on the "lookout."

"Younger Lookout" at Monagaw Bluff, where the Youngers often visited. From the bluff, the Osage River and the fields of St. Clair County can be seen.

In June 1866 Frank James left to visit friends and family in Kentucky until talk about the Liberty robbery died down. He encountered some problems near the town of Brandenburg, Kentucky. When an altercation with four federal soldiers turned into a deadly gunfight, Frank killed two soldiers and wounded a third. The fourth soldier managed to shoot Frank in the joint of the left hip. Some relatives took him in, but Frank asked for his brother to nurse him. Jesse was still weak, but he rushed to Frank's side and remained with him until Frank recovered in the fall.

Cole Younger was still encountering the employment problems faced by all ex-Confederates. In 1866 he approached his brother-in-law John Jarrette about investing in a herd of cattle. Jarrette evidently had a good deal of money at this time, probably from the Liberty bank robbery. Cole was free to travel wherever cattle might be bought and sold, but Jarrette's plans had to take Josie and two small children into account. Jarrette proposed instead that they invest in a large farm. He and Cole bid on a parcel of land offered at auction in Lexington, Missouri, but Jarrette was later denied the property. It is probable that the ex-guerrilla was not able to provide acceptable answers to the banker in charge of the sale.

Now Jarrette agreed to the purchase of cattle. Cole would drive the herd to southern Kansas and Louisiana to make the sale while Jarrette remained behind in Missouri. Either or both of them may have had other plans as well about how to increase their income.

Eight months after the Liberty holdup, on October 30, 1866, the bustling town of Lexington, Missouri, where Cole and Jarrette had their unsuccessful business dealings, was the site of a robbery. Two men entered the bank around twelve-thirty that autumn afternoon. One of the men asked to have a bill changed while the other snickered and wondered aloud what the "discount" on the bill might be. Uncomfortable with the strangers' demeanor, cashier J. L. Thomas replied that the bank was not presently buying such bills. At this point two other men came in, pointed their revolvers at Thomas's heart, and demanded one hundred thousand dollars. The robbers told Thomas they knew the bank had the funds; where was the key to the vault? Thomas declared he did not have it. The bandits threatened to kill him, but Thomas pointed out

Jesse and Frank James, Illinois, 1872.

that even that would not produce a key. Eventually the robbers ransacked the office drawers, grabbed at least two thousand dollars, then casually left the bank. They mounted their four horses and galloped away.

A posse was formed within minutes. However, the posse consisted of ex-guerrillas John and Dave Poole, Jesse Hamlett, and Hedge Reynolds. They rode out of town after the robbers but returned shortly, claiming the bandits had disappeared into the countryside. Questions were soon raised about the legitimacy of the posse. The posse leaders, the Poole brothers, had been two of the most dedicated of Quantrill's men, and they did not seem to have tried hard to capture the robbers. It was also reported that all four posse members had been seen before and during the robbery casually standing around, near or in view of the bank. Did the Pooles have prior knowledge of the robbery? Had the four volunteered so that other citizens would not form a posse of their own? The questions remain unsettled.

Among possible suspects for the Lexington robbery, the foremost candidate would have to be Jesse James. If he had been too weak to participate in the Liberty robbery, it is likely that Jesse would have executed another plan as soon as he was able to take part. It is known that Jesse was exhausted when he returned from nursing Frank in Kentucky; his chest wound began to hemorrhage again, and for a while his health took a turn for the worse. It could easily have been late October before Jesse was strong enough to ride.

If Jesse were one of the Lexington robbers, it would be safe to assume that Frank James took part, provided that his leg wound was sufficiently healed. If Jesse and Frank were there it is likely that Cole Younger was with them; almost certainly Cole would not have engaged in another holdup without Frank. And if Cole were in the group, probably John Jarrette was the fourth man.

However, John Jarrette alone may have planned the Lexington robbery and put his own gang together to do so. The Alexander Mitchell and Company Bank may well have been the bank that rejected Jarrette when he tried to take out a loan. Used to giving orders as a high-ranking member of Quantrill's guerrillas, Jarrette may have asked three others to come along under his leadership. Besides the names of Cole Younger and the James boys, George Shepard's name has been mentioned as a possible participant, along with those of Donny and Bud Pence. The money was never recovered and the Lexington robbery was never solved.

A SHOT THROUGH THE DOOR

On the night of February 18, 1867, five horsemen visited the James-Samuel homestead in Clay County. Jesse had taken to his bed in the early evening as his chest wound had given him a good deal of pain during the day. The winter had been hard on Jesse, and he often lacked the strength to go about his usual business.

According to Jesse's later account, five men rode up to the James-Samuel farmhouse, dismounted, and demanded to be let in the house. Reuben Samuel asked the men what they wanted. Their reply was a gruff demand to open the door. Dr. Samuel hurried to Jesse's bedside upstairs to talk with him about what to do. Looking out his loft window Jesse noticed that the strangers' horses tied to the fence bore cavalry saddles. He knew then that the men were militia come to arrest him on the charge of war crimes.

Beating on the farmhouse door with their rifles, the soldiers shouted for Jesse to surrender. Jesse grabbed his revolvers and silently crept down from the loft. His next actions took the militia by surprise. He fired his revolver through the front door, seriously wounding one of the soldiers where he stood. Wasting no time, Jesse threw open the door and fired both revolvers, one shot after the next, into the group in front of him. Two more men were wounded and another was killed as he tried to run from the porch. The group recovered only enough to pick up their fallen comrade and make their escape. Though still weak, Jesse left home immediately, knowing the militia would be back with a larger force in the morning.

COPYCAT CRIMES AND THE RICHMOND HOLDUP

The next big robbery attempt in Missouri may have been masterminded by John Jarrette. This time six men were involved, and things did not go smoothly. A ragtag group of men approached the private banking house of Judge John McClain in Savannah, Missouri, on March 2, 1867. The feisty old judge refused to give up the key to his vault and even attempted to break a window to alert the town that he was being robbed. He continued to try to sound an alarm even after one of the robbers shot him in the chest. The would-be bandits had to leave in a hurry, frustrated and empty-handed.

Cole Younger later wrote that the outlaws were subsequently identified, but he did not mention names other

Jim Younger (l) and John Jarrette (r), ca. late 1860s.

than to say that none of them were Youngers. In a story carried in the Liberty *Tribune*, R. McDaniels, Robert Pope, and someone known only as Fitzgerald were listed as suspects in the crime; none of those are names of former guerrillas. Jim White, Bill Chiles, J. F. Edmunson, Arch Clement, Oliver and George Shepard, and Bud McDaniels have also been mentioned, but no substantiating evidence has been presented. Warrants were never issued.

If the Savannah outlaws did not include the Youngers, it is not likely that the James brothers were involved. Jarrette may or may not have participated. In all likelihood the robbery was a copycat crime patterned after the raid on the Liberty Bank.

The next holdup, in Richmond, Missouri, turned into such a disaster that it became an important event in the history of robberies during Reconstruction. There are reasons to doubt, however, that Cole Younger and the James boys were involved. For one thing, the three took pride in executing their plans without resorting to more than threats and intimidation. Cole and Frank especially were usually careful and deliberate in manner, while the men who robbed the Richmond bank were impulsive and murderous.

In addition, the Richmond robbery involved a large group: between eleven and twenty men attempted together to rob the Hughes and Wasson Bank. It is unlikely that Frank, Jesse, and Cole would return to working with such a large number now that they knew how to go about a robbery more efficiently. So many strangers together in the streets of a small town will arouse suspicion, and even if the robbery is successful the take will have to be divided more ways.

At about three-thirty on the afternoon of May 22, 1867, four men entered the Richmond bank. With an intuition that the men meant trouble, bookkeeper Willis Warriner rushed over to the vault and tried to slam it shut. One of the men shot at Warriner, and he dropped to the floor to get out of harm's way. Cashier George Wasson was told to open the vault and hand over its contents while Robert Sevier, Ben Chipeze, and Ephraim January were held at gunpoint.

In the course of the robbery, someone suspicious of all of the men in the street alerted others in the town as to what might be happening in the bank. The robbers were met with gunfire as they left the building. One of the first on the scene was Richmond Mayor John B. Shaw. Almost immediately he fell forward in the dirt with a fatal bullet in the chest. Lt. Frank S. Griffin also tried to stop the bandits' flight and was shot through the head. William Griffin, the town jailer and father of the lieutenant, attempted to help his son and was soon lying in the street with a hole in his forehead.

Finally the band was able to get out of town. They headed south with Deputy Sheriff Tom Reyburn and his posse in hot pursuit. The posse rode close enough at one point to exchange fire, but the robbers were soon a good distance away again. One group of the bandits crossed the Missouri River near Sibley. One of them was recognized there as having been in the group that committed the Liberty robbery, although the identification might have been based on hearsay rather than observation by a witness at both events. Near the Holt Station of the Hannibal & St. Joseph railroad, the posse again drew close, and one of the bandits' horses was shot. That was the last the posse saw of them that day.

This time there had been too many witnesses to the crime. Eight men were charged with the robbery after a horse thief, Felix Bradley, bragged from his jail cell that he knew who had robbed the Richmond bank. Named in the warrant were former guerrillas Payne Jones, Dick Burns, Ike Flannery, Andy McGuire, Tom Little, James and John White, and Allen Parmer. The demand for revenge grew strong as the people of Richmond tried to find the men responsible for the deaths in their city. The governor of Missouri offered three hundred dollars for each of the robbers, a sum to be added to the five hundred dollars per man offered by the county sheriff. The officers of the bank offered a separate reward in the amount of the money taken from the bank, some four thousand dollars.

Allen Parmer sent a letter to the editor of the *Missouri Democrat* when he heard he had been named as a suspect in the Richmond robbery. Parmer claimed he knew nothing about the robbery and that he had been at his place of employment with the J. E. Shawhan & Co. in St. Louis when the robbery occurred. Included with his letter was an affidavit from Shawhan supporting his claim.

As it happened, Allen Parmer had been seeing Susan James, the eighteen-year-old sister of Frank and Jesse. Twenty-year-old Jesse was not pleased with his sister's choice of suitors and told her so. Evidently it was one thing for him and Frank to participate in crimes against the northern establishment, but another for his sister to be associated with bank robbers.

Allen Parmer, born May 6, 1848, the son of Isaac and Barbara Parmer. As a guerrilla Parmer participated in the Lawrence massacre. He surrendered with Frank James at Samuels Station, Kentucky, on June 26, 1865. Arrested in Texas as a suspect in the 1879 Glendale train robbery, Parmer was released for lack of evidence. In 1870 he married Susan Lavinia James, with whom he had seven children. After her death Parmer married Sarah Katherine "Kitty" Ogden. He died in October, 1927, in Wichita Falls, Texas.

The White brothers were never caught. Some others named in the warrant were not so lucky. Captain P. J. Miserez gathered a posse and went in search of Payne Jones soon after the warrant was issued. The posse's first stop was at the home of Jones's father-in-law near Independence. It was six in the morning, but Payne Jones greeted them with a double-barreled shotgun. Jones then charged from the house blasting the shotgun in the posse's direction. B. H. Williamson was fatally wounded, as was an eight-year-old girl at the scene. Jones then fled across the cornfields with the posse in pursuit. Jones was able to elude the posse and disappear into the woods after being hit in the shoulder by a bullet and temporarily losing his footing. His reprieve did not last long. When Jones was caught several weeks later he was immediately lynched. The possibility that a suspected bank robber would be summarily lynched rather than given a fair trial came to be an important part of the James-Younger Gang's perspective.

Tom Little.

The dogged hunt for the Richmond outlaws continued. Tom Little was arrested with his friend Fred Meyers. Both were charged with the Richmond robbery and other crimes. Fearing that Little would be released when friends of his brought forth signed affidavits that he was in Dover, Missouri, on May 22, the townspeople of Richmond conducted a mock trial and hanged the prisoners. The same fate awaited Felix Bradley when he was jailed. Andy McGuire was located in St. Louis and returned to Richmond for trial, but no one could identify him as a participant. When a posse sent to Crab Orchard, Kentucky, was able to locate Jim Devers, Devers confessed to being an outlaw but did not confess to the Richmond robbery.

Six months after the Richmond holdup, on November 27, 1867, a robbery was committed at the banking house of P. Roberts in Independence. Two men entered, pointed their guns at the president, and demanded he surrender the contents of the vault. Having done so, the president and the teller were then locked inside the vault. A local newspaper account suggested that Jim Devers was involved. Guerrilla Jim Cummins, who later claimed Jim White was also present, may have taken part. A vigilante group took McGuire and Devers from their cells in Richmond at midnight on March 17, 1868, and hanged them both. Former guerrilla Bud Pence had been arrested the previous July on the basis of George Wasson's claim that Pence had taken part in the Richmond robbery. Pence declared, however, that he had been living in Kentucky since 1865 and was released. On November 22, 1867, the body of Dick Burns was found in a field near Independence; Burns lay wrapped in a blanket with his skull crushed. One of the local papers repeated gossip that said Burns had been murdered by Jim Chiles.

Although Cole Younger was not charged in either robbery, he later took the precaution in his autobiography of offering an alibi stating that he had been at the Bass Plantation near Lake Providence, Louisiana, when the robberies took place. Cole had been driving cattle in the South and often stayed with good friends. Cole provided the names of the respected Lea brothers of Independence as witnesses to his presence in Louisiana.

FRANK JAMES HEADS FOR CALIFORNIA

Frank James, ca. 1869-70.

Jesse James was probably in Nashville at the time of the Richmond robbery. Sometime in late May or early June 1867, Jesse arrived in Tennessee, where his lung wound was treated by Dr. Paul Eve. When Jesse felt stronger and publicity about previous robberies had subsided, he slowly headed back toward Missouri. Jesse stopped for several months along the way to visit the Hite family in Kentucky, where he also saw his brother Frank.

Frank James made his trip to Kentucky sometime at the beginning of 1867, according to a letter written later by his brother. Frank apparently left Alexander Sayer's in Nelson County for New York City. It is possible that Cole Younger accompanied Frank on this trip and that the two cashed some of the Liberty bonds along the way. Jesse later wrote that Frank then sailed from New York City; Jesse failed to mention Frank's destination.

Probably Frank James headed to California. Frank later told his family that he had decided to locate his father's grave. Retracing his father's travels in the gold-mining area of Hangtown, Frank was unable to locate the grave of Robert James. He soon left for his uncle Drury James's ranch near Santa Margarita, California. Drury and

The stage stop built by Drury James at Paso Robles, ca. 1869-70.

his partner had built a stage stop and later a fine hotel close to a spring in the nearby town of Paso Robles. Drury's resort was a popular retreat, and Frank enjoyed the atmosphere of El Adobe de Paso Robles. Jesse later wrote that Frank found work at this time on the Labousu Ranch, owned by Drury's friend J. D. P. Thompson, in San Luis Obispo. Frank wrote to Jesse from California, asking Jesse to join him at Drury's ranch as the hot springs might be beneficial to Jesse's health.

Jesse had been recuperating west of Adairville, Kentucky, with his father's brother-in-law George Hite and his family. Jesse wrote back that Frank's idea sounded like a good one, but that he needed money to finance a trip to California. Jesse suggested that Frank come back east and meet him in Kentucky.

THE RUSSELLVILLE ROBBERY

(Top) *The George Hite house, west of Adairville, Kentucky. Hite was the husband of Nancy James, the aunt of Frank and Jesse.* (Bottom) *The Nimrod Long Banking Company, Russellville, Kentucky.*

Bursheba Younger, living with her son Jim in Harrisonville, decided after about a year that her family had been separated too long. She retrieved her girls from Pleasant Hill and sent for John and Bob in St. Clair County. Jim reported to his mother that the atmosphere would probably be more relaxed for the family in Jackson County since Cole was not around. Bursheba took Jim's suggestion that the family return to the house in Strother. Jim probably knew of Cole's involvement in the guerrilla robberies, and John and Bob were no doubt impressed by their eldest brother's daring deeds, but Jim would not discuss the matter with his mother or brothers. When Jim sent word to Cole in Louisiana that the family was currently together in Strother, Cole left his herds in the care of some friends and traveled north for a Missouri visit.

It is likely that Frank James knew of Cole's whereabouts and contacted him in Louisiana to suggest that Cole meet him and Jesse in Kentucky to discuss a business venture. Because Frank was en route from California, Cole was able to visit his mother and brothers in Strother and still get to Kentucky ahead of Frank.

Jesse James, Greenville, Illinois, 1869 at age 21.

Jesse had decided that a good robbery target would be the Nimrod Long Banking Company in Russellville, Kentucky, located just south of where he was staying with the Hites in Adairville. It is possible that Jesse had inside information about the Russellville institution. His father Robert had studied for the ministry at Georgetown College in Kentucky on a scholarship funded in part by the bank's former owner, George Norton, and partly by Nimrod Long himself. That the James brothers would choose as a target the bank of a man who had been so helpful to the James family is intriguing.

(Top) *George Shepard.*
(Bottom) *"Ol" Shepard.*

Cole and Jesse were on more or less friendly terms at this point, but from statements made by both men later it is likely they did not always agree on method and leadership. Cole had little respect for the younger brother of his closest friend; Cole considered Jesse egotistical and often poked fun at his schemes, though not when Frank was around. It is unlikely that Cole would have considered following Jesse's plans had Frank not agreed to participate; Cole went along because Frank was involved. Jesse assumed he was the leader of the operation since he was the one who came up with the initial ideas. Cole was used to leadership, but the group had been successful thus far and Cole saw no reason to cause dissension by offering too much criticism of Jesse's plans.

Soon after Frank joined Cole and Jesse in Kentucky, the three proceeded with the Russellville plan. A few other men were needed as accomplices. Some of what little evidence there is points to John Jarrette as a participant. Cole had been spending time with Jarrette and their mutual friends in Louisiana, and Jarrette had likely already expressed a desire to be included in future robbery schemes. Other ex-guerrilla friends of Cole and the Jameses who might have come along were Oliver and George Shepard. Oliver "Ol" Shepard was acquainted with both Jesse and Cole. His cousin George had served as a captain in Quantrill's unit. Another possibility is Arthur McCoy, a former captain in General Shelby's cavalry division. Jim White was later named as a suspect, but with no supporting evidence.

A man identifying himself as Thomas Colburn from Louisville visited the Nimrod Long Banking Company in the middle of March 1868, a week before the robbery.

Claiming that he was buying cattle and needed money quickly, Colburn asked Nimrod Long to exchange a bond. Long became suspicious and refused to make the cash transaction when Colburn offered him a discount on the bond. Several days later the same Thomas Colburn returned with another man and asked to change a one-hundred-dollar note. Long continued to be suspicious of Colburn and did not like the looks of his friend either. Long again refused to do business.

Then on the afternoon of March 20, 1868, while clerk Hugh Barclay and cashier T. H. Simmons were eating at the back of the bank, three men entered. One of them was "Thomas Colburn." Approaching the counter where Nimrod Long stood watching, Colburn threw down a fifty-dollar note and demanded to know whether this note was good enough for the bank president. Long replied that he thought the note might be counterfeit and refused to cash it.

The incensed Colburn drew his revolver and put it to Long's head. The other two bandits also drew their guns and demanded the funds of the bank. Long bolted from them and rushed toward the back door. He did not get far as a fourth man entered the bank's side door and ordered Long to halt. Long ignored the order and continued toward the back door. The robber at the side door warned him again, then fired a shot at Long that grazed the side of his head. Long went down for a moment but tried to get up again. This time the robber struck him in the head with his revolver. Still Nimrod Long would not give up the attempt to protect his bank. When his assailant turned to see what the others were doing, Long jumped up and this time managed to run out the back of the building.

Long ran to the front of the bank only to meet two other mounted strangers who began firing at him. The three men inside held Barclay and Simmons at gunpoint while they threw more than fourteen thousand dollars into a wheat sack. Quickly exiting the front door, the three then joined two waiting men and mounted their horses. A Russellville citizen, Matt Owens, was shot when he tried to shoot the robbers as they rode away.

The bandits traveled out of town on the Gallatin Road. They were pursued by a couple of townspeople, but were soon out of sight. It is possible they met a sixth companion just outside town. Based on detailed descriptions of five men given to the sheriff, it is probable that the first three men in the bank were Cole, Frank, and Jesse, with Jarrette as the one who came in the side door. Ol and George Shepard were probably waiting in the street while Arthur McCoy was on guard outside town in case extra

Turn-of-the-century magazine sketch of the Russellville bank robbery.

firepower should be needed. The gang was spotted in Bowling Green, Kentucky, soon after their flight. They headed west, toward Glasgow, then evidently split up and rode in separate groups toward Gainesville.

Detective D. T. "Yankee" Bligh of the Louisville police force as well as another Louisville officer, John Gallagher, were called in by Nimrod Long. Bligh asked questions around the area and decided that seven men had been involved: Oliver and George Shepard, as well as some other men from Missouri by the names of Frank and Jesse James, Cole Younger, John Jarrette, and a man named McCoy.

Acting on Bligh's detective work, the authorities arrested George Shepard in a store in Chaplin, Kentucky, within days. He was returned to Russellville where he was identified and eventually tried and sentenced to three years. Shepard's cousin Oliver was tracked to his father's home in Missouri. When he resisted arrest, Ol was shot and killed.

Oddly, Bligh and his posse did not actively pursue the remaining suspects after the death of Oliver Shepard. Frank did not deny being in Kentucky, although Jesse later contended that he was recuperating in Chaplin with relatives and that Frank had come out from California to look after him there. As Jesse wrote, "If Mr. Tom Marshall, Proprietor of the Hotel at Chaplin, Nelson Co., Ky., will say I was not at home March the 20th 1868 the day of the Russellville, Ky, Bank robbery, I will acknowledge I was in the Russellville robbery, and if D. B. Blackburn, ex Sheriff of San Luis Obispo co. Cal. will say Frank James was not at work on Mr. Thompson Ranch on that day in Cal. I will say Frank James is guilty."

Cole later wrote that his name had been confused with the man known as "Colburn." He did not deny having been involved, but focused instead on the innocence of Jim Younger in regard to the events in Russellville. Jim did not require such a defense, however; he had not been named as a suspect and was not in the vicinity of Russellville in March 1868.

Richard Hall, a blacksmith who had married Cole's older sister Isabelle, gave an interview on June 3, 1868, to the Kansas City *Commercial Advertiser* in which he claimed that the Russellville robbery had been the idea of John Jarrette and the Shepard boys. Hall's version was that Jarrette visited the Younger farm and persuaded Cole to go along. Hall also declared that the Russellville bank was the first robbery Cole committed. Hall evidently did not care much for John Jarrette, his relative by marriage. In his efforts to implicate Jarrette, Hall may not have realized how deeply he was also implicating Cole.

THE YOUNGERS MOVE TO TEXAS

The Younger family continued to try to adjust to postwar life in the town of Strother in Jackson County. Eventually, though, Anne Younger Jones and her husband Lycurgus came to feel they did not want to raise their family in Missouri where the aftereffects of the war continued to haunt them. They decided to join the dozens of other Missouri families relocating to Texas. When Anne encouraged her mother to come south, Bursheba agreed.

Isabelle Frances "Belle" Younger, born in 1834 in Jackson County, Missouri. She married Richard Hall in 1856. They had seven children: Richard, Nettie, Nora Lee, Minnie Gertrude, Harry, Frank, and Harden Thomas. Belle died in 1902, soon after the return of her brother Cole to Missouri. She is buried in Lee's Summit.

It may be that Bursheba was coping with yet another postwar persecution of the family around this time. Members of their family have reported that John Jarrette and his wife, Josie, were victims of an ambush sometime in 1867 or 1868. According to the story, the Jarrette home was set on fire while the Jarrettes and their two young children were inside. Cole and Jim Younger were able to rescue the children, Margaret and Jeptha, but John and Josie died in the flames. The children were then sent to live

Laura Helen Younger, born January 1, 1832, in Jackson County, Missouri. She married William H. Kelley, a farmer and mule driver. The Kelleys raised three children: Mary, who was Kelley's daughter by a previous marriage, Coleman, and Ellen. By 1870 the couple had separated. Laura died December 15, 1924. She is buried in Amoret, Missouri.

Martha Anne "Anne" Younger, born January 9, 1835, in Jackson County, Missouri. She married Lycurgus A. "Curg" Jones, a Missouri farmer, on October 5, 1852. When the family moved to Denison, Texas, Curg Jones owned and operated a fine furniture store. Anne and Curg had six children: Mary, Harry, Alexis, Coleman, Charles, and Lena. Anne died in 1918 and is buried in Denison, Texas.

Mary Josephine "Josie" Younger, born in 1840 in Jackson County, Missouri. She married John Jarrette on May 8, 1860.

Emilly J. "Emma" Younger with daughters Lou, Virgie, and Retta. Emma was born in 1852 in Jackson County, Missouri. She married Kitt Porter Rose in 1869. Emma and Kitt had seven children: Henrietta, Ada, Kitt Jr., Coleman, Louise, Virginia, and Herbert. Kitt became the supervisor of the Jackson County Poor Farm, built on land donated to the county by Henry Younger. Emma served there as her husband's assistant. She died in the early 1900s.

with the Jones family. There are, however, other accounts of the end of John Jarrette. Guerrilla Jim Cummins claimed many years later that Jarrette had become the owner of a sheep ranch in Arizona after the war and that Jarrette finally died in the "Frisco Mountains" of California in 1891. Cummins also stated that Jarrette's daughter turned state's evidence against him after Cummins was arrested for a stage robbery. The Jarrette family stands by the word of Margaret Jarrette, who had vivid memories of her parents dying in the fire.

In any event, Bursheba Younger, at age fifty-two, decided to leave the state where she had experienced a decade of instability and trauma. She and her boys would start anew in Texas. Her daughter Emilly remained behind to marry former Confederate soldier Kitt Rose. Shortly after the family decision was made, Cole arrived with more than enough money to finance the move.

Dallas County was selected as the Younger family's destination. The nearby towns of Scyene and Dallas were booming, and Jim thought the area offered many possibilities for the Younger family to rebuild some of their lost wealth. Many former guerrillas and ex-Confederates had relocated nearby. Cole had visited with these settlers often on his cattle drives through Texas and felt that his family could enjoy the company of fellow Missourians while working together in a large cattle-ranching venture.

Cole was counting on help from Jim, John, and Bob. In fact, the Younger family's legitimate cattle business began to prosper. Soon after the family relocated in the fall of 1868, however, a couple of problems developed. Jim found that he enjoyed working with the horses that were necessary for cattle drives, but he later claimed that Bob Younger, now aged fifteen, hated the labor and grime of ranching, preferring a farm life instead. Bob did his fair share of cowboy chores and was able to socialize with young people near his own age, but he was waiting for when he could leave the cattle business and strike out on his own.

John Younger, now sixteen, refused altogether to be a part of the ranch. He visited Dallas soon after his arrival and found employment in a dry goods store. There he worked regular hours as a clerk and stockboy and became a regular in the Dallas night spots as well. He had always been able to make friends easily and was having a great time. This did not sit well with his oldest brother, but apparently others in the family felt that John had earned the right to go his own way after enduring the trials of the war.

Soon the Youngers were living better in Texas than they had for almost ten years.

Bob Younger at about sixteen.

Jim began to allow himself a life that extended beyond the boundaries of caring for the family. The group began to attend church regularly; Jim and Bob sang in the choir. Cole even sang with the choir when he was home. Bob began to see the daughter of the church's minister, and soon the two young people were in love. John spent time with a number of young women he met in Scyene and Dallas.

Among the Missouri pioneers now in Texas was the family of John Shirley. Before the outbreak of the war Shirley had owned a tavern and a livery in Carthage. His son Bud fought in Quantrill's band, and guerrillas often exchanged information or sought solace at Shirley's establishment. His young daughter, Myra Maibelle, became fascinated by the guerrillas and would often serve as a spy or carry messages to men in the bush. Cole Younger with his comrades visited the Shirley place several times during the war. In 1864, after Bud Shirley died during a skirmish with federal troops, John Shirley moved his family to Texas and opened a tavern and inn in Dallas County. Shirley's inn became a place of welcome for guerrillas during their winter restovers and a place ex-guerrillas continued to visit after the war.

Cole had been friendly with Bud Shirley and his brothers and also enjoyed their father's company. Myra Maibelle looked forward to Cole's periodic visits and told her family she was in love with him. Cole later wrote that he never returned Myra Maibelle's interest and had no memory of even meeting her until after she had married guerrilla comrade Jim Reed and was expecting their first child. Nevertheless, Myra Maibelle and her daughter Pearl would become part of Cole Younger's legend, if not his life. Myra Maibelle, better known by her outlaw name of Belle Starr, told her friends after the death of her husband that Pearl's father was none other than Cole Younger.

(Left) *Myra Maibelle Shirley, later known as "Belle Starr."*
(Right) *Pearl Reed, daughter of Belle Starr. Pearl Reed's descendants believe that Jim Reed, Belle's husband at the time of Pearl's birth, was the girl's father.*

WANTED: JESSE AND FRANK JAMES

Joe Wood, Jesse's physician in Kansas City, had advised rest and relaxation for the young man. Now that the spoils of the Russellville robbery provided Jesse with the money for recreation, he traveled east and entertained himself in style. Evidently he had agreed to meet Frank back in Paso Robles after Jesse took a look at New York City. Within a week of his arrival in New York, Jesse boarded a ship to Panama, then booked passage immediately on a ship bound for San Francisco.

The new Hotel Paso de Robles. The original stage stop is in front of the hotel.

Although Frank had been unable to locate their father's grave, Jesse insisted on making another search. Frank joined him, but they were not able to find the unmarked grave of Robert James. The brothers then descended to Paso Robles, where they vacationed at their uncle Drury James's hotel and mineral spa.

It was in the fall of 1869 that the James boys returned from California to their home in Missouri. Jesse's travels must have been expensive; by this date it is likely that he and Frank both were short of cash. At this time Cole Younger was still in the cattle business in Texas. Cole's side trips to Louisiana and Florida kept him busy, and he may not have been aware that the Jameses had returned to the Midwest.

On December 7, 1869, a bank in the sleepy little town of Gallatin, Missouri, two counties north of Clay County, was robbed by two men. One man entered the Daviess County Savings Association and asked cashier John Sheets to cash a one-hundred-dollar bill. A second man entered the bank soon after that and offered to buy the bill himself.

Accounts vary about what happened next. Almost immediately the unarmed John Sheets was shot twice, in the chest and head. A customer in the bank, a lawyer named William A. McDowell, was threatened by the bandits and then shot in the arm as he fled through the door. The robbers quickly scooped out seven hundred dollars from the cashier's drawer. Shots were fired at the two men as they left the bank and tried to mount their tethered horses. When one of the horses bolted, its rider had to scramble up on the back of the second man's horse. Together they galloped out of town.

Looking for a second horse so they could travel faster, the robbers came upon a man on horseback, Daniel Smoot. Smoot gave up his horse without hesitation when the outlaws trained their guns on him. The two then headed south in the direction of Kidder, Missouri, about twenty-five miles from Kearney. It is known that the robbers stopped to ask directions from a Reverend Helm just outside of Kidder, then rode east, away from Clay County in the direction of Honey Creek, Hamilton, and Breckinridge. There the trail ended. The Gallatin robbers were swallowed up by the back roads and farmlands.

Someone who saw the bandits leave the bank claimed that he recognized one of the tethered horses as belonging to "a James of Clay County" and that the two men were probably the James brothers. A group that included the state of Missouri, the Daviess County Savings Association, prominent citizens of Gallatin, and John Sheets's widow immediately offered a reward of three thousand dollars. Complete with descriptions, the names of Jesse and Frank James were given out as suspects for the first time.

It is almost certain that cashier John Sheets was murdered for reasons having to do with something other than being an employee of the bank. The lawyer McDowell claimed that the two bandits whispered together soon after the second one entered the bank and that one told the other that the man behind the counter was S. P. Cox, the man responsible for the death of "Bloody Bill" Anderson during the war. Another, somewhat different report stated that the men knew who Sheets was, but accused Sheets of being with Cox when Anderson was killed. Sheets did look something like S. P. Cox, and Cox was known to be living in Gallatin at the time of the robbery. Sheets had served in the Union Army as a captain and may have somehow been involved in the skirmish that took the life of Bill Anderson. In any event, it is likely that the robbers shot John Sheets in retribution for Anderson's death.

Two Gallatin men soon learned who the suspects were and enlisted the help of Deputy Sheriff John S. Thomason and his son Oscar. The small posse rode to the James-Samuel farm outside Kearney. As Thomason approached the farmhouse door on foot, a small boy ran past him and threw open the barn doors. Frank and Jesse James burst out of the barn on horseback and rode off into the fields. Thomason ran to remount and the posse chased the James boys across the farm. Frank and Jesse exchanged fire with their pursuers and maneuvered their horses around obstacles on their familiar acreage. When the posse approached one of the farm fences that the

Jameses' horses had cleared, only Thomason's horse was able to take the jump. Thomason continued to race after the brothers while the rest of the posse had to stop to dismantle the top rails of the fence.

In close pursuit now, Thomason jumped down from his horse to shoot more accurately. His horse bolted toward the horses of Frank and Jesse, and one of the outlaws shot the horse through the neck to prevent the horse from returning to Thomason. This effectively ended the chase. Thomason, however, was not willing to give up. He returned to the James-Samuel farmhouse, where he procured a horse and continued to Centerville, about five miles away to the southeast. As it turned out, Thomason was mistaken about the direction the outlaws had gone. Liberty mayor F. L. Long later reported that friends of the James boys told him that the brothers returned to their farm shortly after Thomason rode off for Centerville. When Thomason finally returned to Liberty empty-handed, he was surprised by the news that he had been killed in the pursuit.

What with the number of robberies in various Missouri counties in the past several years, Missouri Governor Joseph McClurg decided to involve the state agencies more directly. Newspaper accounts mentioned that the James brothers had a guerrilla background and should be considered desperate men. McClurg now notified the counties surrounding Clay that they should organize posses and alert their militia units that they might be called upon for assistance. These efforts would prove to be in vain; Frank and Jesse had disappeared from the area.

The James boys continued to be the object of media attention even six months later. Jesse had decided to go public with his thoughts on the Gallatin robbery and subsequent gun battle with Deputy Sheriff Thomason. He enlisted the help of General Shelby's former adjutant, John Newman Edwards. Edwards was one of the founders of the Kansas City *Times* and served as editor. In June 1870, through Edwards's paper, Jesse wrote an open letter to Governor McClurg. He denied all charges that he and his brother had been involved in the Gallatin holdup. Jesse asserted it was impossible for him to surrender because he would be mobbed and hanged without benefit of trial, as other former guerrillas had been. Many witnesses, he claimed, would swear he had been nowhere near the robbery site on December 7. Jesse wrote, "The authorities of Gallatin say the reason that led them to suspect me, was that the mare left at Gallatin, by the robbers, was identified as belonging to me; that is false. I can prove that I sold the mare previous to the robbery."

Jesse did not deny having a rough encounter with Deputy Sheriff Thomason. He justified it by stating, "I do not think that I violated the law when I fought Thomason, as his posse refused to tell me who they were." He acknowledged being acquainted with Oscar Thomason, but said that because Oscar's face had been covered Jesse had failed to recognize him. With that, he dismissed the gun battle. Jesse concluded by repeating that he was completely innocent of the Gallatin robbery and that he would willingly surrender if he were assured he could receive a just trial.

This letter was the first of many Jesse sent to the press and the first of many efforts undertaken by editor Edwards on behalf of the James brothers. Edwards had already proven himself a great friend to other Confederate guerrillas. He had become friendly with men under Quantrill, Todd, and Anderson, and he was familiar with their exploits in Missouri and their winter rest spots in the Texas environs. Edwards had been at General Shelby's side when Shelby refused to surrender at the close of the war and instead took a group of his men to Mexico to support Emperor Maximilian. Edwards published *Shelby and His Men* in 1867 to describe and explain their experiences. Edwards had briefly worked as a reporter for the St. Louis *Missouri Republican* after the war, but soon joined with two of his friends to establish the Kansas City *Times*. In its pages Edwards would defend what he considered the necessity of the Confederate cause in a flowery prose that touted the warriors of the guerrilla movement as innocents who turned to lawlessness only when forced to protect their homeland. It is likely that when Jesse approached Edwards with the idea of an alibi letter to the governor, Edwards not only agreed but actually helped Jesse compose the statement.

John Newman Edwards, one of the country's most famous newspapermen, born January 4, 1839, in Front Royal, Virginia. He moved to Missouri in the mid-1850s. Edwards began as a printer and reporter for the Lexington Expositor, *where he was appointed editor. While at the* Expositor *Edwards became a good friend of Joseph Shelby. Edwards joined the Confederate Army in 1862. He later held editorial positions at the Kansas City* Times, *St. Louis* Dispatch, Sedalia *Daily Democrat, Sedalia* Dispatch, *and St. Joseph* Gazette. *He died in Jefferson City, Missouri, in 1889.*

A second letter from Jesse appeared in the *Times* a week later, again addressed to McClurg and again professing complete innocence. Soon after, the *Times* published several affidavits from Clay County citizens who corroborated Jesse's claims. John S. Groom and James M. Gow declared they had known Jesse James since childhood and that he had been in their stores in Kearney the day before the robbery. Alfred R. McGinnis stated that he had seen Jesse the day after the robbery at the home of a woman named Fox. Jesse's family signed statements swearing that Jesse had been at home on the day of the robbery and that the mare identified as his had been sold the previous Sunday for five hundred dollars to a man from Topeka, Kansas. There was no mention of Frank James in the letters or affidavits, but his actions were not considered separate from Jesse's.

The James brothers would remain wanted men in Missouri for many years, but their activities hardly changed. They moved freely about the state and elsewhere thanks to the support of their widely distributed family, friends, and admiring former Confederates.

TEXAS TO MISSOURI AND TEXAS TO MISSOURI AGAIN

Jim Younger was beginning to settle into his new life in Texas. He took a job as census taker for Dallas County, gathering information for the 1870 census. Jim later wrote that he enjoyed meeting people in the area so much that Cole decided it was a job he too would like to have. Soon both of them were being paid for chatting with people throughout the county. Meanwhile, John Younger was cheerfully occupied by day at the dry goods store and by night at the entertainment spots in Dallas. Bob, the youngest brother, still disliked the dust and labor of being a cowboy, but he took solace in his new friends and his girlfriend. Although it is known that Bob's girlfriend was the daughter of a local Sherman minister, her name has never surfaced.

The Youngers' mother Bursheba was not doing well in Texas. The horror of the war and her husband's murder had taken a permanent toll, and her health was rapidly declining. The tasks of cooking and cleaning fell mostly on her youngest daughter, Retta. Despite all her children's efforts, though, Bursheba continued to grieve for her past life with Henry in Missouri. When she fell deeper into depression, the family decided their mother should return to Missouri; there she would be able to revisit the green fields of her married life and have the company of her older daughters and their families.

Jim, Bob, John, and Retta prepared to return to Missouri in the spring of 1870. All the children knew that Bursheba, now aged fifty-three, would not live long. Jim did not look forward to leaving Texas but would do anything for the comfort of his mother. He decided to settle the family into a new home there, then return to Dallas County at his earliest opportunity. Bob, too, told his girlfriend he would be back. Cole decided not to go: he claimed that because he had never surrendered after the war, he was subject to arrest if he ever touched foot in Missouri again. Although that had not stopped him in the past, he evidently did not want to actually live there. So in the company of the ever-faithful Suze, most of the family returned to their home state.

A small posse showed up looking for Cole and Jim almost immediately after the Youngers arrived in Jackson County. John told the posse Cole was not there and that they had no business with Jim Younger since Jim had served time in the Alton Penitentiary for his Confederate service and was now a free man. The posse still wanted to talk to Jim and told the family they would be back. When Jim returned that day and was told about the posse, he decided to go back to Texas at once so as not to cause further trouble for the family.

The posse did return, soon after Jim left. They refused to believe that Jim was not in the area. The posse leader reasoned that Cole was probably somewhere around, too, since so many of the family were there. Bursheba and the boys insisted they were mistaken, but the posse pulled John outside to question him further. Bob Younger, trying to follow his brother, was struck unconscious. Bursheba ran to her youngest son while John was wrestled to the ground and a noose placed around his neck.

When Bob regained consciousness he ran again to his brother's aid, only to be knocked down once more and held to the ground while John was taken to the barn. There John was repeatedly hanged from the rafters, then lowered and ordered to give up his brothers. The young man was hoisted four times until he eventually passed out. The posse had to leave empty-handed, but before they left the leader warned the family that if Cole Younger were indeed in the area, he would be found and killed. John was taken in the house and placed on a bed to recover. Bursheba then collapsed and lay helpless in a bed beside her son. She died a few weeks later, on June 6, 1870. It was her fifty-fourth birthday. Bursheba was buried in her daughter Laura Hall's family plot in the Lee's Summit Cemetery.

After their mother's death, John and Bob reunited with Jim when Jim returned to St. Clair County to decide with his brothers where the family should live. The deci-

(Top) *Jim Younger in Texas, ca. 1870.*
(Bottom) *Bursheba Fristoe Younger, ca. 1866–70.*

sion was made that they all should go back to the haven of Texas. Retta joined their sister Anne in Denison, Texas, while the boys set up a home for themselves in nearby Sherman.

Cole continued to travel throughout the South with his cattle herds. Under his instruction, Jim bought some acreage in Grayson County, Texas, to be used as a place to allow their cattle to graze. Other land that Cole purchased under an alias brought in an income for the family when it was leased to tenant ranchers. For a while life was peaceful for the Youngers.

Within months of the family's return to Texas, Cole became embroiled in a gunfight in Louisiana having to do with a friend's involvement in a rigged horse race. News of this reached the residents of Sherman along with rumors that Cole Younger may have been involved in the robbery in Russellville, Kentucky, a couple of years before.

This new light on Cole Younger came as a shock to

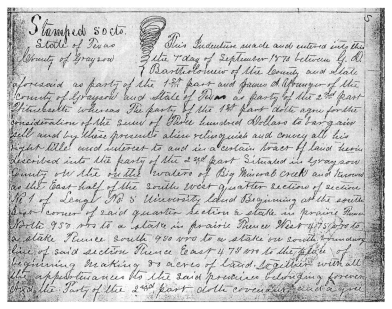

Land grant issued for acreage in Texas purchased by Jim Younger.

Bob's girlfriend. She broke off their informal engagement without allowing Bob an opportunity to explain. Later Cole was able to convince the young woman's preacher father that Cole had not been involved in Russellville by offering to produce receipts from a business trip he said he was on at the time. The daughter remained unconvinced. She was used to hearing Bob complain about his older brother, and she felt that Cole was probably guilty. She refused to have anything more to do with Bob Younger.

Furious at the way his older brother's illegal activities haunted his new life, Bob Younger left Sherman and went to stay for a while with his sister in Denison. Jim later claimed that while he was sympathetic, he knew there was little that could be done. Jim said that John Younger had felt little optimism about Bob's relationship in the first place because of the Youngers' past and because he knew what activities Cole was

currently engaged in. For his part, Cole considered that he had made an effort on Bob's behalf and that Bob was better off without the girl if she would not trust him.

John continued working at the dry goods store and having the good times he felt he had been robbed of as a boy. He was surprised when Jim suggested one day that John and Bob return with Jim to St. Clair County. Jim later wrote that he viewed it as an opportunity to spend time in each other's company again in a place where he knew John and Bob had strong, positive memories. Bob jumped at the idea. John, deciding he was bored with clerking, welcomed the chance to relax for a while.

Telling Cole they would return, Jim, John, and Bob Younger once again left Texas, arriving in St. Clair County in the fall of 1870. Bob was soon enjoying the tranquility of the area. He lazed atop the old lookout and probably daydreamed of possibilities that awaited him. John took up where he had left off in Dallas by frequenting entertainment spots at the local resort at Monagaw Springs. There he met people from all over the country. Jim took long walks in the country and often joined Bob on the bluffs above the Osage River.

(Top) *Cole Younger (l) with John Younger (r), ca. 1871–73.* (Bottom) *Cora McNeill. Cora remained close to her former sweetheart Jim Younger throughout his later incarceration. She married Minnesota legislator C. P. Deming. After Deming's death Cora married George M. Bennett. Both men had been involved with the Younger parole drive.*

One day, while visiting in nearby Osceola, Jim was introduced to Cora McNeill, the daughter of a prominent local physician. Cora was a lovely young woman who soon discovered she enjoyed the company of Jim Younger above all others. The Younger brothers were delighted that Jim, who had been frustrated and unhappy for a long time, had found happiness with someone who could appreciate him. Jim later recounted that he wasted no time asking Cora to marry him, but Cora felt the proposal was premature. She told Jim that she loved him but felt it best that they wait a while. Anxious to establish a stable, comfortable relationship and a life of his own, Jim reluctantly agreed.

JOHN YOUNGER IN TROUBLE

Deciding he was bored with the quiet life he was living in Missouri, John Younger made plans to return to the excitement offered in Dallas. The twenty-year-old renewed his employment at the dry goods store in the winter of 1870–71. With no one to supervise him, John then took up with some of the rowdier personalities, men whom Cole and Jim had advised him against. One of these, Tom McDaniels, the brother of one of Cole's guerrilla comrades, was in Texas under the alias of "Tom Porter."

Trouble developed on the night of January 15, 1871—coincidentally the date of Cole's and Jim's birthdays—when John was passing the time with McDaniels and some other acquaintances in a saloon in Scyene. John's companions began urging him, for a prank, to shoot the pipe out of the mouth of a slow-witted man named Russell who hung around the saloon doing odd jobs. John did fire a shot or two, but even in his drunken state he realized he was frightening the man, and he stopped. His friends were disappointed and suggested as another joke that Russell swear out a warrant for John's arrest on the charge of attempted murder. Russell went to the office of Sheriff Jeremiah Brown and did just that.

Brown assigned the task of arresting John Younger to Deputy Charles H. Nichols. Brown knew that John was a friend of Nichols from Missouri. He also knew that John Younger could be rowdy but probably had not intended to harm Russell. Russell, though, had a right to ask for John's arrest for his foolish prank. The next morning

Main Street, Dallas, ca. 1871-73.

Deputy Nichols and his friend James McMahon went looking for John Younger. They found him eating breakfast at the hotel. Told he was under arrest, John asked if he could finish his meal before turning himself in. Nichols, knowing John Younger was reliable, agreed and told John to report to him at the dry goods store.

What happened next has been the subject of speculation and folklore. The most likely version seems to be that when John and his drinking buddy McDaniels left the hotel together, John was startled to see that a guard had been placed on his horse. Angry that Nichols had not taken him at his word, John entered the dry goods store with McDaniels and demanded to know why Nichols had seen fit to place the guard. Becoming incensed, John shouted at Nichols that he was no friend. James McMahon drew his revolver at John's angry words. An enraged John Younger drew his gun as well, and the two exchanged fire. As McMahon went down, Nichols shot John in the arm. Now McDaniels entered the fray by drawing his gun. Either John Younger or Tom McDaniels shot Nichols, then the two ran from the store. They mounted Nichols's horse and together rode as fast as they could out of Scyene.

Charles Nichols died from his wounds four days later. He was the first lawman to be killed in Dallas County. Warrants were issued at once for the arrest of John Younger and the man known as Tom Porter. By the time of Nichols's death John was back in St. Clair County to ask the advice of his brothers. Jim suggested that John not frequent the resort spa or any places where he was known.

John decided to look for a job in Little Rock, Arkansas. Soon after he found employment in a dry goods store there, however, John discovered that the owner had been a friend of his father, Henry. Jim later wrote that John feared his presence might prove a danger to his father's friend, so John returned to Missouri to take his chances.

CLELL MILLER JOINS THE JAMES-YOUNGER GANG

While their descriptions had appeared in Missouri newspapers in 1870, the James brothers—Frank aged twenty-seven and Jesse aged twenty-three—spent their time traveling, visiting family and friends, keeping out of trouble, and avoiding the law. It was while Jesse was visiting his Kentucky cousins, the Hite family, in 1870 that a doctor was called to the Hite house to care for him. Folklore has it that Jesse felt so depressed and angered by his sister Susie's decision to marry Allen Parmer that Jesse attempted suicide. Considering that Parmer was a former guerrilla and that Jesse later visited

Susan and her husband several times, the story lacks credibility. Jesse may not have been pleased with his sister's choice of an ex-guerrilla since many of them were dangerously protesting their treatment after the war in ways similar to what Jesse and Frank were doing. There is no evidence, however, that Jesse and Parmer did not get along.

It is more likely that Jesse had to be treated for an accidental overdose of pain medication. Jesse suffered from his chest wounds throughout his life and apparently turned often to laudanum for pain relief. Laudanum, a powerfully addictive opium derivative, was widely prescribed at the time. Jesse's frequent use of this opiate might also partly explain his sometimes poor judgment, his suspiciousness, and his impulsive behavior later on.

One of Jesse's new associates at this time was Clell Miller. Clelland D. Miller had been born not far from the James farm, in Holt, Missouri, on January 9, 1850. At the age of fourteen he joined "Bloody Bill" Anderson's guerrilla outfit, the same organization that teenager Jesse James had joined. Just three days later, Clell was captured by Union soldiers during the encounter that took the life of Bill Anderson. For the next six months Clell was detained in the Jefferson Barracks in St. Louis before being released at the close of the war to return to Clay County. No doubt frustrated that he had not been able to make much contribution to the Confederate cause, Clell Miller was probably enthusiastic about joining Jesse, Frank, and Cole to protest the current Missouri regime.

On the night of June 2, 1871, young Miles Alcorn was interested in the four men spending the night in his father's barn in southern Iowa. He admired their fine horses and sophisticated dress. One of the men

(Top) *Clell and Ed Miller's parents, Moses and Emaline Miller.* (Bottom) *Clell Miller, born January 9, 1850. He died September 7, 1876, and is buried in Holt, Missouri.*

made a present of a silk handkerchief to Miles when they left the next morning. The men then proceeded to the town of Corydon, Iowa, whose citizens were excited by the visit that day of noted orator Henry Clay Dean. The Methodist Church was hosting Dean's visit in conjunction with a proposal to install a railroad to serve the area. While Dean waxed poetic before a large audience in the church, the four strangers entered the Ocobock Brothers' Bank. They found the cashier alone. Brandishing their revolvers, the bandits informed the teller that he was about to be robbed. Tying him up, the outlaws then removed a sum estimated between six and ten thousand dollars.

Ocobock Brothers' Bank, Corydon, Iowa.

The bandits could have ridden out of town without attracting attention. Instead it appears that Jesse, with his sense of humor and theatrical daring, suggested the four pay a visit to the town meeting. Accordingly, they stepped into the church and one of the bandits, likely Jesse, interrupted Henry Clay Dean's speech to inform the townsfolk that their bank had been robbed. Some members of the crowd grew irritated, thinking the men had appeared as part of a hoax to disrupt the meeting. The strangers were told to leave. The Gang smiled and did as they were told. Then someone at the meeting decided that perhaps the bank should be checked after all. The cashier was found bound and gagged and the robbers long gone.

A Corydon posse was organized. The bandits' trail became easier to follow after Tom Stevens, a farmer living halfway between Corydon and the Missouri border, reported to the sheriff's posse that someone had exchanged a heated horse for a horse Stevens had left tied to a hayrack near his road. Next, a farmer near Woodland, Iowa, described finding a cache of pennies under a tree in his grove; this might have been where the spoils from the bank had been divided. With the trail pointing to Missouri, it was not long before the now-familiar names of Jesse and Frank James were mentioned. Someone else along the trail suggested the other two men might have been guerrilla captain Cole Younger and a Clay County fellow named Clell Miller.

The earlier involvement of the Missouri governor in the search for the Gallatin robbers had not gone unnoticed by the Pinkerton Detective Agency in Chicago. William A. Pinkerton later claimed that his services were solicited by Corydon, Iowa, but the town's small size and resources suggest that Pinkerton himself might have offered help in tracking down the robbers. Robert Pinkerton was sent to Corydon, where he followed the bandits' trail into Missouri. Another Pinkerton detective by the name of Westphall eventually arrested Clell Miller on suspicion of robbery. Miller was brought to trial in Wayne County, Iowa, but was released when he was able to produce several witnesses to testify that he had been nowhere near the town of Corydon on the day the bank was robbed. Soon another letter from Jesse appeared in the Kansas City *Times* in which Jesse claimed he had nothing to do with any robbery in Iowa or anywhere else.

JOHN, BOB, AND JIM GET INVOLVED

Still eluding the arrest warrant for Charles Nichols's death in Dallas, John Younger probably learned of the Corydon robbery while visiting his sisters in Kansas City. No doubt worrying that the incident would bring additional lawmen into the area, he traveled down to St. Clair County a few days later.

John's uncle, Jeff Younger, had recently married a woman named Emma Barmour, and the new couple was planning to relocate to California. Jeff suggested that John accompany him to Los Angeles, where Jeff felt certain John could find employment in the hardware and saddle shop of his friend, Philip Ruiz. John readily agreed.

In the past, Cole had suggested once or twice that John and Jim join him and the James boys in one of their robberies. Jim later wrote that he was appalled at the idea and refused to discuss it further. John found the notion interesting but thought the right time had not yet presented itself. As for Bob, Cole had never made such a proposition to him. Bob was the baby of the family and Cole probably felt their mother would have been furious if he were to involve the boy in his illegal activities.

It was Cole, in fact, who decided to send Bob to the College of William and Mary to provide Bob with the education the others had been denied. Bob thought the idea ridiculous since his formal education had ended abruptly years ago, but Cole insisted, informing his brother that he would personally escort him to Virginia before Cole went on to Florida. Soon after Cole dropped him off at the college, Bob headed to the Carolinas. Cole had neglected to enroll Bob at the school

Bob Younger.

since Cole assumed that if Bob were to show up with a bundle of money he would be admitted. Bob figured out that was unlikely, so Bob now had Cole's money and a lot of time on his hands. He had never done extensive traveling or spent much time on his own. He felt the time had come to do some exploring.

Bob soon longed for the company of someone familiar and decided to locate Cole in Florida. When the brothers were reunited, Bob invented a sad story about how he had been ostracized at the college because of his association with Cole and the Missouri guerrilla war. Bob said he had no option but to leave in order to save face. To ease his little brother's humiliation at the hands of strangers, Cole suggested that Bob accompany him on his own travels in the cattle business for a while.

The docks of New Orleans at the time of Bob Younger's employment there.

Bob later told Jim that as he spent time alone with Cole for the first time in many years, he began to chafe under the controlling and self-serving nature of his oldest brother; he grew tired of Cole's bragging about his wartime exploits. In the meantime, Bob had been asked by a boyhood friend from Missouri to join him in New Orleans to work among the ranks of the Gulf Shipping firm on the docks of the Mississippi. Bob Younger, aged eighteen by October of 1871, decided to strike out on his own again. He spent the next year in New Orleans loading seabound ships and becoming more his own man.

Having disengaged himself from the responsibility of his youngest brother, Cole headed back to Missouri to visit Frank James. Clell Miller had not yet been arrested, so there was nothing hanging over the quartet's heads other than rumor and innuendo. They were all used to being careful about their movements and thought their new life more than worth the risks involved in robbery. The members of the Gang had learned to enjoy such luxuries as fine clothes, beautiful horses, and dining in hotel restaurants in the larger cities they visited. They traveled freely whenever they felt the urge to explore and often rode first class on the very trains they would later rob. Jesse enjoyed bestowing small, special gifts on his family, but his sister Sallie recalled years later to Jesse's son that she never remembered receiving a gift from Frank.

It is probable that Cole, Frank, Jesse, and Clell made the next bold move in the growing number of robberies. On April 29, 1872, four men entered the picturesque town of Columbia, Kentucky. Two of the men sauntered into the Bank of Columbia while their two companions stood guard on horses outside. At the sight of the strangers, cashier R. A. C. Martin became alert. Bank robberies in Kentucky and Missouri during the past few years had garnered a lot of publicity. When Martin thought he saw one of them reach for a gun, he did not wait for the men to state their business. He shouted, "Bank robbers!"—and was immediately shot dead.

There were three other customers in the bank at the time. Two of them jumped through a window. The third ran out the door, pushing his way past another robber who was entering the bank after hearing the gunfire. The first two bandits grabbed six hundred dollars from the cashier's drawer, ran into the street, and rode away from Columbia with their companions before anyone was able to confront them.

A posse was quickly called together and the pursuit began. The four men drove their horses hard away from the bank, then tricked the posse by circling back around the town. After the posse failed, Detective D. T. Bligh of Louisville, who had pursued the Nimrod Long Bank robbers at Russellville, Kentucky, four years before, was again called in to investigate. Bligh took reports from various people in Columbia who had observed the four men posing as cattle buyers in the area. Given the descriptions, Bligh determined that three of the robbers must have been Jesse and Frank James and Cole Younger.

Soon information about the suspected outlaws began to appear in the papers. A report in the St. Louis *Missouri Republican* stated that a man matching the description of Frank James had stayed at the home of a well-respected farmer in the Columbia area the night before the robbery. According to the story, Frank had borrowed a copy of *Pilgrim's Progress* from the farmer's mother and had returned it, almost completely read, the following morning. The old woman believed that a man with such breeding and such interest in literature could not possibly be a bank robber. Cole later wrote that he and his cattle herd had been in Neosho Falls, Kansas, at the time of the robbery. In another letter to the *Missouri Republican* Jesse accused detective

An etching of the Bank of Columbia robbery.

Bligh of being a "Sherman bummer"—that is, someone who supported W. T. Sherman and condoned his sometimes brutal actions during the war—who had conspired to frame the James and Youngers of such crimes because they were known to be staunch Confederates. Jesse declared, "I am in constant communication with Governor Hardin, Sheriff Groom, of Clay Co., Mo., and several other honorable county and state officials, and there are hundreds of persons in Missouri who will swear that I have not been in Kentucky."

Cole Younger, ca. 1869–72.

John Younger in the meantime had grown restless in southern California. Writing to Jim in Missouri, he said he was homesick and claimed that Philip Ruiz was so pleased with his work that Ruiz had offered him a partnership in the saddle business. John invited Jim to join him in California for a while. Never one to deny the needs of his family, Jim arrived in Los Angeles to find John living at the impressive Pico House. He also found John in a quandary. Philip Ruiz was suggesting that John marry Ruiz's daughter. John needed help to extract himself from a sticky situation without offending the man who had been so good to him.

During their discussions, Jim revealed to John his long-time dream of raising and training cavalry mounts for the government on a ranch he wanted to set up near Dallas. John humored his brother, and Jim later claimed that John said the idea sounded good and perhaps all four brothers could make it a reality. Jim got caught up in the fantasy and, apparently forgetting that John could not safely return to Texas as he was a wanted man there, wrote about their plans to Cole. Cole wrote back that Jim and John should meet him in St. Clair County to discuss the future. Jim then rode to the San Gabriel Valley to buy horses from Carlos Ruiz for the trip back to Missouri. He and John left Los Angeles after informing a disappointed Philip Ruiz of their plans.

The two headed north up El Camino Real and reached San Francisco in twelve days. There they boarded a train bound for the Black Hills of the Dakotas and eventually found their way to St. Clair County. Joining Cole in Monagaw Springs, the three enjoyed a brief reunion. Jim was disappointed when his plan for the horse ranch was hardly discussed. Cole and John went off to visit their sisters in the Kansas City-

Independence area while Jim stayed in St. Clair near Cora McNeill. The two lovers were glad to be reunited, but evidently felt they could not make permanent plans yet for the future.

An unusual event took place while the Youngers visited Kansas City and while the James brothers were probably visiting their own family in nearby Clay County. On September 26, 1872, the annual Kansas City Exposition was in full swing at the fairground when three men rode up to the fair's ticket office. In view of the crowd waiting in the ticket line, one of the men jumped off his horse and grabbed the money box from cashier Benjamin F. Wallace. After stuffing the money into a bag secured to his waist, the robber threw the box on the ground and turned to remount. Wallace had run out of the booth and now scuffled with the robber, but then backed away at the sight of a gun drawn by one of the other men who waited on horseback. For reasons that are unclear, a shot was fired at Wallace. The bullet struck the leg of a little girl standing in line with her mother. In the resulting confusion the three men disappeared. Their spoils amounted to a mere $978.

Pico House, Los Angeles, California, 1872.

Several years later, an article published in the *Neosho Times* in Missouri claimed that the man who grabbed the money box declared that he was Jesse James. The Kansas City fair robbery has been ascribed many times, then, to the James-Younger Gang. It seems unlikely, though, that the three bandits included a James or a Younger brother. Any of them might have been easily recognized by friends or family in so public a place in Kansas City. The style of the robbery was not that of others committed by the James-Younger Gang. Robbery had become casual, almost a way of life to Cole, Jesse, and Frank, but it would have been out of character for them to display such a disregard for the safety of bystanders, especially children and families. Although the threat of Wallace's actions might have encouraged a robber to retaliate, the James boys and Cole were seasoned military men who would not react without quickly assessing the situation. While Jesse did enjoy the attention his previous robberies afforded him, he had never been so foolish as to announce his identity, especially when he was so often denying any guilt through his vigorous letter-writing campaign. The robbers certainly would not have considered all the people attending the fair to be Union sympathizers, whereas revenge in the name of the Confederacy was the foremost motivation of the Gang at this time.

Whether members of the James-Younger Gang did or did not seize the cashbox, John Newman Edwards soon got into the act by composing a rousing editorial for the Kansas City *Times*. Edwards did not at first bring politics into his description of the robbery, but even as he denounced the crime he hailed the robbers as heroes. Edwards

James "Jim Crow" Chiles. Chiles served with Shelby and operated a gambling house and saloon in Kansas City after the war.

claimed the incident was "a deed so high-handed, so diabolically daring and so utterly in contempt of fear that we are bound to admire it and revere its perpetrators." Suspicion that the Jameses and Youngers had been involved grew deeper after this editorial, and public speculation increased after Edwards published a glowing editorial extolling the virtues of the Confederate guerrillas two days later. In October the *Times* published a letter purporting to be from the Exposition robbers. Perhaps intending to increase suspicion that the robbers were the James-Younger Gang, the letter asserted that the robbers were to be admired for their daring deed and that their actions had certainly been more moral than some of the deeds perpetrated in the name of the Union government. The authors of the letter then offered to pay the little girl's medical bills. Signatures at the bottom of this letter were those of three well-known historical figures: Jack Shepard, Dick Turpin, and Claude Duval.

When Jesse read this in the paper he evidently felt that a reply was necessary. On October 20, 1872, Edwards published Jesse's declaration: "I can prove where I was at the very hour the gate was robbed." Jesse told the *Times* readers that James Chiles of Independence was the one who had named Jesse, Cole, and John Younger as the Exposition robbers because Chiles had seen Jesse on the road that day. Chiles's identification was impossible, Jesse asserted, because Chiles in fact had not seen Jesse for at least three months. By way of proof, Jesse requested that Chiles contact the paper and state that fact. A week later a letter from Chiles was published in which he denied seeing Jesse or the Youngers at any time close to the day of the robbery.

Cole later claimed that he was furious that Jesse had seen fit to offer an alibi for John and himself. Prior to Jesse's printed remarks, no one had suggested John Younger might be involved. The *Pleasant Hill Review* carried Cole's response: "My name would never have been used in connection with the affair had not Jesse W. James for some cause best known to himself, published in the Kansas City Times a letter stating that John, he and myself were accused of the robbery." Cole acknowledged that he and John had been visiting their sisters in the area at that time, but denied they had anything to do with the robbery. Cole later wrote in his autobiography that he and Jesse had not been on good terms at the time and that Jesse's letter was the main reason why the public began to join the names of James and Younger in a robber gang.

Despite Jesse's lack of discretion, the James-Younger Gang planned another robbery soon. Cole surprised both Jim and John by telling them about this, but Cole probably had decided that if his brothers were going to be accused anyway they might as well enjoy the spoils. Jim reminded Cole about the Texas ranch, but Cole shrugged off the topic and told him it would have to wait.

Jim must have realized that none of his brothers was interested in his idea. He decided to return to Texas alone. During the winter of 1872–73 Jim arrived in Dallas. In a move no doubt intended to distance himself from his brothers' tainted reputations, Jim joined the Dallas police department under Marshal Tom Flynn and began saving his salary toward his ranch.

Disassociation from the stigma attached to "Younger" proved to be difficult. When a robbery took place in Dallas in February 1873, Jim and fellow officer J. J. L. Hollander were accused and indicted. It may be that Hollander provided Jim's name as an easy target so that Hollander's actual accomplice could remain unknown. In any event, Jim later wrote that he felt he would not be given a fair trial, and he fled Texas before he could be arrested. Jim returned to St. Clair County where he was welcomed by family and friends. Hollander stood trial and was sentenced to five years in prison.

Jim Younger, ca. 1872–73.

Two family members Jim did not see in St. Clair upon his return were Cole and John. The James-Younger Gang was busy again: Cole's invitation that John join the Gang the next time they rode had been met with enthusiasm.

On May 27, 1873, the Mississippi River town of Ste. Genevieve, Missouri, welcomed four strangers. Two of them entered the Ste. Genevieve Savings bank, where they encountered cashier O. D. Harris. At gunpoint Harris was told to hand over whatever money he had. The take amounted to about four thousand dollars.

Sam Hildebrand, sometime during his Confederate service.

What the bandits may not have noticed was a young man who moved stealthily toward the front door, then darted out to alert the town. Hearing the outcry, the two robbers pushed the cashier in front of them and made their way out to join two accomplices waiting in the street with their horses. During the confusion one of those horses bolted. A local farmer watching the drama was ordered by the robbers to hand over his horse and promptly did so. The bandits, riding out of town with guns blazing, shouted "Hurray for Hildebrand!"—advertising their allegiance to the ferocious Sam Hildebrand, a local guerrilla who was something of a hero to those in the town who supported the Confederate cause. It is almost certain that the Rebel-yelling robbers were Frank, Jesse, Cole, and John.

The James boys headed north to Clay County while Cole and John returned to St. Clair, where they were surprised to find their youngest brother. Bob had grown bored with work on the docks of New Orleans and told his brothers he had decided to take up farming in Missouri, his ultimate goal being to become as successful as his father. Cole laughed and told the boy he was a fool to think he could ever live so openly in Missouri, considering that Cole, Jim, and John were all wanted men. Jim later recounted the incident, saying he was told that John showed off his share of the cash from the Gang's recent robbery and wasted no time in suggesting that Bob, too, make a little money with the Gang. John had a ready answer when Bob voiced concerns about the illegalities of such action and the dangers involved: John and Bob had gotten acquainted with Jesse James when they lived in Texas; both had been impressed by Jesse's intelligence, and surely Jesse would not be involved in anything that was actually foolhardy. As for breaking the law, weren't the Yankees getting exactly what they deserved? Northern supporters had made life miserable for the Younger family. If the Youngers attempted to rebuild their lives on Yankee money, what good Confederate could fault them?

John's arguments made sense to the younger man. John was parroting what he had often heard from Cole and Jesse, but he was also repeating a widespread sentiment. Those in Missouri who had been aligned with the Union still wanted to drive out Confederate sympathizers. After Order Number 11 destroyed the business communities of western Missouri, investors from the East arrived and were now ensconced in the banking centers. For the most part these newcomers controlled the investment money needed for rebuilding farms and businesses destroyed or damaged during the war. Without access to low-cost funding, many pro-Confederate farmers had been forced to find new homes and take up farming elsewhere. Resentment ran deep against this, although the average Missouri family was too busy trying to eke out an existence to fight the establishment. The retributive actions of the James-Younger Gang were welcomed by many of their former comrades-in-arms as the Gang seemed to be making a statement on their behalf. If the methods used by the Missouri boys lay outside the law, there remained the fact that the law was protecting those who were greedy and corrupt. For as long as they rode, if the James-Younger outlaws needed an alibi or a place to hide or rest, they found such assistance freely given.

Officers in Eastern power circles, having gained control of the majority of Midwest banking institutions, were now seeking to expand by backing the development of railroads into the Western frontier. Many people along that frontier considered this another attempt by the powerful Eastern establishment to usurp their rights. Members of the James-Younger Gang may well have agreed with such an assessment, but they saw something else in the ever-expanding railroad enterprise: lots of money. Small-town banks controlled by carpetbaggers were one thing, but the transfer via railroad of great sums of money to the West meant that the take from a single robbery would be multiplied threefold.

The James-Younger boys were not the first to think of this. Seven years before, in September 1866, the Ohio and Mississippi Railroad had been relieved of more than twelve thousand dollars by robbers later determined to have been the Reno brothers. The same siblings robbed a second train shortly thereafter and were eventually captured. Such a robbery, however, had never been attempted west of the Mississippi. The senior members of the James-Younger Gang decided they would be the first to bestow that honor on the railroads.

Studying the logistics of train robbery, Jesse, Frank, and Cole focused on the Chicago, Rock Island & Pacific Railroad line. Since this new venture would require additional men, Cole proposed that John and Bob accompany them. The Jameses agreed. Clell Miller, too, was asked to join, and Cole suggested that Charlie Pitts, the young man who had found Henry Younger's murdered body, be invited. Pitts was smart and aggressive and a trustworthy Confederate sympathizer.

Jesse suggested a fellow he knew to have some similar qualities: Bill Chadwell. Chadwell was born William Stiles in Monticello, Minnesota. He had been arrested as a horse thief and had served time in jail in his home state. After his release he appeared in Missouri using the name "Chadwell." He had an engaging personality and had somehow become friendly with Jesse, possibly through mutual friends.

Cole suggested that Jim, too, contribute his talents as a horseman to this next effort. At first Jim wanted nothing to do with the plan, but the idea of robbing a train must have intrigued him. Jim's brothers knew that he had been depressed by the indictment brought against him in Dallas, which had meant the end of Jim's life there. Proposing that Jim might experience some of the excitement without seriously breaking the law, Bob suggested Jim come with the group and perhaps hold the horses. In a burst of defiance against the system that was holding him down despite his own actions and desire to fit in, the frustrated and disillusioned Jim agreed. The next venture of the James-Younger Gang would turn out to be the first, and only, time that all four Younger brothers would participate together in a robbery.

Mary Grant, who inadvertently entertained the Adair train robbers. Mrs. Grant was 102 years old at the time of this photograph. She died three years later, in 1938.

THE ADAIR TRAIN WRECK

Frank and Cole visited Omaha, Nebraska, in July 1873 to scout the area. Through information supplied by friends, they learned that a shipment of gold worth more than seventy-five thousand dollars was to be shipped by rail from the Cheyenne region later that month. On July 21, Mrs. Mary Grant provided dinner for two men who claimed to be visitors to the Adair, Iowa, area. No doubt it was not a coincidence that Mrs. Grant's husband oversaw the section house and activities of the Adair railroad station. While the two guests were raving about Mrs. Grant's pie, several of their colleagues were breaking into the handcar house, from which they removed a spike-bar and tie hammer. The two groups reunited on the tracks a mile and a half west of town several hours later while the good folks of Adair were eating their supper. Using the spike-bar and hammer to pry off the fishplate connecting two rails, the Gang then pulled out the spikes. A rope was tied to the west end of the disconnected north rail and a rope was passed beneath the rail on the south. At a place called Turkey Creek, the men waited hidden in a cut in a nearby bank and held fast to the rope.

A short time later, the train approached, a locomotive with several cars traveling at about twenty-five miles an hour. The remaining rail was jerked away a few seconds before the train reached the disconnected rail. Intending only for the suspended rail to force the train to stop, the outlaws were not prepared for what happened next. The train cars remained on track, but the engine slammed into the rail break, plunged into a ditch, and toppled on its side. Des Moines engineer John Rafferty died instantly and fireman Dennis Foley was seriously injured. In the ensuing alarm and confusion among the passengers, the Gang reacted quickly. Two jumped into the express car, where they forced guard John Burgess to open the safe. To the robbers' chagrin they discovered the gold shipment had been delayed; the strongbox contained only about two thousand dollars. Frustrated, the bandits passed through the cars and took what they could from the frightened passengers. This netted them only another thousand dollars.

(Top) *The section house where Mary Grant served pie to two of the Adair robbers.* (Bottom) *The site of the Adair train robbery is marked by this piece of rail and a train wheel. A large sign proclaims the spot as the "Jesse James Train Robbery Site."*

From the nearby town of Casey, Iowa, railroad employee Levi Clay sent telegraphed alarms to Omaha and Des Moines. Soon, armed men were on their way by train from Council Bluffs. Before reaching Adair, the posse was dropped off at a spot where a group with horses was waiting for them. From there the robbers' trail was traced until it split in different directions and disappeared into the Missouri countryside. The posse had to give up.

The Youngers rode to St. Clair County while the James boys headed west. Cole later sent a letter intended for publication to his brother-in-law, Curg Jones. Writing that he and John had been in St. Clair County on the day of the Adair robbery, Cole claimed they both had attended religious services there. He went so far as to name other worshippers who could provide alibis for them. In December 1873 Jesse wrote another of his now-familiar letters of denial, this one bearing a return address of Deer Lodge, Montana Territory. Once again Jesse declared the James brothers had nothing to do with any robbery. He told his readers that he and Frank had not been in Missouri since October of that year, nor had they been closer to the state than "Denver City." He did not mention Iowa.

If Frank, Jesse, and Cole felt little remorse for the death and injury they caused at Adair, Jim Younger later said he was sickened by events that day. Jim claimed that Bob also felt bad about the death of Rafferty. Things had not gone as smoothly as his brothers had promised. Causing deaths during the war had been for a purpose, but the train engineer certainly had not deserved to die. Jesse argued that although Rafferty's death was unfortunate, the fact that he worked for the railroad made him fair game. Jim said that Bob accepted Jesse's reasoning because he wanted to ease his conscience. Jim himself remained not only upset but disgusted.

"Younger Lookout" from the Osage River.

The Youngers did not know what repercussions to expect from the Iowa affair. Throughout the fall and early winter of 1873, they hid in St. Clair County, close to family and friends they could trust and whose company they enjoyed. Jim was probably glad to spend more time with Cora and see as little of his brothers as possible. The other three brothers lay low, sometimes just sitting and talking at the cave near the river. That year the four had Christmas dinner in Roscoe, Missouri, with their friends, the Snuffer family. Shortly after Christmas, Jesse visited the Youngers and went to the cave.

The James-Younger Gang was not overly concerned about their safety at this time. Though their names had been mentioned in conjunction with several robberies, it was not the procedure of law enforcement agencies to circulate photographs of suspects; the general public did not know what the Jameses or Youngers looked like. Citizens of Clay and St. Clair counties knew of the brothers' notoriety, but people there who could have identified them to authorities were either friends, Confederate supporters, or those who feared reprisals might be taken should they point a finger.

It did come to the Gang's attention that the Pinkerton Detective Agency, which worked closely with railroad officials, had been hired again to smoke them out. Even so, the Youngers heard and saw nothing unusual during their stay in St. Clair. The Jameses, too, noticed nothing out of the ordinary when they went home for Christmas. The robbers continued to enjoy their proceeds with none of the consequences that had been promised them by the press.

In fact, in a special supplement to the St. Louis *Dispatch* on November 22, 1873, their supporter John Newman Edwards published a lengthy article exonerating them. Edwards had joined the staff of the *Dispatch* in August of that year. Entitled "A Terrible Quintet," the essay addressed the alleged crimes of Frank and Jesse James, Cole and John Younger, and another outlaw, Arthur McCoy. McCoy was a St. Louis tanner who joined Shelby's regiment after participating in the battle of Shiloh. McCoy was suspected of being a member of the James-Younger Gang, but hard evidence of that fact has never surfaced. Edwards presented short biographies of the five based on information Edwards claimed to have gathered from interviews with the men's friends and families. Edwards also provided detailed alibis for every robbery since the Russellville holdup in 1868, but then asserted that even if any of the five had been involved in robberies their actions would have been justified. Insisting that each of them had been driven to their participation in the war because of constant harassment of their families and that each had served the Confederacy loyally and gallantly, Edwards claimed that the quintet had been made ferocious as a result of diabolical deeds by Union forces. Edwards maintained that if the war had never taken place these same men, who had fought for the rights of the common man, including their neighbors, friends, and families, would be leaders in their communities now, instead of being labeled outlaws. He went on at great length about society being at fault for allowing such an abhorrent campaign as was being waged against these courageous sons of the South.

Before the end of 1873 a friend of the Youngers in St. Clair County, Augustus C. Appler, began a series of articles defending the Youngers using information derived from their mutual friend, Owen Snuffer. The articles appeared first in the Osceola *Democrat* and were later collected in book form. According to Jim, most of the Gang relished this publicity. The fact that the stories contained little of the truth did not matter to them. John Younger was delighted to have been included. Bob and Jim, though, were happy to have been left out.

Soon after these eulogies by the press, in January 1874, a stagecoach enroute between Malverne and Hot Springs, Arkansas, was robbed. Relieving those on board of their currency and jewelry, the bandits then questioned the passengers as to whether any of them had served in the Confederate Army. Money and a watch were returned to Memphis resident G. R. Crump when he replied in the affirmative. John A. Burbank, former governor of the Dakota Territory and a Union supporter, was not as fortunate.

Could these stage robbers have been the James-Younger Gang? The bandits' respect for supporters of the "Lost Cause" indicated as much to many people at the time. On the other hand, the James-Younger Gang had not made a practice of robbing stagecoaches; the take was hardly worth the effort. It cannot be ruled out that the coach robbery was the Gang's work, but by this time, thanks to wide publicity, any group of bandits could stop a stage, spout pro-Confederate rhetoric, and be presumed to be the James and Younger brothers.

THE GAD'S HILL TRAIN ROBBERY

Though the train no longer stops at Gad's Hill, Missouri, the site near the 1874 robbery of the Iron Mountain Railroad is still marked.

The James-Younger Gang was not content to rest on its reputation for boldness. They laid plans now for a dramatic robbery that would demonstrate just how daring they could be. No train had ever been robbed in their own state of Missouri, and Jesse and Cole liked the idea of the attention and fame that would result from such a feat. The selected target was the Iron Mountain Railroad, specifically the small flag station at Gad's Hill, a site possibly named from the legend of Robin Hood. The site of the robbery may have been suggested by the well-read and sardonic Frank James.

The Gad's Hill station was located about one hundred miles south of St. Louis on the downgrade into the piedmont. Five men walked into the little station at about five-thirty on the evening of January 31, 1874. The group most likely included only Frank, Jesse, Cole, John, and Bob. Several local men were talking together inside the small building when the five strangers entered the station with guns drawn. One of the strangers held the startled bystanders at gunpoint while the others went back outside to place a flag on the track to signal the train to stop at the station to take on passengers. Then they all waited.

Obeying the flag, the train slowed to a stop. As soon as he stepped down, Conductor C. A. Alford was placed under guard by another bandit. The three remaining robbers boarded the train and began their collection activities. Baggage Master Louis Constant was ordered to keep his hands high while the express safe was looted. Enjoying the fact that this robbery was going smoothly, the outlaws decided to have some extra fun. Strolling through the train, their guns pointed at the ceiling, the three examined the hands of the male passengers. Smiling, congenial, they explained that they were not going to take anything from either ladies or hard-working men of the soil. They delighted, though, in taking money and jewelry from the more affluent passengers. One man who either looked or sounded suspicious—the robbers declared the man was possibly a Pinkerton guard—was taken to a private compartment and strip-searched.

Two other well-dressed gentlemen were forced from the train and made to strip to their underwear in the January weather. Both men, the robbers noted, looked like bank and railroad officials. They were probably right. It is likely, in fact, that these victims were John F. Lincoln, superintendent of the St. Paul & Sioux City Railroad, and Lincoln's friend John L. Merriam, founder of the Merchant's Bank of St. Paul. Lincoln was robbed of two hundred dollars and Merriam gave up his watch and seventy-five dollars. What the outlaws could not guess was that their public humiliation of Lincoln and Merriam would have dire consequences in the future.

Banker John L. Merriam. His humiliation at the hands of the James-Younger Gang at Gad's Hill had grave consequences for some of its members.

Through with their pranks, the robbers mounted up, but then handed a note to Engineer William Wetton before they rode away. The note turned out to be an account of the robbery, obviously intended for publication. Describing the events of the evening with superlatives, the authors left a space for the amount taken in the robbery to be filled in by the authorities.

A posse was formed after the train reached Piedmont, some seven miles down the line, but by then the bandits were far away. This time valuable hours were not wasted in organizing another posse. Railroad officials realized that an alarming pattern was beginning to develop. First in Iowa and now in Missouri, western trains were becoming outlaw targets, sources of money and notoriety. Because part of the booty taken during the Gad's Hill holdup included registered mail packages, the Pinkertons were called in immediately to search for the robbers on behalf of the federal post office.

Frank and Jesse returned to western Missouri and the comfort of alibis provided by friends and family. The three Younger brothers returned to St. Clair County, but after visiting briefly with Jim, Cole and Bob then left for Hot Springs, Arkansas. Had it been the James-Younger Gang who robbed the Malverne-Hot Springs stagecoach a few weeks earlier, it is not likely that they would have returned to the area after so short a time.

John did not go with Cole and Bob. John had probably been celebrating his new wealth with too much spirit, and he fell ill around the time of his brothers' departure. Telling Cole and Bob he would join them when he felt up to the trip, he remained in Monagaw Springs with Jim.

The St. Louis *Dispatch* ran an article describing the Gad's Hill robbery while John Newman Edwards was in the state capitol on business. The paper unequivocally accused the James and Younger brothers of being the perpetrators and detailed all the Midwest robberies since the Liberty bank holdup in 1866. The article included a statement by an anonymous St. Louis policeman who said he had been in Richmond, Missouri, on the day of that robbery in 1867. Evidently unaware that Bud and Cole Younger were the same person, the policeman confidently identified the Richmond robbers as Jesse and Frank James as well as "Budd and Cal Younger."

John Newman Edwards was furious when he learned of the article. He immediately wired his editor to publish nothing further about the Gad's Hill incident.

Several campaigns were being organized to arrest the band of outlaws committing robberies all over the Midwest. Missouri Governor Silas Woodson went so far as to name names: a reward of two thousand dollars was offered for the arrest and delivery of the bodies of Frank and Jesse James for their involvement in the Gallatin robbery and murder.

THE DEATHS OF JAMES WHICHER AND JOHN YOUNGER

Other posses and lawmen had failed to bring in the James-Younger Gang, but the Pinkerton Agency was certain it could succeed. An aggressive campaign was mounted to flush out the outlaws. Pinkerton agents in 1874 were not yet impressed by the intelligence, cunning, and deadliness of the men they were hunting. They would soon change their minds.

Rather than wait for another robbery, the Pinkertons decided to seek out the outlaws in their home territory. A twenty-six-year-old Pinkerton detective by the name of James W. Whicher arrived in Liberty, Missouri, on March 10, 1874. Ahead of his arrival, the Chicago agency got in touch with several Liberty businessmen and other local authorities. Whicher met with former sheriff O. P. Moss and Commercial Bank president D. J. Adkins early on the morning after he arrived. Whicher confided to them that his plan involved his going alone to the James-Samuel farm, where he would pose as a drifter seeking work as a farm hand. Once employed, he would gain the confidence of the family and eventually surprise Frank and Jesse by arresting them in their own home.

Robert and William Pinkerton in the field against the James-Younger Gang.

It was later reported that the two Clay Countians were astonished at Whicher's naivete. Moss and Adkins warned Whicher that it was absurd to think the James boys would welcome a stranger into their private lives without grave suspicions. Nevertheless, Whicher boarded a train bound for Kearney at five-fifteen that afternoon. He arrived around dusk and left the Kearney train station to begin the four-mile walk to the James-Samuel farm. That was the last that was seen of James W. Whicher that evening. The next morning his body was found beside the road outside Independence. He had been shot twice, through the head and the heart.

Under later questioning, the Blue Mills ferry operator disclosed that four men had awakened him to operate the ferry at about three in the morning. One of the four had been bound and gagged. A spokesman for the other three told the operator they were officers in pursuit of horse thieves; they had captured this man and were looking for his partner on the other side of the river. Bearing in mind that the ferryman had seen the men only briefly in the darkness, Deputy Sheriff Thomason, who had chased the James boys around their property after the Gallatin robbery, asked the operator for descriptions. The Deputy was then able to tentatively identify the men as Jesse James, Arthur McCoy, and "Bloody Bill" Anderson's brother Jim. The bound and gagged prisoner, Thomason believed, was probably James Whicher.

At the same time Whicher was making his ill-fated journey to Clay County, two other Pinkerton detectives arrived in the Youngers' stomping grounds in St. Clair County. Twenty-nine-year-old Louis J. Lull was a former Union Army soldier from Illinois. He had graduated from Annapolis in the class of 1866 and was serving as a captain on the Chicago police force when the Pinkerton Detective Agency offered him the assignment of arresting the Younger brothers in Missouri. Accompanying him was a former Confederate soldier from St. Louis, James Wright, who often went by the name of "Boyle." Since he once served alongside some men from St. Clair County, Wright seemed a natural for this assignment.

Under the name of "W. J. Allen," Lull checked into the Commercial Hotel in Osceola, where he and Wright met a third operative. Ed Daniels was a constable of Osceola Township recruited by the Pinkertons as a man familiar with the terrain of St. Clair County.

By this time John Younger had recovered from his excesses and was getting ready to join Bob and Cole in Hot Springs, Arkansas. Before leaving, John persuaded Jim to accompany him to a dance held at the Monagaw Hotel on the night of March 16. They stayed at the hotel until quite late, finally retiring to the cabin of their nanny Suze's sister, Hannah McFerrin, and Hannah's husband, John. Late the next morning they arose and made plans to take their afternoon meal with their friend Theodrick Snuffer, who lived outside Monagaw Springs in the small nearby settlement of Roscoe.

(Top) *Edwin B. Daniels, born in Boston, August 5, 1843. He served the Union in the First Regiment of the Massachusetts Volunteer Cavalry, and moved with his parents to Sedalia, Missouri, at the height of the war. Daniels sat on the civic committee to incorporate the City of Osceola. He is buried in Osceola, Missouri. (Bottom) Monagaw Hotel.*

John and Jim had just sat down to eat when they heard the sound of approaching horses. Sensing trouble, the two scrambled up into the attic under Snuffer's direction and watched from between the slats of their hiding place while Snuffer went outside to greet the strangers. Lull and Daniels approached the house. Wright hung back, out of sight about three-quarters of a mile up the road. Lull asked Snuffer directions to the house of the Widow Simms. Lull explained that

John and Hannah McFerrin in front of their Roscoe cabin.

they were cattle buyers and that Mrs. Simms might have several head they were interested in buying. Snuffer gave directions to the widow's place, then watched as they rode off in the opposite direction, back toward Wright.

John and Jim scrambled down from the attic to talk over the situation. Jim later detailed what happened next; much of his statement was substantiated by remarks made by witnesses during the coroner's inquest following the incident. John thought the two men were too well armed to be cattle buyers, and he had noticed that the younger of the two looked nervous. It was his idea that he and Jim follow them. Jim told his brother they had no need to look for trouble; they should finish their meal and deal with the men later if the need arose. John insisted, declaring that he was going to see what the men were doing in the area even if he had to do it alone. Reluctantly, Jim agreed to go with him.

Lull and Daniels were talking as their horses walked along the Chalk Level Road. Wright rode slightly ahead of the pair. They were discussing their next move when they suddenly heard hoofbeats behind them. Turning, they saw John and Jim approaching with their weapons drawn. Wright fled,

Chalk Level Road was the site of the Roscoe gun battle.

spurring his horse in the direction of town as soon as he saw the pair. Jim called to him to halt, but Wright rode on through the fields. Jim fired his revolver and Wright's hat went flying from his head, but the detective did not even slow down.

(Top) *John Harrison Younger. John never married and had no known offspring. He died at the hand of Pinkerton detective Louis Lull on March 16, 1874, and was buried in the Yeater Cemetery, Roscoe, Missouri.* (Bottom) *The grave of John Younger. For many years the grave was marked only by this iron rail.*

John now ordered Lull and Daniels to drop their guns, and Jim gathered up their weapons from the dirt. Lull's revolver, an English-made .43 caliber Trantor, brought a smile to Jim's face, and he thanked Lull for the present. John now demanded that the two strangers identify themselves. Lull answered that they had come from Osceola. Asked what they were doing in Roscoe, Lull replied that they were "Just rambling around." Two farmers nearby, "Ol" Davis and Speed McDonald, looked up from their chores to watch this exchange. John trained his double-barreled shotgun on Lull and Daniels and asked them point-blank whether they were detectives. Lull again answered, saying they were not. In that case, Jim wanted to know, why were they so heavily armed? Lull's cocky response was that they had the right to be.

At this point John aimed his shotgun at Daniels's chest and asked whether he had anything to say. While John and Jim waited, their attention on Daniels, Lull reached under his coat and withdrew a small No. 2 Smith & Wesson pistol. Before either of the Youngers could react, Lull shot John Younger through the neck. Lull's horse lurched forward at the sudden report. John turned to fire at Lull and hit him in the shoulder and arm. Jim also fired at Lull as Lull's horse bolted down the road, but that bullet missed the detective. Seizing his chance, Daniels now spurred his horse in the direction Lull had taken. Jim turned his gun on Daniels and fired. Daniels fell to the ground with a mortal wound through the neck.

Infuriated and bleeding heavily, John Younger took off after Lull and chased him through a grove of trees. When Lull was knocked from his horse by a low-hanging branch, John fired his shotgun at the detective who lay sprawled on the ground. That shot missed its mark. John was swaying in his saddle, but fired again. This time he hit Lull squarely in the chest. Turning his horse, John tried to get back to where Jim was examining Daniels's dead body. Seeing him approach, Jim called out John's name in alarm. John looked at Jim, then fell from his horse and landed on the far side of the nearby fence. John Younger lay dead at the age of twenty-four.

Jim briefly held his brother's body in his arms, then removed John's revolver, watch, and personal effects. Farmer Speed McDonald had reached John at about the same time as Jim, and Jim now ordered Speed to take Jim's horse and ride to tell Snuffer what happened. Jim also asked Speed to "take care of John." Jim then flung himself on John's horse and took up the chase after James Wright.

As McDonald headed to the Snuffer place, farmer John Davis examined the dead body of Daniels, then walked over to where Lull had fallen. The detective, alive but seriously injured, had propped himself against a tree. Lull was moved to the front porch of Hannah McFerrin's cabin while the bodies of John Younger and Ed Daniels were carried inside. Later that evening Lull was moved to the Roscoe House hotel, where Drs. A. C. Marquis and L. Lewis were called in to care for him.

Meanwhile, James Wright escaped from Jim Younger and reported the shootout to Sheriff James R. Johnson in Osceola. Deputy Simpson Beckley organized a posse upon hearing Wright's account of the Pinkerton operatives being "captured" by the Youngers. Wright himself did not join the gathering posse, but galloped away. He was never seen in St. Clair County again.

A friend of the Youngers, David Crowder, guarded John's body throughout the night. He was buried in the morning in a temporary, shallow grave in the Snuffer's yard, as Jim had directed when he returned to Roscoe the night before. The body was transferred that night to the Yeater Cemetery a few miles southeast of Snuffer's farm. There John's body was laid at an angle with his head to the northwest. It was a final resting place that would be noticeable only to those who knew what to look for.

On March 18, 1874, a coroner's jury determined that John Younger had been killed by W. J. Allen and that Ed Daniels had been killed by James Younger. Soon another determination of death would be necessary. Although Lull's doctors at first were optimistic that Lull would survive, his condition took a turn for

(Top) *Arthur Younger and wife, Cordia Leota Lovelady. In 1921 Arthur and Melburne Younger attended a carnival in Berryville, Arkansas, where a side show barker displayed a mummified body said to be that of John Younger. Declaring that the body was not their cousin John, the young men ordered the barker out of town. When he learned they were Youngers, the barker left in a hurry. Berryville officials notified Arthur and Melburne that it was up to them to dispose of the corpse, whose identity was never discovered.*
(Bottom) *Melburne Younger.*

the worse. His mother and wife arrived in the company of Pinkerton official Robert J. Linden, and Lull continued to weaken. Care of the detective was then turned over to

Dr. D. C. McNeill, who, ironically, was the father of Jim Younger's sweetheart Cora.

It was too late for a change in treatment. Linden announced Louis Lull's death soon after the shooting. Lull's body was placed in a wagon, transferred to a train in Clinton, and returned to Illinois. Many people in St. Clair County, however, continued to believe that Lull was still alive. It was popularly thought that Lull's death had been faked by the authorities so that he could escape from western Missouri before the Youngers avenged the death of their beloved brother. Cora McNeill's later version of events expressed some of these suspicions. Cora recalled that whenever her father was asked about the incident he would always reply, "You must learn to keep the game in your lead." If the Lull death were not a hoax, Dr. McNeill could have easily denied the allegation rather than issue so cryptic a statement. Nevertheless, if Louis Lull were not dead when he left Missouri, he did die shortly thereafter. He was given an impressive funeral attended by hundreds of Chicago police officers, then buried in Rose Hill Cemetery in Chicago. The date on Lull's tombstone reads May 6, 1874, a date some weeks after Lull's "body" left Missouri.

Dr. D. C. McNeill. Serving the Confederacy as a surgeon, Dr. McNeill later became a highly regarded physician in St. Clair County.

Jim Younger was unable to reach his brothers in Arkansas for several days. Jim later wrote that Bob and Cole were having breakfast in a Hot Springs hotel when Bob noticed that Cole, who was reading the local newspaper, suddenly looked stunned. When Cole showed the paper to Bob, the younger man was equally horrified. An article announced the death of John Younger and reported that Jim Younger was missing. Cole declared they had to find Jim at once.

They came upon Jim somewhere outside Hot Springs. Numbly he described the recent events. After sitting for hours in shocked silence, the three began to make plans. The Pinkertons would be more eager than ever to find them now. Cole decided to go to Lake City, Florida, where he was involved in a cattle venture. Jim decided to put as much distance between himself and Missouri as possible, but in the opposite direction. He would not return to Los Angeles but would try to find work as a rancher somewhere inland from the coast. Cole suggested Jim contact their Uncle Coleman, head of the San Jose Horticulture Society. Jim was unwilling to involve their family in his flight, however, so Cole then suggested Jim contact an uncle of the James boys, Drury James, living in San Luis Obispo, California.

Bob was confused about what to do. He could leave with either brother, but in the past whenever there had been trouble he had always stayed with John. He no doubt felt lost. He could not get on with his life until he saw John's grave for himself, even though he knew his brothers would not agree to his returning home. Telling Cole and Jim he would stay with their sisters in Texas for a while, Bob parted from his brothers and headed back to Missouri.

Allan Pinkerton was pleased that his detectives had flushed out and eliminated one of the Youngers, but he was furious that he had lost Whicher, Lull, and Daniels. As for James Wright, Pinkerton had nothing good to say; he was quoted as saying that had Wright not fled the scene in Roscoe, Louis Lull might still be alive.

Meanwhile, back in Clay County, James Whicher's death had aroused suspicions in the press and among the Pinkertons. There was talk that Sheriff George E. Patton of Clay County must have alerted the James boys and that others in the area had collaborated to protect Frank and Jesse after the murder.

There was no evidence linking Sheriff Patton with Whicher's death, but attacks on him continued in the St. Louis newspapers until Patton was forced to file libel suits against both the *Globe* and the *Republican*. The *Republican* responded by running a small piece extolling Patton's abilities as a law enforcement official. Using the same papers, the Pinkertons and their supporters accused the people of Clay County of harboring outlaws, a matter that soon became a national issue. The Missouri citizenry was referred to as cowardly for continuing to allow the actions of a handful of lawless men to run their state and terrorize anyone passing through it.

(Top) *The grave of Louis Lull in Rose Hill Cemetery, Chicago.* (Bottom) *Marker designating the site of the Roscoe gun battle.*

In response, Governor Silas Woodson suggested to the Missouri General Assembly that a military unit with secret agents be organized and funded by the state to rid the area of the bands of cutthroats roaming the region. Woodson's call for a militia was denied, but the House and Senate did vote to appropriate ten thousand dollars to hire secret agents to locate and capture the outlaws. One-third of the Missouri House abstained from this vote, but the bill passed. Another bill, calling for money to be provided to the widows and orphans of those killed while attempting to arrest the James and Younger brothers, was tabled.

John Newman Edwards and other media supporters of the outlaws continued to offer alibis, explanations, and excuses for the James-Younger boys, even as their readers were called upon to take a stand against lawlessness. Articles were printed describing the prominent backgrounds of both the Younger and James families. Wartime records of bravery and persecution were again emphasized. By way of alibis, the Youngers were said to have been living in Texas since the war.

Wedding portrait of Jesse James, 1874.

MARRIAGE, ROMANCE, AND MORE ROBBERIES

Perhaps because he thought it would promote an appealing "family man" image, Jesse James decided, at the age of twenty-seven, to finally marry his cousin, Zee Mimms. Aged twenty-eight now, Zee had selflessly stood by Jesse through all the years of his outlawry.

Zee's parents had not been as understanding. Although they liked their nephew, they did not approve of Zee's relationship. Zee and Jesse had continued to see one another when they could, and Zee at one point had threatened to elope with Jesse. After the death of Zee's father, her mother reluctantly agreed to the marriage.

On the morning of April 24, 1874, friends of the couple gathered at the Kearney home of Zee's sister, Lucy Mimms Browder, on South Jefferson Street. Jesse rode down the main street of town before the ceremony, greeting friends and announcing the pending wedding. He arrived at the house at about nine o'clock, only to be met by an unhappy "Uncle Billy" James, a Methodist minister having second thoughts about committing his niece, whom he was fond of, to life with an outlaw. Jesse explained to his uncle that he was blamed for far more than he was guilty of, and eventually the reverend relented.

The couple left to visit the James-Samuel farm after the wedding and about three weeks later, on May 11, Zee boarded a train bound for the Sherman/Wichita Falls area of Texas. Jesse had arranged for her to meet him there at the home of his sister Susan. The couple continued their honeymoon in Galveston, then spent some time in Dallas. Eventually they returned to Kansas City. A reporter from the St. Louis *Dispatch* said he had talked with Jesse in Galveston and that Jesse had told him, "You can say that both of us married for love." This same reporter recalled the new Mrs. James as a young woman "with an elegant form, beautiful eyes and a face that would be attractive in any assembly."

Frank James was also having thoughts of marriage. About a month after Jesse's wedding, on June 6, 1874, Frank eloped with Anna "Annie" Reynolds Ralston. Annie's father, Samuel Ralston of Jackson County, was a prominent citizen of Independence. Annie had graduated from the Independence Female College in 1872 with a Bachelor of Arts degree in Science and Literature. The popular and lovely Annie then decided to teach school and took a job in Little Santa Fe, Missouri.

It is not known with certainty how Annie came to be acquainted with Frank James. Samuel Ralston had allowed his home to be used as a haven for guerrillas during the war; perhaps it was then the two met. Regardless of Frank's wartime affiliations, though, Annie knew that marriage to the notorious Frank James would not be well received by her parents. As part of her elopement plan, Annie told her

Anna "Annie" Reynolds Ralston. Annie married Frank James in 1874 and lived with the outlaw until his death. She died July 6, 1944, and is buried beside Frank in the Hill Park Cemetery in Independence, Missouri.

parents she was going to visit her brother-in-law, Ezra Hickman, in Kansas City. Hickman did meet her when she arrived at the depot, but Annie told him she wanted to speak with a friend still aboard the train and that she would take a buggy and meet Hickman at home. At some point Annie met up with Frank. A note Annie left for her mother, which was not discovered for some time after Annie had gone, read simply, "Dear Mother, I am married and going west."

Frank and Annie traveled northwest by train and were married upon their arrival in Omaha, Nebraska. The Ralstons had no idea whom their daughter had married until an uncle of Frank's ran into one of Annie's brothers in Kansas City and informed him about his new brother-in-law. By that time Frank and Annie were in Texas visiting with Jesse and Zee. Two years later, Frank visited the Ralston home alone to reassure Annie's parents that their daughter was well. Frank fell into an argument with Samuel Ralston when Annie's father demanded to know the whereabouts of his daughter. Frank refused to tell him and rode off to reunite with his wife.

Romance was in the air for one of the Youngers as well. Bob met a young widow named Maggie on his way back to Missouri to see John's grave. Maggie's last name has never been revealed; she has been described by those who saw her in Bob's company as a gentle, beautiful woman. Maggie was originally from New England, but was now living alone with her son on a farm outside Jackson County. Bob fell in love with Maggie after he recovered from his initial distrust of anyone "Yankee." He promised to return to her after he got his life in order.

Susan Lavinia James. Susan married Allen Parmer on November 24, 1870. They lived first in Boonsboro (later Cane Hill), Arkansas, where Susan taught in the Bethesda Community School. When the Parmers moved to Sherman, Texas, Susan taught school and Allen worked with cattle and in railroad construction. The Parmers also lived in Archer City and Wichita Falls, Texas. They had seven children: Robert, Flora, Zelma, Allen Jr., Susan, Kate, and Feta. Following complications from the birth of a stillborn son on March 3, 1889, Susan died at the age of forty-one. She is buried in the Riverside Cemetery in Wichita Falls.

After visiting John's grave, Bob headed for Texas as he had told his brothers he would. He heard in Denison that the honeymooning Jesse James was visiting Susan James a few miles away from Sherman. Bob decided to visit the couple to offer his congratulations and to get to know Jesse a little better.

Jim Younger at this time was settling into the life of a rancher near Santa Margarita, California. He had taken Cole's advice and had asked Drury James for a job on Drury's La Panza ranch. Jim later wrote that he enjoyed the serenity of the hills surrounding the Santa Margarita-San Luis Obispo area and was happy to be ranching again. He began to revise his earlier dream of a ranch in Texas for that of owning a spread in California some day. He wanted to bring Cora west to settle with him.

Neither love nor marriage had a restraining influence on robberies in the Missouri area, though the James-Younger Gang might have been innocent of some of them. On the Sunday afternoon of August 30, 1874, two events took place in Lafayette County. Three masked men stopped the Waverly-Carrollton omnibus and robbed the passengers. A second omnibus, on the opposite side of the Missouri River near Lexington, was stopped and robbed shortly thereafter. Three armed and mounted men had been observed in Lexington earlier that day and had been seen to board the ferry taking the omnibus across the river to North Lexington. Strollers along the high road by the river watched three horsemen emerge from behind a house to stop the omnibus. The bandits shouted to the passengers to get off the bus, then robbed each one at gunpoint. Mollie Newbold, witnessing the event while walking in the area, ran to the ferry to report the robbery. The ferry quickly crossed the river while pedestrians watched the conclusion of the robbery from the banks. Professor J. L. Allen, a bus passenger, later declared that he was pleased to have been robbed by men of such national reputation as that of the James-Younger Gang.

There is, however, reason to believe that the omnibus robberies were not the work of the James-Younger Gang. Professor Allen might have jumped to a conclusion based on wishful thinking. Another bus passenger, Mattie Hamlet of Lexington, did tell reporters she was well acquainted with the James and Younger families and that she recognized the robbers to be Frank and Jesse James and "Will Younger." She further claimed the men recognized her and that when she asked them why they were stooping so low as to rob citizens on a Sunday afternoon ride on an omnibus, they had admitted the deed was a bit small for them. Lexington was close to the Clay County home of the Jameses, there were relatives of the Youngers in the city as well, and any number of people along the river that day might have recognized the three men. It

(Top) *The Drury James adobe home on La Panza Ranch, built in the 1860s near Santa Margarita, California. It was visited by Frank and Jesse James and Jim Younger.* (Bottom) *Site of the Waverly-Carrollton omnibus robbery.*

is not entirely plausible that the Jameses and Cole Younger would rob neighbors with whom they were acquainted and endanger bystanders to do so. Mattie Hamlet was not even aware that Cole Younger's name was not Will. She in fact refused to sign an affidavit swearing that the three were Frank, Jesse, and Cole. Miss Hamlet also wrote a letter to Zerelda Samuel claiming her identification of the robbers was made in haste. It is more than likely that the omnibus robberies were one of the copycat robberies taking place all over the Midwest.

St. Louis police detective Flourney Yancey was assigned the task of investigating the robbery on behalf of the state of Missouri, but Yancey was unable to find firm evidence with which to charge the James-Younger Gang. Yancey did claim that at one point in his search he battled with Jesse James and Jim Younger in the brush near the Clay-Ray County line. Although Jesse might have been back from Texas by that time, however, Jim Younger was still in California.

Bob Younger on his Jackson County farm, 1875.

Another robbery occurred later that year, on December 7, when the Tishimingo Savings Bank of Corinth, Mississippi, was robbed of five thousand dollars. It was reported that two men entered the bank and, brandishing knives rather than revolvers, demanded the money. Two accomplices waited outside. During the course of the holdup, the cashier was slashed across the forehead. One of the men was later identified as resembling Cole Younger. This holdup may well have been another copycat crime. For weapons, the James-Younger Gang preferred guns to knives, and the identification of Cole is unreliable since few people in Mississippi knew what Cole Younger looked like.

Bob Younger, after visiting with Jesse and Zee in Texas, returned to Missouri and Maggie. Asking her if she would be interested in starting a farm with him, he said they would be married some time in the future if things went well. Maggie agreed and joined Bob in Jackson County, where he was able to lease a farm by using an alias.

Even though he had fulfilled his desire to start his own farm, Bob's outlaw days were not over. On December 8, 1874, one day after the robbery in Corinth, Mississippi, five men robbed the Kansas Pacific Railroad near Muncie, Kansas. There has been some controversy regarding the personnel involved, but the professionalism of the job points to the James-Younger Gang—probably Jesse, Frank, Cole, Bob, and Clell Miller. The men first ordered the section hands to load the track with ties. The railroad workers were then tied up inside a shed and the robbers flagged down the train. Crewmen of the train were ordered to decouple the baggage and express cars. The thirty thousand dollars inside the two cars was quickly extracted and the Gang disappeared.

Other culprits have been suggested for the Muncie robbery. One James family member claims that the James-Younger Gang interrupted the robbery as it was being committed by Bud McDaniels and Bill Ryan. The names of Ed Miller, Jim Cummins, and Billy Judson have also been mentioned in conjunction with this scenario. The personnel would number at least ten if that were true. Jesse allegedly later issued a denial, writing in a letter addressed mysteriously only to "My Dear Friend" that "Clell Miller, Tom McDannial, Wm. McDannial, Jack Kene and Sol Reed are the five men who robed the Muncie Kan R R train the 8th of Dec 1874 . . . When those scondrals robed the train at Muncie they took a horse and rode it to Clay county and turned it out to leave the impression that it was the James boys."

The Muncie robbery was so successful that irate railroad officials offered a five-thousand-dollar reward and asked the governor of Kansas to match the reward with state funds. The governor more than agreed; he threw in an additional thousand dollars for any of the robbers,

A period etching showing railroad workers stacking ties to stop the train in Muncie, Kansas.

dead or alive. Kansas did not want to become known as an outlaw state like Missouri.

A few days after the robbery, Bud McDaniels, the brother of Tom McDaniels (who had been involved with John Younger in the killing of lawman Charles Nichols in Scyene, Texas), was arrested in Kansas City on a charge of public drunkenness. When patted down by the sheriff he was found to have more than a thousand dollars and several pieces of jewelry in his pockets. The jewelry was thought to be some of that taken from the safe aboard the Kansas Pacific Railroad. Charges of train robbery were filed against Bud McDaniels, but he escaped from jail before he was tried and then was killed in a field when a farmer tried to capture him. While in custody Bud McDaniels never acknowledged that he was guilty or admitted who his accomplices might have been. The code of the guerrillas once again held firm.

THE PINKERTONS AND THE BOMB

With state agencies and railroad companies throughout the Midwest becoming involved in the hunt for outlaws, the Pinkerton detectives were beginning to look incompetent. The agency had been touted as the best in the field, but so far they had produced nothing except the body of John Younger, which had cost the agency two men. Moreover, aside from the incident of the Kansas City Exposition, John Younger's name had never even been mentioned as an important suspect. The Pinkertons were desperate now to prove they could capture the famous bandits. Pinkerton agent Jack Ladd was sent to take a job on the farm of Daniel Askew, adjacent to the James-Samuel spread. Ladd was working with the Pinkerton office in Chicago as part of an intricate plan to flush out Frank and Jesse James.

During the dead of night on January 26, 1875, the occupants of the James-Samuel household were awakened by the sound of a window breaking. Jumping from his bed, Reuben Samuel ran into the main room and discovered a large ball of material aflame on the floor in front of the fireplace. He pushed the object into the fireplace, but the fire spread to other parts of the room. Then the house suddenly rocked with a tremendous explosion.

Zerelda had just entered the room, followed by her eight-year-old son, Archie. As large pieces of the bomb flew across the room, Archie was struck in the side and Zerelda had part of her right hand and arm blown away. Reuben Samuel beat at the fire, family members screamed in terror, and the men who had perpetrated the attack fled into the night. Reuben was able to subdue the flames at last, but he could not repair the human damage. Archie Samuel died within an hour. Zerelda's right arm had to be amputated at the elbow.

It was determined in 1992, through examination of a portion of the shell that remained at the James-Samuel farm and extensive research by historians Fred Egloff and Ted Yeatman, that the bomb was a Berney liquid incendiary shell filled with Levi Short's concoction of coal tar and gun powder. The crude shell, filled with materials commonly called "Greek fire," had been made at the United States Rock Island Arsenal for Allan K. Pinkerton on orders from Lt. Gen. Philip H. Sheridan. The Pinkerton Detective Agency evidently had friends in high governmental places and were anxious to eliminate the ex-guerrilla outlaws at any cost.

Public sentiment in support of the James-Samuel family ran high after this attack. Within days the Missouri legislature authorized an investigation into the matter. Governor Charles Hardin assigned Adj. Gen. George Caleb Bingham to lead the investigation. Bingham was able to discover that a train on the Hannibal and St. Joseph and the St. Louis, Kansas City and Northern railroads had brought a specialized team of detectives to a station near Kearney on the night of the attack. The engineer of the train either waited while the Pinkertons made their attack or returned to pick them up after the explosion. A pistol bearing the initials P.G.G. (Pinkerton Government Guard) was later found near the James-Samuel farm's fence. The attack, however, was not as successful as the Pinkertons had hoped: Frank and Jesse were safe. It was once again the innocent members of their family who paid the price for the desperation of their enemies.

A Clay County grand jury indicted Robert J. King, Allan Pinkerton, Jack Ladd, and five other unknown participants for the murder of Archie Samuel. The case never came to trial. Jesse's reaction was printed in the Nashville *Banner* on August 4, 1875. His letter, giving a return address of Kansas City, read in part, "Oh, Pinkerton (if you have got a heart or conscience), I know the spirit of my poor little innocent brother hovers around your pillow, and that you, never close your eyes, but what you see his poor delicated & childish form around you & him holding his shattered arm over you and you looking at the great wound in his side and seeing his life blood ebb away. You may vindicate yourself with some people, but God knows if you did not do the deed it was by your force."

(Top) *Zerelda Elizabeth Cole James Simms Samuel, born in Woodford County, Kentucky, January 29, 1825. She died February 10, 1911.* (Bottom) *Archie Peyton Samuel was the half brother of Frank and Jesse James. Born July 26, 1866, Archie died January 26, 1875, from a bomb thrown by Pinkerton detectives.*

Earlier, in March, an editorial in the St. Louis *Dispatch* suggested amnesty be extended to the James and Younger brothers on the grounds that the Gang had been driven to their crimes by extenuating circumstances. A resolution calling for complete amnesty for Cole, Jim, and Bob Younger as well as for Frank and Jesse James, was introduced into the Missouri House of Representatives by Jefferson Jones of Callaway County on March 17, 1875, on the first anniversary of the death of John Younger. A pardon for their wartime activities was proposed, while amnesty proceedings would guarantee a fair trial for any crimes they had been charged with since the war. Jefferson Jones may have been instrumental in dictating the legal content of the resolution, but other wording in the document resembled the style of John Newman Edwards. Legislators opposed to the bill pointed out that other men in positions similar to those of the James and Younger brothers during the war had found ways to lead productive, nonviolent lives. A subsequent resolution, presented by Gen. James Shield on behalf of the Commission on Federal Relations, proposed only that the five be given a fair trial and be promised full protection during any such proceeding. Neither bill met the two-thirds margin required to pass.

606 Boscobel Street, Nashville. Jesse and Zee lived here in 1875.

Shortly after the pardon and amnesty drives failed, vigilante justice was exercised in Clay County. Daniel Askew, the neighbor who had "hired" Pinkerton detective Jack Ladd and who probably had knowledge of the plan to attack the James-Samuel homestead, was murdered on the evening of April 12. That act of revenge undermined much of the good will previously extended toward the Jameses. A letter regarding Askew's death, dated June 10, 1875, and said to have been written to someone named "Jim" from Jesse James in Comanche, Texas, declared, "I hear they are making a great fuss about old Dan Askew, and say the James Boys done the killing. It's one of old Pink's lies, circulated by his sneaks."

Jesse James decided that he and Zee would be safer if they stayed out of Missouri for a while. The couple moved into a house at 606 Boscobel Street in Nashville while they awaited the birth of their first child. Jesse had been in Nashville before, when he sought medical attention after the war. There he had come under the care of Dr. Paul Eve, who treated him for his serious chest wound.

Cole Younger also did not want to stay in Missouri during the legislative debate concerning his liberty. He informed his family that he was off for a brief trip to Cuba. Bob, though, was fulfilling his dream of starting a farm with Maggie and was determined to see it through. He laid low and minded his own business while remaining in Jackson County.

ROBBERY, FATHERHOOD, AND MORE ROBBERIES

It is possible that the four Gang members were reunited in Missouri by May 13, when the dry goods store of D. B. Lambert in Clinton, Missouri, was robbed. Eight young people playing croquet on the lawn beside the store were invited inside, at gunpoint. More than three hundred dollars in goods were stolen, including firearms and jewelry. Later reports described the robbers as well-dressed, well-mounted gentlemen. No names were specified until Clinton farmer Matthew Dorman mentioned that he had seen and spoken with two of the Youngers and two of their friends a couple of days before the robbery. No effort was made, though, to bring a formal accusation against the Youngers or the Jameses.

Whether the dry-goods robbery was another copycat crime or the work of the James-Younger Gang remains uncertain. Jesse later laid the blame on Clell Miller, Tom McDaniels, Jack Keene, and Sol Reed. In the letter allegedly from Jesse which was addressed to "My Dear Friend," a plan was proposed to smoke out these men. "I have positive proof Clell Miller was riding his fathers iron Gray mare in the henry co. store robbery. . . . Clell or this mare can be identified as being in the store robbery."

A few months later, on August 31, 1875, Zee James gave birth to Jesse Edwards James, in Nashville. It was not a surprise to his friends that Jesse named his son after John Newman Edwards. The next day, Jesse probably remained at home enjoying his new fatherhood while Frank and Cole were busy robbing a West Virginia bank.

The two eldest brothers recruited John Younger's old drinking buddy, Tom McDaniels, who was still wanted in Texas and who had returned to Missouri. Another Missouri friend, Tom Webb, was asked to come along. The four men entered the town of Huntington, West Virginia, on September 1, 1875. One of the men occupied himself in Sanburn's Blacksmith while another stood stationed near the horses. The other two entered the town bank, where Cashier Robert T. Oney was ordered at gunpoint to open the safe. Oney denied knowing the whereabouts of the key to the inner vault. The robbers soon located it for themselves. At least nine thousand dollars was removed from the vault while another thousand was taken from the counter. Before leaving, the bandits asked the cashier whether any of the money in the bank was his own. When Oney replied that his account balance was about seven dollars, that amount was returned to him with the explanation that the bandits did not believe the robbery should cost the employee money.

A messenger named Jim entered the bank at that point and was put to use as a shield. Moving quickly with Oney and the messenger in front of them, the bandits exited through the front door and crossed the street to their waiting horses. Oney and Jim were then released unharmed.

A posse formed immediately and the chase was on. Since the robbers were not familiar with West Virginia terrain, a local man named Barbour, whom the bandits came upon several miles outside Huntington, was asked at gunpoint to serve as a guide. Barbour traveled with them only about an hour before being released unharmed.

As soon as the robbers crossed into the state of Kentucky, Detective D. T. Bligh of Louisville was once again called upon to lead the posse. A farmer named William Dillon watched as the outlaws, pursued by the posse, approached his farm outside Pine Hill. Dillon called out to ask them their business. Shots were fired at the farmer, Dillon returned the fire, and one of the bandits was seriously wounded. With the posse close behind, the outlaws tried to hide their wounded comrade in a cornfield; then they continued their flight. The wounded robber was delirious and close to death by the time Bligh arrived. Asked for his name, the outlaw answered only that he was "Charley Chance."

A rumor soon circulated that the wounded man was none other than Jesse James. The man's pockets were searched and he was identified eventually as Tom McDaniels. It was reported that among McDaniels's last words were, "Did they get Bud?"—possibly referring to his dead brother Bud or possibly to Cole Younger, called Bud by his friends.

The other three robbers fled into Tennessee with the posse close behind. The pursuers managed to surround one of the bandits in Fentess County, Tennessee, when the bandit's horse threw a shoe and the robber was forced to dismount. He was quickly seized. His pockets were found to contain almost forty-five hundred dollars taken from the West Virginia bank. When questioned, the outlaw said his name was Jack Keene. Bligh at first believed that he had captured Cole Younger, but it was soon determined that the outlaw was really Tom Webb. Webb was returned to West Virginia, where he subsequently was convicted for his part in the robbery and sentenced to twelve years. Cole Younger and Frank James escaped without further incident.

Later, Jesse took it upon himself to defend Cole Younger in relation to the West Virginia robbery. In a move meant also to discredit Detective Bligh, Jesse asserted, "I and Cole Younger are not friends, but I know he is innocent of the Huntington robbery and I feel it is my duty to defend him and his innocent and persecuted brothers from the false and slanderous reports circulated about them. I think the public will justify me in denouncing Bligh, and I now do, as an unnecessary liar, a scoundrel and a poltroon." This letter was published in the Nashville *American*.

With the exception of miscellaneous and unfounded reports, including a rumor that Frank James had been captured and sent to the Missouri penitentiary, the Gang was not heard from again for nine months, until early the following summer. A bank robbery did take place in Baxter Springs, Kansas, on April 19, 1876, but the suspects were not the usual members of the James-Younger Gang. They were two men by the names of Charlie Pitts and Bill Chadwell, both of whom had been accomplices in the deadly train robbery at Adair, Iowa. Pitts and Chadwell would soon be part of the Gang again, when they would ride in the most well-known robbery attempt in the James-Younger Gang's career.

BOB BACKS A BAD PLAN

Bob Younger, 1876.

Bob Younger and Jesse James had become close friends during Bob's visit while Jesse and Zee were honeymooning in Texas. Jesse, aged twenty-seven then, seemed to take an almost paternal interest in the younger man. The twenty-year-old Bob was impressed by Jesse's accomplishments and looked to his new friend for direction and advice. Bob missed the guidance of Jim and John but sometimes resented the heavy hand of Cole. Two years later, in 1876, Bob was still open to suggestions from Jesse. He was enjoying his new family life with his fiancée Maggie, yet he never seemed to have enough money to realize his dream of a big, successful Missouri farm.

According to Zee James's account, Jesse and his family moved to Baltimore, Maryland, during the winter of 1875-76. Some time the following spring, Jesse visited Bob's farm to ask whether Bob would like to "earn" some extra money. Bob was agreeable; if the spoils from another robbery were exceptionally large, he would invest the money in his farm and retire from outlawry. Jesse supported Bob's ambition and told him he would contact him as soon as he worked something out. Within the week Jesse sent word to Bob to meet him in a hotel in Kansas City.

During that hotel meeting, Bob was astonished to hear Jesse's idea that the Gang's next target should be in Minnesota. How would the Gang find their way around such foreign terrain? Jesse explained that Bill Chadwell had been born in Minnesota and had offered to serve as their guide. Taken aback by the bold scheme, Bob hesitated and said he would have to discuss it with Cole. The two made plans to meet in Monagaw Springs, Missouri, the following week. Jesse would bring Clell Miller along.

Cole Younger was in Texas at the time. Bob sent a letter asking Cole to meet him at Monagaw Springs, but by the next week's meeting Cole had not arrived and Bob could not be sure his letter had even been received. Again Bob refused to commit to

Jesse James, 1876.

the plan until he could talk it over with his brother. It was agreed that Bob would contact Jesse after locating Cole. Bob then returned to Jackson County, where after almost another week he mailed a second letter to Cole. A day or two later Cole arrived in Monagaw Springs. Hearing he was there, Bob quickly rode to meet Cole and outline Jesse's plan.

Jim Younger later wrote that Cole was outraged that Jesse had approached his little brother with such a foolhardy idea. Cole considered Jesse's attempt to circumvent Cole in the Gang's decision-making process to be a sneak tactic, especially since Jesse had used the young and inexperienced Bob to do so. An argument ensued, with Bob Younger declaring that his position in the Gang was just as important as Cole's. He was probably repeating what Jesse had told him. Realizing this, Cole grew more angry that Jesse's influence over his youngest brother had become greater than his own. When Bob declared that Chadwell would serve as their guide through Minnesota, Cole pointed out that they hardly knew Chadwell and that Chadwell was a friend of Jesse's, not theirs. Cole thought it foolish to rely on one man for their safe passage, and he reminded Bob that Minnesota was a long way from home.

Bob became more determined as he struggled to assert his independence. Finally Cole asked Bob to wait a while longer before giving his answer to Jesse; he would not say why. Bob responded that he was over twenty-one and could do as he pleased, and what he pleased to do was go with Jesse. He claimed it did not really matter to him if Cole participated or not. Finally, in a compromise, Cole agreed to meet with Bob and Jesse at the end of June if Bob would guarantee that Frank James would be there as well.

"COME HOME. BOB NEEDS YOU."

Unknown to Bob, Cole sent a cryptic wire to Jim Younger in California: "Come home. Bob needs you." It was Cole's hope that Jim could use his influence to talk Bob out of going along with Jesse's wild plan. Jim did not make further inquiries but left La Panza ranch immediately.

When all three Youngers met with Jesse and Frank in Kansas City at the end of June, Jim was also astonished by Jesse's plan. Years later Jim wrote to a friend that he was furious with Jesse for involving his brother in such a dangerous scheme. At one point the Youngers broke away from the Jameses to talk in private. The arguing continued. Cole finally played his last card, a kind of coercion: if Bob was set on going to Minnesota, then Cole and Jim would have no choice but to accompany him. Cole was hoping that if Jim had to be included in

Ruins of the La Panza Post Office where Jim Younger received Cole's telegram saying Bob needed help.

the ill-advised plan, Bob would change his mind. After all, Bob was aware that Jim was happy in California and Bob respected Jim's desire to make a new life for himself. Bob did say to Jim that he did not want him to come along. Picking up on what Cole was up to, Jim replied that he would have no choice but to go if Bob insisted on going with Jesse.

Bob Younger held fast and said he was committing. Now Cole and Jim had no choice but to join in, if only to look out for Bob's best interests. Bob apologized to Jim for his stubbornness but said it was important to him to stand up for himself and make his own decisions.

The James and Younger brothers then began laying out detailed strategy for their northern robbery. First on the list was how to finance the trip. Jesse, Bob, Cole, and Frank came up with a plan for a train robbery in Missouri that would bring in the necessary funds. Jim informed them that he would not go along with that. It was one thing that he had agreed to ride along to Minnesota, but he would never commit a robbery in his own home state. Everyone but Bob was disappointed at Jim's declaration. The others thought the train holdup should be committed by the same men who

Bruce Younger, allegedly. Born in Osceola, Missouri, in 1853, Bruce Younger was the son of Parmelia Wilson, Charlie Younger's mistress. By age seventeen Bruce was known throughout the Midwest as a horse breeder. Often seen at racetracks with Louis Dalton, his brother-in-law and father of members of the future Dalton Gang, Bruce eventually incurred large debts. He indulged in a colorful life among the boomtowns of Kansas. After relocating to New Mexico he disappeared. A mummified body found in the Guadalupe Mountains was identified as Bruce by his sister Sophia.

would go on to Minnesota. Nevertheless, it was agreed that a fellow named Hobbs Kerry would be contacted to stand in for Jim. Kerry had been an associate of the Youngers' uncle Bruce, and the James brothers knew him as well.

THE ROCKY CUT TRAIN ROBBERY

The Gang learned that a railroad bridge was being built over the Lamine River near Otterville, Missouri, for the Missouri Pacific Railroad line. A dissection in the bank near the construction site was known as Rocky Cut. There the trains passing through were forced to slow to a crawl as they moved through the construction area. One of those trains would be the target.

The group of seven, including Charlie Pitts, Hobbs Kerry, and Bill Chadwell, assembled at Rocky Cut on the night of July 7, 1876. First they seized the night watchman as he waited at the bridge to guide the train through the area. His red lantern was used to bring the train to a full stop and the Gang jumped on board. Passengers and crew were held at gunpoint while two safes containing more than fifteen thousand dollars were emptied.

While the Gang was busy, a minister on board worked some of the other passengers into a state of frenzy; soon the passengers were singing hymns and the preacher was praying aloud for the souls of those he believed in danger. The bandits, who had no intention of molesting the passengers, seemed amused. They completed their robbery, mounted, and rode off. A small posse was formed. Its leader was Bacon Montgomery, a former commander of a post-war unit of the state militia in Lafayette County. The posse came up empty-handed.

Governor Hardin offered a reward of three hundred dollars for any of the outlaws who had taken part in the Rocky Cut robbery. Another official, St. Louis Police Chief James McDonough, was called into the case. McDonough was unable to bring in the robbers in Missouri, but he would figure importantly in the lives of the James-Younger Gang later on.

It turned out that the Gang made the first of several grievous errors that summer by including Hobbs Kerry in their number. Kerry returned to his favorite retreat of Granby, in southern Missouri, and there made little effort to disguise the fact that he had come into some easy money. Somehow it became known that he wrote to the Youngers' uncle Bruce, probably asking him for help in purchasing a thoroughbred horse. When one of McDonough's informants learned of Kerry's actions, detectives were sent into southern Missouri to investigate. They spoke with a farmer who stated that Kerry had been among a group of men who stopped by his farm for a meal prior to the robbery. A warrant was prepared for the arrest of Bruce Younger, and Kerry himself was arrested and charged with participation in the Rocky Cut holdup.

Almost immediately, Kerry confessed everything, even volunteering the information that Frank and Jesse James, Cole and Bob Younger, Bill Chadwell, and Charlie Pitts had been his accomplices. No evidence could be found to implicate Bruce Younger in the crime.

Before an official posse could be effectively organized, the James-

This recently discovered marriage license of Bruce Younger and Maibelle Reed (Belle Starr) reveals a unique association. The rowdy crowd around Bruce Younger in Kansas included Maibelle Reed, although the two may have become acquainted earlier through their families. Bruce and Belle were married on May 15, 1880. The marriage appears to have lasted about three weeks.

Younger Gang was on its way to Minnesota. Jesse, however, did dash off one of his famous communications with the media before his departure. On August 18, 1876, the Kansas City *Times* published Jesse's declaration that he had heard that Confederate enemy Bacon Montgomery was actually the leader of the group who robbed the Rocky Cut train. Montgomery responded in print that he would gladly participate fully in any investigation of his involvement if Jesse would agree to the same and present himself in Sedalia for that purpose. Jesse offered no further accusation or remark about Montgomery.

On August 11, a group of detectives descended on the Jackson County farmhouse of Frank James's father-in-law, Samuel Ralston. The Ralston home was searched at dawn in an unsuccessful effort to take Frank or Jesse by surprise. A neighbor of the Ralstons, Joseph Connelly, was then escorted by detectives on a train to Pomeroy, Kansas, where the detectives had been told by an informant that they might find the James boys at the home of C. E. Wells so that Connelly could identify them. Connelly eventually was released when the Jameses were not found in Pomeroy.

Jesse feigned disgust at Hobbs Kerry's confession and at the entire affair. As he wrote to the Kansas City *Times* on August 14, "this so-called confession is a well-built pack of lies from beginning to end. I never heard of Hobbs Kerry, Charlie Pitts and William Chadwell until Kerry's arrest."

Cole Younger later wrote in his autobiography that since he and his brothers were being confused with young upstart train robbers, they decided they might as well actually enter the world of thievery themselves. Cole claimed that it was Kerry's pointing the finger of guilt at them that convinced the James-Younger brothers to "make one haul, and with our share of the proceeds start life anew in Cuba, South America or Australia."

RECONNOITERING IN MINNESOTA

Their financing now secured, the outlaws made their final preparations and first moves toward Minnesota. Accounts of the James-Younger Gang's experiences in that state, by those who participated and those who only observed, have produced any number of controversial speculations—not to mention discrepancies, misplaced accusations, confusion, and deceit—in the more than a century that has elapsed since the crime. Certainly, though, events of the summer of 1876 followed from egotistical, desperate, and foolhardy decisions, the sum of which brought to a close the reign of the James-Younger Gang.

Frank and Jesse left their mother's farm sometime around August 10, hidden under a tarpaulin in the back of a wagon, probably driven by Bill Chadwell. They rendezvoused with the Youngers, Clell Miller, and Charlie Pitts north of Clay County, where eight horses were being held. The men then rode on to Council Bluffs, Iowa, and sold the horses. Dividing into small groups, they boarded separate trains for Minnesota.

It was on August 15 or 16 that the entire Gang met again, in Minneapolis. Deciding it would not be a good idea to be seen as a group, they split up again but encountered each other often and kept tabs on everyone's whereabouts.

Bob Younger and Charlie Pitts played poker for a while on the evening of their arrival in Minneapolis. Months later, in the fall, an account was given that Bob and Charlie had been seen sleeping on the river bank near Sibley and Fifth streets that night. If true, it is possible that the two young men had gambled away the money allocated for that night's lodging.

The next day the entire group arrived in St. Paul and divided into small units again. Cole and Bill Chadwell put up at the Merchants Hotel on Third and Jackson streets while the others selected hotels

Third Street, St. Paul, Minnesota, at the time of the arrival of the James-Younger Gang. The Merchants Hotel and the gaming house were located on Third.

nearby. Cole and Chadwell later engaged in some poker playing of their own at a gambling parlor owned by Guy Salisbury on East Third Street. Since Bob had lost so heavily the night before, Cole refused to play with Bob and Charlie when they appeared at Salisbury's to join the game.

Cole had assigned Jim Younger the task of keeping an eye on Jesse, as Cole wanted to limit Jesse's interaction with the impressionable Bob. Jim was with the group of Jesse, Frank, and Clell Miller when they traveled outside St. Paul to stay at the Nicollet House. They were soon joined by Bill Chadwell, who was friendly with Mollie Ellsworth, the manager and madam of the house, and with Kitty Traverse, one of her employees. What with the transient nature of the house of ill-repute, the men did not draw much attention. They gambled and drank and talked freely with other patrons, especially those having information about Minnesota, its people, and its banks. Kitty Traverse later stated that one of the men appeared ill and never left his room. That probably was Jim Younger; Jim did not care much for the company he was forced to keep, and he was not one for raucous activities.

Cole and Charlie Pitts soon caught up with the group at the Nicollet. On August 20, Bob and Charlie went out to try to purchase some exceptional horses. The others were later described as being either bored or relaxed while they bided their time, doing things such as tossing coins from the balcony to a little girl in the street. Bob and Charlie purchased two McClellan saddles and a bridle from the Hall and McKinney Livery in St. Paul, and bought a bit from Nortons & Ware on Robert Street. They found horses that suited their purpose at the establishment of William A. Judd on Fourth Street.

The group at the Nicollet House then rode back into St. Paul. By accident there, Bill Chadwell ran into Patrick Kenny, a police officer he knew. Kenny asked after Chadwell's health and wondered what he was doing in St. Paul. Chadwell told him he

National Hotel, Red Wing, Minnesota. Frank and Jesse James, Jim Younger, and Charlie Pitts were guests of the National before the Northfield raid. The wooden structure of the hotel was later destroyed by fire.

was preparing to leave on a trip to the Black Hills. Later it was reported that Jesse had been seen purchasing a map at a local bookstore.

On August 26, Jesse, Frank, Jim, and Clell took a train to Red Wing, Minnesota, where they registered at the National Hotel and posed as cattlemen. The register recorded them as Ed Everhard, A. L. West, Chas. Wetherby, and J. C. Hortor. This group of four went over to J. A. Anderberg's Livery after dinner, and Frank James purchased a dun horse. Two more horses were purchased from a man by the name of A. Seebeek. A fourth horse was obtained somewhere along the way.

Meanwhile, Cole and Charlie took the train to St. Peter, Minnesota. Soon after their arrival they purchased two unbroken horses from a man named Hodge and bought reins, saddles, and bits at Moll & Sons. While in St. Peter, the two men stayed at the American House, where they registered as J. C. King and J. Ward. Before leaving St. Peter, Cole and Pitts took their new horses to a stable where they began breaking them in and teaching their horses the maneuvering tricks that can be useful in outlaw activities. During this interval, Bob Younger and Bill Chadwell remained in St. Paul.

Frank and Jesse had separated from Jim Younger and Clell Miller and were exploring the area in the vicinity of Northfield. By August 28, they were in Brush Prairie. The two were able to learn a good deal about the nearby community of Northfield under the guise of being prospective farmers who might purchase farmland owned by John Mulligan. Frank and Jesse even went so far as to negotiate a price. Informing Mulligan that their money was in a bank in Red Wing, they assured him they would return soon to close the deal.

Northfield was of great interest to Jesse as a possible robbery site. The rapidly expanding town had been settled by New Englanders after its establishment by John W. North, a prominent Republican and businessman who had been appointed Surveyor General of the Nevada Territory by Abraham Lincoln. North was one of those entrepreneurs who moved briefly to the South after the war to take advantage of financial opportunities available to those held in esteem by leaders in the federal government. When North brought his money back to Minnesota, he constructed a mill and a hotel. The establishment of Carleton College and St. Olaf College soon drew more people to the town, now named Northfield in honor of its founder. In 1876 it was a prosperous community but at the same time a quaint, quiet college town.

A turn-of-the-century parade passes Anderberg's Livery in Red Wing, Minnesota. Frank James's dun horse was purchased from Anderberg.

Bob Younger and Bill Chadwell intended to join Cole and Charlie Pitts in St. Peter on August 29; however, they missed their train. In general, Bob's experience in Minnesota was one mishap after another. Cole and Charlie did not waste time waiting for Bob and Chadwell but proceeded to investigate the area for themselves.

The two rode through the small community of Hanska and asked if they could rest for the night at the farmhouse of Mads and Granhild Ouren. The Ourens found the pair to be charming guests. Mads would later remember that Cole admired and asked about the splendid rifle that hung above Mads's door. It was a rifle that Cole would encounter again, and soon.

While Cole and Charlie Pitts were reconnoitering in Hanska, Jesse and Frank were exploring Northfield. They ate at a restaurant and walked about the town posing as potential buyers of Mulligan's place. They spoke with a man named Trussel about roads in the area. They also looked over the First National Bank of Northfield.

Bob Younger and Bill Chadwell finally arrived in St. Peter and registered at the local hotel as G. H. King and B. T. Cooper from Illinois. The Gang remained in small groups: on August 30, Cole and Charlie Pitts arrived in Madelia, where they once again posed as cattle buyers. The two stayed at the Flanders Hotel and enjoyed a long conversation with proprietor Thomas L. Vought over dinner. Vought, too, would reappear in the Gang's lives, in just about two weeks.

All eight outlaws reunited in Mankato, Minnesota, on September 1. After a brief rendezvous, two of them checked into the Gates House while two others registered at the Clifton House. John Jay Lemon, a Mankato resident, later stated that two of the outlaws visited Jack O'Neil's saloon that evening.

The next day, two strangers entered the First National Bank of Mankato and asked to change a fifty-dollar bill. They looked over the bank while they waited, but left as soon as their business was done. They joined two associates outside while their other companions watched on horseback from a short distance away. There were a number of people in the town that day due to a meeting of the local Board of Trade. Construction of a new building next to the bank was being watched by groups of bystanders. With so many people around, Jesse decided it would be best not to conduct their business in

(Top) *Mankato, Minnesota, 1876. Two members of the James-Younger Gang stayed at the Clifton House (l) the night before the aborted robbery of the First National Bank of Mankato.* (Bottom) *First National Bank of Mankato, Minnesota.*

Mankato. He signaled and both groups quickly left town. He told the others later that he thought he had been recognized in Mankato by a man he believed to be someone named Charles Robinson.

The Gang regrouped outside Mankato to discuss their next move. Jim later wrote that Cole was disgusted with Jesse and was convinced that it was only Jesse's vanity that led him to think someone so far away from Missouri had recognized him. Ignoring Cole, Jesse described the town of Northfield and suggested the bank there as their target. Bill Chadwell was familiar with Northfield and provided the Gang with some additional background information.

Chadwell told them that Adelbert Ames and Benjamin Butler were prominent citizens of the town. Both men were known to Southerners as carpetbagging scoundrels who had taken repeated advantage of people after the war. Ames had served as governor of Mississippi and had been impeached by that state's legislature earlier in the year for various improprieties. He had been cleared of all charges but had decided to relocate to Northfield, where his father and brother lived. Ames purchased an interest in the Northfield mills with money said by those sympathetic to the South to have been obtained from his carpetbagging activities. Benjamin Butler, too, was known to have a carpetbagger background in Mississippi. Southerners had even nicknamed him "Spoons" to indicate that he would steal his grandmother's silverware if given the chance. Butler soon made Northfield his home as well.

(Top) *Ames Mill, Northfield. Jesse Ames purchased John North's sawmill in 1869 and converted it to this flour mill. His son Adelbert joined him in Northfield in 1876.* (Bottom) *Gen. Benjamin "Spoons" Butler.*

Bill Chadwell believed that both these men kept their money in the First National Bank. The Gang agreed that this would make a splendid mark. The James-Younger Gang divided into two groups and began to make their way toward Northfield, some forty miles away to the east from Mankato.

THE NORTHFIELD DEBACLE

Jesse and Frank, along with Bob Younger and Charlie Pitts, arrived in Janesville, Minnesota, on September 4. Posing this time as railroad engineers, they registered at the Johnson House under the names of "Dave Smith," "George Pryor," "Jno. Jones," and "James Johnson." Cole, Jim, Clell Miller, and Bill Chadwell stayed in Le Sueur County that night, probably at the Adams Hotel in Cleveland, Minnesota. By September 5, the James group had moved on to Waterville. It was later reported that someone in Waterville answering Jesse's description was seen having a confrontation with a local resident. The two argued as to whether Jesse was someone the man recognized, although the man did not think then that he was talking to Jesse James. The discussion calmed down when Jesse finally convinced the fellow that Jesse was not who the man thought he was.

On the night of September 5, Cole, Jim, Clell Miller, and Bill Chadwell checked into the Dampier House in Cordova. Available rooms at the Dampier must have been scarce; two of the Gang, one of them later identified as Bill Chadwell, shared a room that night with a man named W. W. Barlow of Wisconsin. Barlow later reported that his roommates had been polite and he was pleased to have been in their company.

Bridge Street, Northfield. From this bridge Cole Younger and Clell Miller watched their accomplices cross the street to enter the First National Bank of Minnesota.

The following night, Jesse, Frank, Bob Younger, and Charlie Pitts stayed at the farm of C. C. Stetson, five miles outside Northfield on the Faribault Road. The other four outlaws put up that night at the Cushman Hotel in Millersburgh. It was later reported that one of the men said he was ill and remained in his room during dinner. Jim Younger's better judgment was evidently putting a strain on him.

On the morning of September 7 the Gang met up a few miles west of Northfield, outside the town of Dundas. They reviewed their plan.

The Gang would take up three initial positions, then move forward in sequence. As the main organizers of the robbery, Jesse and Bob would be the ones to enter the bank. Frank would go with them. Cole and Clell Miller would watch from a nearby bridge as the three secured their horses. The men in town would enter the bank as Cole and Clell came across the bridge. While Jesse, Bob, and Frank were doing their work inside, Cole and Clell would take up positions near the bank door. At the same time, Charlie Pitts, Bill Chadwell, and Jim Younger, waiting about a quarter of a mile away, would move forward to take up guard positions at the bridge. In the event of trouble, Charlie, Bill, and Jim were to holler their loudest Rebel yells and fire their revolvers into the air to divert attempts to interfere with the robbery. Jim later claimed that it was agreed by all participants that no civilians were to be shot. Money in hand, the Gang would then leave town as quickly as possible, Bill Chadwell leading the way.

It was about one o'clock when Jesse James, Frank James, and Bob Younger rode into Northfield. They tethered their horses outside J. G. Jeft's restaurant down the street from the bank and went inside to eat. They left about fifty minutes later. Strolling over to Lee & Hitchcock's Dry Goods, they casually sat down on some boxes stacked in front of the store. Talking quietly and laughing, there was nothing in their behavior to suggest they were anything other than the same two farmers who had been talking about buying a local farm and who were having a conversation with a friend.

At exactly two o'clock, the three entered the First National Bank of Minnesota. Cole later wrote that while he and Clell Miller waited at the bridge he was surprised to see so many people in the town. He did not feel it was safe. Aloud to Clell he wondered why their men had not simply passed through the town when they saw all the townsfolk going in and out of the shops and walking in the street. Clell Miller meanwhile was smoking a pipe while he waited. When Cole saw the three start for the bank door he advised Clell, "If they do [go into the bank] the alarm will be given as sure as there's a hell, so you had better take that pipe out of your mouth."

Division Street, Northfield. The Lee & Hitchcock Dry Goods Store fronts the Scriver Building. At the rear of the building is the First National Bank of Minnesota. Bob Younger was shot in the arm as he ducked under the outside staircase.

As Cole and Clell crossed the bridge and rode slowly down Division Street, they came upon none other than Adelbert Ames, out for a stroll with his father and his son. It was later reported in the Rice County *Journal* that Cole motioned to Ames and said to Clell, "Look, it's the governor himself." Ames, overhearing the remark, watched the two men continue on their way and said to his son, "Those are Southerners. Nobody up here calls me Governor."

Riding up to the front of the bank, Cole and Clell noticed that the door had been left ajar. Cole dismounted slowly and stood adjusting his saddle girth while he waited. Clell got off his horse and sauntered over to close the bank door. Just as Clell put his hand on the door, a hardware merchant, J. S. Allen, attempted to enter the bank, and Clell put his hand on Allen's arm to stop him. Immediately Allen realized what was taking place. He took off down the street shouting, "Get your guns! They're robbing the bank!" Henry Wheeler, a medical student home on vacation from the University of Michigan, had been watching Cole and Clell from the sidewalk in front of his father's drugstore on Division Street. As soon as young Wheeler saw Clell grab the merchant's arm, he also began shouting "Robbery!"

Cole and Clell scrambled up on their horses. Looking down the street they saw Jim, Charlie, and Bill charging up on their mounts. To keep the townspeople at bay, the five of them galloped their horses up and down the street, fired their revolvers into the air, and whooped and yelled.

Things inside the bank were not going much better. At first it had looked promising: there were no customers inside, only three employees. Immediately after the trio entered, Jesse demanded that bookkeeper Alonzo E. Bunker throw up his hands. There would be no play-acting this time. Bob and Frank held their guns on teller Joseph Lee Heywood and clerk Frank J. Wilcox as Bunker lifted his hands. Jesse then shoved Bunker beside the others and announced, "We're robbing this bank. Don't any of you holler. We've got forty men outside."

Their guns still trained on the bank employees, the robbers climbed over the counter. Heywood was asked if he was the cashier. He replied that he was not—which was true inasmuch as Heywood was only the acting cashier while his employer, G. M. Phillips, was away in Philadelphia attending the Centennial Exposition. The robbers refused to believe Heywood. One of them told him to open the safe door "damn quick" or he would blow off his head. Heywood replied that he could not open the safe inside the vault. When the order was given to the other employees, they said they did not know the lock's combination.

(Top) *Interior of the First National Bank, Northfield, as it was in 1876. The front desk is where Joseph Heywood was killed.* (Bottom) *Bank clerk Frank J. Wilcox.*

At this point Frank James decided to inspect the vault more closely and walked over to peer inside. In a brave and foolish move, Heywood broke from the others and tried to push Frank into the vault and close the door. Frank resisted and his arm and hand were almost crushed by the heavy door. Frank was enraged, but it was Bob who grabbed Heywood away from the vault and threw him roughly to the floor. Jesse knelt, put a knife to the cashier's throat, and ordered him to open the safe or "I'll cut your damn throat from ear to ear."

Heywood would not be swayed. He looked Jesse in the eye and told the outlaw that his throat would have to be cut. He was not able to open the safe, Heywood told him, because the safe had a chronometer lock. Now the robbers were puzzled: they had not heard of this new type of lock, which was preset to open only at a specific time. They asked Heywood what he meant and as Heywood explained, Bob Younger's attention shifted away from Alonzo Bunker. Seizing his chance, the bookkeeper dashed toward the back door. Bob shot Bunker in the shoulder, but the bookkeeper stumbled out, ran from the bank's back door to the street, and began shouting, "They're robbing the bank! Help!" Cole, who had dismounted, poked his head in the door as the robbers tried to decide what to do next. "Hurry up!" Cole hollered to his associates, "They've given the alarm."

As the citizens of Northfield became aware of what was taking place inside their bank, they ran to get their revolvers, rifles, and shotguns. The outlaws in the street were still firing only into the air, but the angry civilians fired directly at the robbers with whatever weapons they were able to find.

Cole remounted and yelled at everyone to get off the street. An immigrant by the name of Nicholas Gustavson continued up the street and seemed oblivious to the danger. Cole looked directly at him and told him again to "Get off the damn street!" What Cole did not realize was that Gustavson could not understand English. Caught in the subsequent crossfire, Gustavson was mortally wounded and died four days later.

Henry Wheeler, the medical student from the drug store, had hurried to the Dampier Hotel directly across from the bank. Armed with an old Army carbine, Wheeler took up a posi-

(Top) *Bookkeeper Alonzo E. Bunker. Bunker was able to escape through the back door of the bank after being shot in the shoulder.* (Bottom) *From one of these Dampier Hotel windows Henry Wheeler shot Clell Miller and wounded Bob Younger.*

tion at a second-story window and joined in firing at the outlaws. Clell had dismounted near the bank to see what was taking the men inside so long, but now changed his mind, deciding it would be safer on horseback. As he tried to remount, Elias Stacy, who had been handed a firearm by J. S. Allen, aimed in Miller's direction with a small fowling piece. Stacy's aim was true: he peppered Clell's face with shot.

Anselm Manning was born in Canada and moved to Northfield in 1856. He worked as a blacksmith and carpenter, then as a surveyor when the railroad was laid through Northfield. He eventually established a hardware store in town.

Anselm Manning, owner of a hardware store on Bridge Street, had armed himself with a breech-loading rifle. He now inched closer to the outlaws from his position at the corner of Bridge and Division Streets. Manning saw the three horses tethered outside the restaurant and correctly reasoned that they belonged to the bandits inside. Taking careful aim, Manning shot Bob Younger's mount. As Manning reloaded, Cole ran again to the door of the bank. Manning took a shot at him, but missed and set about reloading. Bill Chadwell was still spurring his horse up and down the street, and Manning now fired at him from a distance of about seventy yards. His rifle bullet pierced Chadwell's heart, and the outlaw toppled from his horse.

Meanwhile, Henry Wheeler continued shooting from the second-story hotel window. One of his carbine shots hit Jim Younger in the left shoulder. Wheeler paused only briefly, then resumed firing. Another of his bullets struck Clell Miller, severing Miller's subclavian artery. As Cole, still on foot, ran over to help Miller, Anselm Manning fired again and Cole was hit in the left thigh. Seeing that Clell was dead, Cole limped toward the bank door, yelling, "They're killing our men! Get out here!"

Inside the bank, the bandits refused to give up. Jesse dragged Joseph Heywood over to the vault and demanded that the cashier open the lock of the safe. Heywood again refused. What Heywood did not reveal was that the chronometer lock of the safe had not been set. Any of the outlaws could have opened the safe themselves at any time.

Frustrated, Jesse fired a shot into the floor. Bob Younger, realizing that their time was up when he saw Cole at the door, ran out of the bank to help his comrades in the street. Jesse and Frank heard the gunfire outside and watched Bob go out the door. Jesse scooped up what little money was lying on the counter and followed Bob Younger out the door. Frank, however, did not immediately join the others. He glared at the teller. Wilcox watched in horror as the bandit aimed his revolver at Heywood and

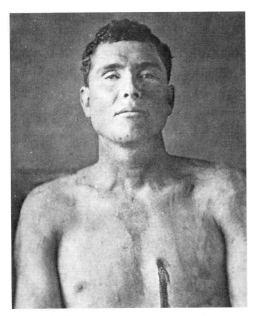

Bill Chadwell as seen in death, shot through the heart. Born "William Stiles" in Monticello, Minnesota, Chadwell was arrested as a horse thief in St. Paul. He relocated to Missouri after his release from jail and began using the name Chadwell. Bold, congenial, and sly, Chadwell was a welcome addition to the James-Younger Gang.

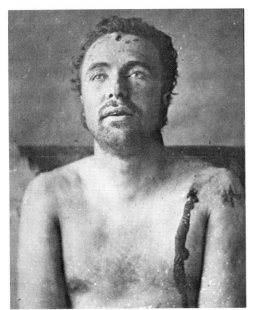

Clell Miller in death.

Joseph Lee Heywood, born August 12, 1837, in Fitzwilliam, New Hampshire. He left his family's farm in 1857. In 1862 he joined the 127th Illinois Regiment of the Union Army. He participated in the Battle of Vicksburg and later served as a druggist at the Union Army Dispensary at Nashville. Relocating to Minnesota, Heywood became bookkeeper at the Northfield First National Bank of Minnesota in 1872. He also served as treasurer of both the City of Northfield and Carleton College. He and his wife Mattie Buffum had one daughter. After Mattie's death Heywood married Lizzie Adams. More than $12,000 in gifts were received by his family after his murder, and his daughter attended Carleton College on scholarship. A Joseph Lee Heywood Library fund was established and a window bearing his name was placed in the Congregational Church of Northfield.

fired. That shot missed as Heywood sank down into his chair. According to Wilcox's later account, "as the robber made over the desk railing he turned and placing his revolver to Heywood's head, fired." Then the outlaw calmly, almost nonchalantly, exited the bank as blood and brains spread over the teller's desk.

A few moments before, when Bob Younger had run out the bank door, he saw that his horse had been felled. He also saw that Clell Miller and Bill Chadwell lay dead in the street. He now ran through a downpour of bullets as he tried to catch one of his dead comrades' horses. That task proved too difficult and Bob returned to the wooden sidewalk, exchanging fire with the determined Anselm Manning as he ran toward the corner. Bob ducked under a staircase near the corner of Division and Bridge, opposite of where Manning was continuing to fire at the Gang. Henry Wheeler, watching from his perch across the street, was able to see Bob only when the outlaw reached out to return Manning's fire. Wheeler took careful aim and shot Bob in the right arm, breaking it at the elbow. The ambidextrous Bob shifted his gun to his left hand and resumed firing.

Henry M. Wheeler, born June 23, 1854, in North Newport, New Hampshire. He moved to Northfield with his family in 1856. Wheeler earned his undergraduate degree at Carleton College. He graduated from the University of Michigan Medical School in 1877 and from the College of Physicians and Surgeons in 1880. He practiced medicine in Grand Forks, North Dakota, from 1881 until his death.

Cole, on horseback now, rode by Bob's location and yelled to him. Bob staggered out and Cole grabbed his brother by the belt and pulled him up behind him. Meanwhile, Frank and Jesse had been able to mount their horses in front of the restaurant. They looked around to see whether everyone who was still alive was able to leave. Cole's saddle horn was ripped loose by a bullet as the signal was given for the outlaws to thunder out of the town. Cole held on to the mane of his horse as Bob clutched his waist. Once again Cole was assaulted by a barrage of bullets. One hit his side and another tore into his thigh. Charlie was also shot, although it has not been determined precisely where, as he waited to make sure Cole and Bob would be able to get out of town. Several accounts tell of Jesse James being hit in the thigh as he began his retreat, and it is possible that Frank was slightly wounded in the leg as well. As for Jim Younger, shot in the shoulder, he was waiting now at the bridge. He started to turn his horse back to help Cole rescue Bob, but Cole gave him the sign that he was on his way.

THE RIDER OF THE DUN HORSE

In a cloud of dust and gunfire, the James-Younger Gang retreated west from Northfield. They did not know that their attempt had gained them only the $26.70 that Jesse had been able to grab from the counter. Most of them did not know that Nicholas Gustavson lay dying, and only one of them, the rider of the dun horse, knew that the brave bank teller had met a bloody end.

Several elements of the Northfield robbery continue to be controversial. One point of contention concerns the identities of the men who actually entered the bank. Bob Younger later readily admitted that he was one of the robbers who had gone inside, but he refused to identify his accomplices. When Jesse James was assumed to have been involved, the authorities took for granted that Jesse would not have been one of the men who waited outside. Cole Younger later asserted in his autobiography, a document of limited truthfulness, that Charlie Pitts was inside the bank.

Another point of contention concerns the identity of the man who murdered Joseph Heywood. It was assumed by many that the killer must have been the malicious Jesse James, although Frank James may have been so frustrated and furious at Heywood for injuring him that Frank might have shot him. Cole's autobiography states that Charlie Pitts killed the cashier. It was not until Cole lay dying, several decades later, that he revealed the identity of Heywood's killer and confirmed that the murderer had been the rider of the dun horse.

Part of continuing speculation results from Cole's various contradictory accounts. Cole claimed in letters written to friends in his later years that the fiasco at Northfield happened because all the men who went inside the bank had been drinking whisky, Cole adding that he never had confidence in a man who drank. It is likely that Frank James shared this sentiment, as he had undergone the same guerrilla training as Cole. What is not likely is that Frank would drink before a robbery or place his life in the hands of drunken accomplices. Jesse James drank on occasion but he was never known as a heavy drinker. Bob Younger was certainly nervous about the upcoming events, but there is nothing in his history to suggest he would drink to the point of impairing his judgment and endangering his brothers and friends. Nevertheless, in Cole's last account, he told Harry Hoffman that it was originally decided that Bob would stay at the door of the bank and that Cole had sent Bob inside when he realized Bob had been drinking. This statement contradicts two of Cole's other descriptions. He had said he was waiting on the bridge when he saw the three men enter the bank; if true, he could not have directly contacted Bob before Bob went in the bank. Cole also stated earlier that he was not aware of any drinking and if he had been, he would not have gone into the town.

The James-Younger Gang was well practiced in bank robbery. Jesse was prone to erratic judgment at times and might have felt he had to prove the merits of his disputed robbery plan, but that the Gang would jeopardize themselves by proceeding if even one of them were drunk is at odds with their usual style. Cole did not bring forward the drunkenness story until after Bob Younger's death. It appears likely that Cole put the blame on whisky in order to save face for his part in the debacle.

RETREAT TO DUNDAS AND SHIELDSVILLE

The people of Northfield did not know who had tried to rob their bank, but knew they wanted them captured. Part of the robbers' original plan had been to cut the Northfield telegraph wires when they left town so that news of the robbery could not be transmitted rapidly. There was no time, though, to cut wires when the Gang had to ride out of Northfield at breakneck speed. While only a handful of men chased the robbers immediately after the holdup, the message went down the wires immediately that the bank had been robbed and that three men were dead. Mayor J. T. Ames, Adelbert's son, also telegraphed the state capitol for help.

In the meantime, the outlaws retreated southwest through Dundas without incident. They stopped at the Cannon River to clean their wounds and consider the situation. Bill Chadwell, their only guide, was dead. Frank's hand and arm had been injured in the vault. Bob's bloody right arm hung limply at his side. Jim, Charlie, and Jesse had all been shot. Cole himself had been hit at least three times.

While the Gang regrouped, a farmer named Philip Empey appeared near the river bank, leading a horse pulling a cart loaded with rails. Empey was unaware of the afternoon events. He soon made the acquaintance of the surviving members of the James-Younger Gang when they demanded his horse for Bob to use.

News of the robbery had not reached Millersburgh by the time the Gang passed through that town. Two men traveling the road outside town had seen the Gang confront Empey and steal his horse. Outnumbered by six dangerous men, they did not confront the strangers but followed them and waited for an opportunity to alert others.

Bob Younger's arm was bleeding so profusely the group decided to stop at the farm of a man named Robert Donaldson to get clean water and tend to the injury. Donaldson provided a bucket of water and asked how the young man's injury had happened. One of the outlaws answered that there had been a fight with a "blackleg" back in Northfield. Bob had been shot but the professional gambler had been killed. When Donaldson asked the name of the blackleg, the reply was "Stiles."

Soon the men were on their way again, but Bob had lost so much blood he was lightheaded and weak. He had trouble staying in the saddle, and the Gang was forced to travel slowly, Cole leading Bob's horse by the reins.

The group stopped near Shieldsville to water their heated horses. They watched a group of local men hang their guns outside before going into a house. The same men, noticing the strangers at the watering trough, came back out to see what was going on. Ordering the men not to touch their weapons, the Gang rode off. They made about four miles before the men were able to catch up with them. Shots were exchanged, but the robbers eluded the men from Shieldsville for the rest of that day.

TWO-WEEK MANHUNT

A torrential rain began soon after the Gang disappeared into an area known locally as the Big Woods. That downpour turned out to be just the beginning of a two-week deluge. Rain would continue every day as the men made their way over the unfamiliar terrain.

It soon became obvious that they were in trouble. None of the Gang could be sure which direction might lead them to safety. They had no friends in the area, no easy access to fresh horses, no way to arrange for medical treatment, and they could not afford to stop and rest. Frank and Jesse may have had minor leg wounds, but the Youngers' injuries were more serious. All of them had lost blood. An infection settled in Bob's injured elbow and Jim's shoulder wound began to fester. Cole's bleeding thigh wound was so painful he had to wrap his leg tightly and lean on a tree branch when he walked.

Early in their retreat, by the time the outlaws encountered the four men in Shieldsville, more than two hundred men in the area had answered the authorities' call for a posse. By the second day the number of men in the field had grown to more than five hundred.

Parts of this huge posse were led by local sheriffs and deputies, some smaller groups by local Civil War veterans. Most of the volunteers, however, had no experience to bring to an organized hunt for criminals. Dozens of men, and boys as well, were drawn into the pursuit by the fifteen-hundred-dollar reward offered by Minnesota Governor J. S. Pillsbury. Others in the posse were only thrill seekers, unreliable participants who joined late in the hunt. The improvised nature of the posse created serious problems for leaders who had to make detailed plans and manage the men under their command. As George Huntington of Northfield later wrote about his fellow posse-members, "their failure at critical moments and places to do what they had been depended on to do made them more than useless, worse than enemies." Reports of outlaw sightings came in from all directions, many reports contradicting information received only a short time before. Nevertheless, the units of the large posse persevered, setting up picket lines of men throughout the area in an effort to block every route of escape.

Steady rainfall day after day gave the six hunted men one advantage: tracking their horses was all but impossible. The posses also did not know what the robbers looked like. Several times, in fact, the outlaws would cross paths with small posse groups only to identify themselves as members of another posse also looking for the Northfield robbers. The tired mounts of the Gang went unnoticed as many of the legitimate posse members rode equally used horses, and the outlaws hid their wounds.

On September 8, the day after the Northfield holdup, two men approached the wife of a farmer named George James and asked the woman whether she had seen two mules in the area. Saying they were worried that their mules might have wandered into a marshy area, the men asked Mrs. James about the local terrain. Satisfied with her answer, the two tipped their hats and left.

Later that day the Gang attempted to cross the Cannon River, but found the water too high. They then proceeded on Cordova Road along the river and, posing as a posse, stopped to ask a group of road workers where they might safely cross. They were directed to a nearby bridge. Close to the bridge, however, they spotted another posse and decided not to press their luck. The Gang detoured around Tetonka Lake only to come face to face with another posse, led by a Civil War captain named Rodgers. There was an exchange of gunfire and the outlaws, plunging into the lake on horseback, crossed over and vanished into a dense wood.

Later that same afternoon the Gang stole two horses from farmer John Laney.

Two more horses were commandeered from Ludwig Rosenau, whose son Wilhelm was ordered to lead the group across the river. The Gang then turned south toward Janesville. Two more fresh horses were acquired by forcing two boys at the Rosenhall farm to unhitch their plowing team. Following the boys' directions, the Gang then tried the Elysian Road again, the same road on which, not far away, they had abandoned their original mounts at the Kohn farm near Waterville. Not much progress had been made away from Northfield. That evening two of the least injured of the Gang members were able to trick another posse into giving them a meal, and they brought back extra food for the others.

Employing evasive action, the Gang continued to wander for days. By the evening of September 10, as the Gang hid on an island on Lake Elysian, they were surrounded by a posse of more than two hundred. In the morning, though, the outlaws escaped again, this time by releasing three horses as a diversion, tethering the other three to a tree, then proceeding through the boggy woods on foot. Evidently they stopped to dress their wounds about one mile west of the lake; bloody rags were found at the scene several days later.

The Gang was now in dire need of rest. They holed up in a deserted farmhouse ten miles northeast of Mankato for the next day and a half.

On September 12, the six hunted men crossed paths with a farmhand named Jeff Dunning. Rather than kill the man in cold blood because he would be able to reveal their whereabouts, the Gang let Dunning go free on the condition that he tell no one of having sighted them. Dunning remained silent for about three hours after he arrived back home. L. M. Demarary, summing up Dunning's failure to expose the fugitives, noted that "Of course by that time the gang was several miles away."

The outlaws fed themselves the next day by stealing chickens from Demarary's farm. Then they crossed the Blue Earth River at a railroad bridge and followed the tracks around Mankato.

Bob Younger's severely injured arm and the infection in Jim Younger's shoulder were taking a toll on both men, who by September 14 were unable to keep up with the others. Realizing that he and Jim were slowing down the group, Bob suggested the five others ride on and leave him behind. The Gang refused to abandon Bob but did agree it would be a good idea to split up so as to confuse the posse. Those who could travel faster would probably be followed, but it was possible the slower group might be able to travel undetected.

Popular stories about the Northfield robbery and the subsequent retreat of the outlaws often claim that Jesse James suggested shooting Bob Younger so that the Gang could make good its escape. Accounts by the Youngers about the Northfield robbery varied a great deal across the years, but both Cole and Jim Younger consistently denied this charge against Jesse. As Cole told Jackson County Marshal Harry Hoffman many years later during Cole's deathbed confession, "No, Jesse James nor any person ever made that request or suggestion." Cole went on to tell Hoffman that the night before the decision to split up, Jesse and Frank went off in search of horses. When they were able to locate only two fresh mounts, it was Jesse, according to Cole, who suggested that Bob Younger take one of the new horses to ride. Cole in fact declared that the decision to split up the Gang was his own: "During this night Bob's arm had taken a turn for the worse and he was suffering great pain and I told Jesse and Frank to take the horses and go. And this they did. Their acts and treatment of us were honorable and loyal."

The Youngers turned over most of their personal effects to the James boys, and the Gang parted company. Loyal Charlie Pitts chose to stay with his longtime friends, the Youngers. It would prove to be a costly decision.

Frank and Jesse James decided to follow the Blue Earth River west. That evening as they approached Lake Crystal they noticed a small group of men sleeping on a bridge at the lake. Hoping to cross, they approached quietly but were spotted by one man who then took a shot at them. The two outlaws galloped off before the sleepy posse could get organized. Later the brothers stole two horses which they were forced to ride bareback. Even so, by riding hard they were able to reach the South Dakota border within forty-eight hours. Near the border, on September 17, they stole two horses to replace their exhausted mounts. Very likely they had a good laugh later over the fact that one horse was blind in one eye while the other was partially blind in both. Frank and Jesse soon procured other horses and continued on their way. The ploy of splitting up had worked, at least for the James boys. As they had predicted, most of the posse had pursued their trail.

Meanwhile, the Youngers and Charlie Pitts followed the railroad tracks south. They stopped briefly along the Crystal Road near Linden, where they were able to steal and prepare some corn, chickens, a small turkey, and a watermelon. Before they could eat, though, they heard voices above them on the bank. Correctly assuming that the voices meant a posse, the four scrambled up the bank and ran toward the woods. They were pursued but were able to disappear again, near the top of Pigeon Hill. The posse, returning to the embankment where they had first spotted the four, discovered two leather bridles, a small piece of carpeting, a blood-soaked handkerchief, a shirt with the initials G. S. O., a ripped shirt with no back, and two of Bob Younger's coats: a blue gossamer coat and a new brown linen duster.

The next day Cole, Jim, Bob, and Charlie were seven miles outside Madelia, still on foot. They tried to push westward but the denseness of the forest and the number of boggy areas and small lakes and ponds were confusing. Early on the morning of September 21, as the four were following a road along Lake Linden, they came upon a farm where a teenaged boy was milking cows. Nonchalantly, the four outlaws greeted the boy with "Good morning," then walked on and disappeared into the woods a short distance from the farm. Oscar Sorbel watched until the men were out of sight, then ran to tell his father about the suspicious foursome. The boy wondered aloud whether the men might be the Northfield robbers. He was told to get back to work and stop letting his imagination run wild.

Axle Oscar Sorbel was born of Norwegian parents in the United States. He received $56.25 for alerting the authorities to the Northfield robbers near his family's farm. Sorbel later moved to Webster, South Dakota, where he worked as a veterinarian.

About an hour later, two of the outlaws returned and asked young Oscar if they could buy some bread. Having paid for the bread, they walked back into the woods. This time Oscar was able to convince his father that the men really might be the Northfield robbers. Mounting his horse, the young man rode quickly to get the sheriff, seven miles away in Madelia.

Sheriff James Glispin was in the company of T. L. Vought. Vought had conversed with Cole Younger earlier in the month, when Cole and Charlie Pitts stayed in Vought's hotel, The Flanders House. The two had used different names, but Vought remembered the larger of the two men (Cole) asking him about the roads and terrain of the area. Now Vought wondered whether his guests that night had staged the Northfield robbery. Glispen coordinated the forming of a posse with Civil War veteran W. W. Murphy. The posse was large: almost the entire male population of Madelia responded to the call and headed out with Sheriff Glispin and Oscar toward the Sorbel farm.

The outlaws, still on foot, were sighted within an hour's distance from the farm as the four attempted to cross a slough south of Hanska Lake. However, the posse led by Sheriff Glispin was unable to pursue the outlaws as the horses were too heavy to cross the boggy ground. Glispin and his men had to watch as the robbers ran into the woods above the Watawon River.

Four other men joined Glispin and Vought as they walked their horses slowly around Hanska Slough. Then, about a quarter mile from the river, the outlaws were spotted again. Glispin called to them to surrender. His call was ignored. At Glispin's command the posse opened fire. The outlaw band shot back at the posse as they continued to run.

At the bottom of a marshy thicket, the four decided to take a stand. By now they had little choice. The terrain was so dense and muddy and the men's exhaustion so great after two weeks on the run, it was useless to continue. They took up positions out of sight in a thickly wooded area and prepared themselves to meet Glispin and his men head-on. According to Cole's later account to Harry Hoffman, when Charlie Pitts suggested that the four surrender, Cole looked at his friend and said, "Charlie, this is where Cole Younger dies." The tenacious Charlie shrugged and addressed Cole by his Confederate title. "All right, Captain. I can die as game as you can. Let's get it done."

Bob Younger was sitting with his back propped against a tree. Too weak to aim his revolver, he would reload the others' guns. Minutes passed as the four men waited for the fight to begin.

The posse of seven to whom the Youngers surrendered. Left to right: Sheriff James Glispin, Capt. W. W. Murphy, George Bradford, Benjamin Rice, Thomas L. Vought, Charles Pomeroy, Jr., and James Severson.

W. W. Murphy called out for those in the front ranks of the posse to group together. Glispin, Vought, and Murphy, along with Benjamin Rice, George Bradford, Charles Pomeroy, and James Severson, got ready to descend toward the thicket. Murphy advised them not to shoot first since they wanted to take the outlaws alive. If there was shooting to be done, the posse should shoot low.

The seven men began to scramble down the slope into the marsh on foot. More than a dozen others watched cautiously from a short distance above. The group entering the slough tried to follow the river as they inched closer to the spot where they believed the outlaws waited. George Bradford later recounted, "I became convinced that we were getting away from the river and leaned down to look under the brush and told Mr. Glispin that I thought he was getting away from the river, when something drew my attention to the front and glancing that way saw some of the men we were after and just then one of them [Pitts] jumped up and fired. Almost simultaneously with his shot two men at least fired and Pitts dropped."

Charlie Pitts had fallen dead with a bullet in his heart. As a volley of shots was exchanged, Bradford was grazed by a bullet across his wrist. Cole's gun was shot from his hand. Murphy called out for the outlaws to surrender. By way of response Cole grabbed Charlie's gun and resumed firing. During the next volley a bullet struck Cole near his right eye, and Jim Younger was struck in the mouth with a rifle ball that smashed several of his teeth and lodged at the rear of his jaw. Another bullet lodged close to Jim's spine. As Cole and Jim went down, Bob Younger, his back to the tree, called to the posse to stop firing. "I surrender!" he yelled. "They're all down but me!"

Glispin immediately ordered his men to hold their fire. As Bob Younger staggered out of the thicket holding up a handkerchief, a shot rang out from the bank behind Glispin's group, and Bob was struck in the chest. He stumbled to the ground. Glispin yelled to the group behind him that he would shoot the next man who fired his weapon. Bob, shaking his head, muttered an exhausted protest, "I was surrendering. Somebody shot me while I was surrendering."

Charlie Pitts in death. Born in 1844 near Commerce, Oklahoma Territory, Pitts was one of twelve children. He was informally adopted at the age of sixteen by affluent Missouri farmer Washington Wells, on whose farm he worked. Pitts does not appear to have been a member of the guerrillas, but folklore has it that he served as a spy for Quantrill's movement. Pitts spent some time in the Ozark Mountains and with the Cherokee Indians after the war.

Slowly the posse walked toward the fallen outlaws. They helped Bob up from the dirt and watched closely as Jim Younger released his weapon and rose. Cole called to the approaching strangers and challenged them to fight him hand to hand. Bob looked over at his brother and told him resignedly, "Cole, it's all over. Give it up or they will hang us for sure."

Not willing to endanger his brothers in that way, Cole allowed himself to be taken into custody. Bob asked his captors for a plug of tobacco to help ease the pain in his arm and was given one. The Youngers then watched sorrowfully while Charlie's body was removed from the mud.

The Youngers were helped out of Hanska Slough and guided toward a wagon. As

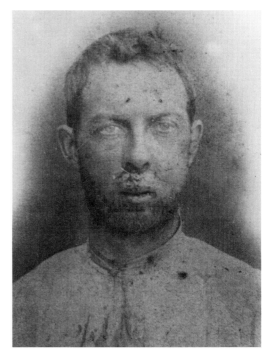

(Above) *Bob,* (Top Right) *Cole, and*
(Bottom Right) *Jim Younger, hours after
their surrender.*

Vought assisted Bob into the wagon, Cole recognized Vought as the owner of The Flanders House hotel. Affable even in the worst of circumstances, Cole greeted him as "Landlord." Jim was bleeding profusely and held his chin over the side of the wagon as the outlaws were taken back to town. On the way, the family of George Thompson approached in a buggy and Mrs. Thompson insisted the wagon stop so that she could give Jim a handkerchief to hold over his wound. Cole acknowledged to George Thompson that, yes, they had met when Cole and Charlie had visited Thompson's store in St. James.

News of the capture preceded the arrival of the outlaws, and the people of Madelia cheered as the wagon entered the main street. Cole Younger rose from his place on the floor of the wagon and tipped his hat to applause. The Youngers were then installed on the second floor of the Flanders House.

Cole encountered another acquaintance when Mads Ouren greeted him in the hallway. Bleeding from numerous wounds,

Flanders House in Madelia, Minnesota.

Cole chatted with Ouren, saying he had recognized Ouren's fine rifle, the one he had admired in Ouren's home, as one that had been used against him. Cole noted, though, that Ouren had not been the one who had fired that rifle. Ouren nodded and told Cole he had loaned the gun to a member of the posse.

Cole and Jim were placed in a bed together while Bob was taken to a room down the hall. Soon, Drs. Cooley and Overholt were called in to examine the outlaws' wounds. The trio was in wretched physical condition. During their two weeks on the run the men had been exposed to the basest elements of late-summer days and nights in the harsh Minnesota terrain. The heat, downpour of rain, and cooler nighttime temperatures had taken a toll on their bodies. The three had wrapped pieces of clothing around their feet in a useless effort to keep them dry. When Cole's boots were pulled off, his toenails came with them.

The town doctors determined that Cole had twelve bullet wounds, although not all of them were recent. Jim had five. Bob had a seriously wounded elbow and a fresh chest injury from the shot fired at him in the slough. Jim's badly injured mouth was cauterized, a painful procedure that Jim silently endured. This process was to be repeated several times during the next few days as Jim's mouth continued to bleed.

After their wounds were cleaned and dressed, the men were allowed to rest. Women from the town had promptly organized to donate fresh clothing to the outlaws. The men's other possessions did not amount to much. The three had only their weapons and their billfolds. Jim's billfold held a hundred and fifty dollars; Cole and Bob each had five dollars.

Guards were posted in and around the hotel to thwart escape attempts from the men inside or by accomplices who might still be in the area. Soon people from around the county began to pour into Madelia to catch a glimpse of the captured bank robbers. People gathered in the streets, eager to hear gossip about the robbery or speculations about the outlaws' future.

The foremost topic of discussion was the identities of the captured men. Before the robbery the Gang of eight had agreed not to reveal each other's identities whether alive, dead, or absent, a promise that would be kept across several decades. Police Chief James McDonough of St. Louis had traveled to Northfield as soon as he heard about the robbery. From descriptions gathered after the Rocky Cut robbery, he had determined that the two men killed in Northfield were Clell Miller and Bill Chadwell. It was McDonough's guess that the men who escaped Northfield included the James brothers and Cole and Bob Younger. In St. Paul, when McDonough later examined the body of the man killed in Hanska Slough, he was able to identify him as Charlie Pitts.

Bob and Cole freely admitted who they were but authorities were at a loss to identify the third man in their possession. It was known that he had not participated in the Rocky Cut robbery, but Cole and Bob would not identify him at first. Jim himself was unable to speak and chose not to deal with the issue immediately. A rumor began to circulate that the third man was none other than the infamous Texas outlaw Cal Carter. Confronted with this Jim shook his head, but the rumor persisted. When Jim was finally able to state his name a few days later, he was not believed. As for knowledge of the James boys, Cole and Bob denied ever having anything illegal to do with Frank or Jesse.

In addition to guards posted in the hallways and outside the hotel, each prisoner was provided with a personal guard. There was to be no vigilante justice in Madelia. It was posse member George Bradford who guarded Bob Younger that night. He reported in the morning that Bob had little to say.

In St. Paul, when he heard that Cole and Bob identified themselves, Chief McDonough felt certain that the two escaped outlaws must have been Frank and Jesse James. He had learned that the two had been tracked as far as Dakota Territory but there the trail had been lost. McDonough now ordered a small posse to be posted near the James-Samuel farm in Clay County, Missouri, in case the James boys returned to their home base.

That second day, the press was allowed to interview the prisoners. Cole immediately began citing events and justifications that might have come verbatim from John Newman Edwards's editorial, "A Terrible Quintet." Cole and Bob also expressed surprise and gratitude to the press about the courteous manner in which they had been treated since their surrender. Bob added that he had expected they all would be lynched. Bob chose not to describe events in his past, but when asked why the Gang had chosen to rob a Minnesota bank he replied candidly, "We tried a desperate game and lost. But we are rough men used to rough ways and we will abide by the consequences." Bob admitted that he had been one of those who had entered the Northfield bank, but steadfastly refused to name the men with him or disclose who had fired at cashier Joseph Heywood. Bob stated only that the murder of Heywood was "an act of impulse" and was something the entire group regretted.

A reporter from the St. Paul *Pioneer Press* asked Bob whether he liked the new sport of baseball. Bob answered yes he did, and noted that he had seen the St. Paul Red

Cole Younger at the time of his transfer to the Faribault jail.

Caps team as they left the Merchants Hotel in St. Paul. A copy of the *Pioneer Press* for September 22, 1876, carrying a story announcing the capture of the Northfield robbers the day before, made Bob smile. The young outlaw remarked that he had heard that hundreds of the papers had been sold; he was glad, he said, that somebody was making money off the bungled affair as he himself was "out five hundred dollars" after the robbery attempt.

Cole had been questioned by Sheriff Glispen soon after his arrest. When Glispen asked who had been Cole's accomplices, Cole told him he would provide a statement in the morning. True to his word, when approached by the sheriff the following day, Cole handed him a written statement. It was one sentence long: "Stay by your friends even if heaven falls." It was clear by that point that none of the prisoners would reveal the names of their Northfield accomplices. Preparations were made to move the trio to the Rice County seat of Faribault for arraignment and trial.

As for the robbers who had not survived the Northfield debacle, their bodies were being disposed of elsewhere in Minnesota. Charlie Pitts's body was sold to a doctor named Murphy in St. Paul for use as a skeleton. Bill "Chadwell" Stiles's body ended up in the possession of Henry Wheeler, the medical student who had fired on the Gang in Northfield. Clell Miller's corpse was embalmed and put on display for a while. Eventually Miller's family in Missouri was able to obtain a court order to retrieve his body for burial at the Muddy Fork Cemetery in Clay County.

THE YOUNGERS IN JAIL

On September 23, 1876, the Youngers were turned over to Sheriff Ara Barton of Faribault, Minnesota. Under heavy guard, the party boarded a car on the St. Paul & Sioux City Railroad to begin the trip to Rice County. Hundreds of people had gathered at the train station in St. Paul the day before, on Friday, because of a rumor that the notorious felons would be moved at that time. The transfer did not take place until Saturday, but even so there were still large crowds. The train arrived in Faribault at about noon. Another large group of onlookers there greeted the train and watched as the Youngers were taken directly to the county jail.

The outlaws were housed in separate cells measuring seven feet long and three-and-a-half feet wide. Once the outlaws were settled, visitors were permitted to look in at the prisoners. Bob at one point was accused of being impertinent when, because of his height and the narrow quarters of the cell, he rested his feet against the bars. Cole was allowed at first to sit on a cot near the doorway into the sheriff's quarters. By September 26, some four thousand spectators had walked through the little jail. Jim at first was too miserable to care much about the unwanted attention, but later he turned his back to the gawkers. Bob hunched as far back in the tiny cell as he was able.

Cole, however, enjoyed conversing with the sightseers, though he would say nothing on the topic of outlawry. He answered questions and narrated his distinguished family's history of persecution and was able to win some sympathy. A heavy guard was placed on the prisoners when anonymous threats of retaliation against those who had imprisoned the Youngers began to be received.

Within days the surgeon general of the state of Minnesota arrived at the Faribault jail to examine Jim Younger. He discovered that the bullet that had smashed through Jim's mouth was still embedded in front of his left ear. The doctor decided to leave the bullet in place for the time being as the wound was quite inflamed and painful. Meanwhile Bob Younger, who had granted some interviews, grew tired of talking to the press. He continued to be polite but said little. The *Pioneer Press* had dubbed him "The Knight of the Bush."

Soon after the Youngers took up their temporary residence in Faribault, C. B. Hunn, the superintendent of the United States Express Company, arrived along with St. Louis police chief James McDonough. The two men were accompanied by a party of seventy-five curious citizens from Missouri. McDonough had come from St. Paul, where he had identified Charlie Pitts's corpse. In Faribault McDonough confirmed that Cole and Bob Younger were indeed who they claimed they were. McDonough was convinced, though, that Jim Younger was Cal Carter of Texas. Bob and Cole had finally told the authorities that the man was their brother Jim, Cole even going so far as to offer McDonough a bet of five hundred dollars on the point, but McDonough continued to assert that the third prisoner must be Carter.

Jim Younger, shortly after his incarceration in Faribault.

Mayor Ames of Northfield soon paid the Youngers a visit. He informed them of the death of Nicholas Gustavson, the immigrant who did not understand English and who had been caught in the crossfire in the Northfield street. During his questioning Ames accused Cole Younger of firing the shot that killed Gustavson. Cole denied the charge, the two argued, and Cole finally asked that Ames be removed from his cell. What Ames had not told Cole or the others was that a Northfield coroner's jury had already determined the cause of Gustavson's death: "a stray bullet which had been fired by an unknown party."

Other visitors were also eager to interrogate the Younger boys. Louisville detective D. T. Bligh, whom Jesse James had once denounced in print as "an unnecessary liar, a scoundrel and a poltroon," showed up and tried to persuade Cole to admit to the Huntington robbery in West Virginia the year before. Cole denied any knowledge of the affair.

John F. Lincoln, superintendent of the St. Paul & Sioux City Railroad, also called at the jail, in the company of Minnesota state legislator John L. Merriam. The two had come to discuss with the Youngers the subject of the Gad's Hill train robbery in

1874, about which they shared a particular personal interest. Cole Younger asked John Merriam as they were introduced if they had not met somewhere before. Merriam smiled. It must have been a satisfying moment when he informed the outlaw that yes, they had met before, that he and John Lincoln had been passengers on the Gad's Hill train. It is more than likely these two men were the official-looking gentlemen who had been forced out of the train and made to strip to their underwear. Cole immediately denied having anything to do with the Gad's Hill events. As to where he had been on that night in early 1874, Cole declared that he and Bob had been in St. Clair County, Missouri. Bob Younger at that moment was responding to John Lincoln's questioning and did not hear Cole's stated alibi. Bob declared that he and Cole had been in Arkansas at the time of the Gad's Hill holdup. Need-less to say, the Youngers' stories were not believed.

Henrietta "Retta" Younger, born January 9, 1857 in Jackson County, Missouri, the youngest of the Younger children. Financed by her brother Bob and sister Anne, Retta was studying at the Baptist School in St. Joseph at the time of the Northfield robbery. She became a teacher and married prominent businessman A. Bledsoe Rawlins on April 1, 1894. The couple settled in Lancaster, Texas, where Retta helped the widower raise seven children. She had no children of her own. She died May 13, 1915, and is buried in Lancaster.

On September 26, 1876, formal warrants were delivered to each of the Youngers in their cells by Justice John B. Quinn and Judge Samuel Lord. Attorney Thomas Rutledge of Madelia had been appointed counsel for the outlaws. Acting on behalf of him-self and his brothers, Cole waived a preliminary hearing. The brothers remained in their cells for a few more weeks as the pros-ecution prepared its case. Meanwhile the authorities remained nervously alert to the possibility of an attempted rescue of the Younger boys. In one unfortunate incident, a deputy by the name of Henry Kapanick was shot and killed outside the jail when a guard, Frank Glaser, mistook Kapanick for someone attempting to break the Youngers out of jail.

During those weeks of imprisonment in Faribault, the story of the capture of the Youngers remained big news throughout the Midwest. The Younger family back in

Missouri read the first announcements with despair. The boys' nineteen-year-old sister Retta and their sister Belle's husband Richard Hall left immediately for Faribault and arrived on October 5. The family was hoping that the three men taken into custody had been misidentified. It was such a shock when Retta first caught sight of her brother Jim that she broke into tears. Seeing the young woman's obviously sincere distress, the authorities reluctantly had to accept that the man they had been referring to as Cal Carter was indeed Jim Younger.

For more than a month the Youngers remained in the Faribault jail before their day in court. Retta and Richard Hall remained in town to consult with the boys' attorney. The Youngers were model prisoners, even though the steady flow of un-wanted visitors and the glare of relentless over-head lights allowed them little privacy or rest. Young women sent the handsome Bob Younger gifts of candy and nuts. Cole and Bob became quite friendly with Sheriff Ara Barton. Their warm relationship with Barton would continue, in fact, throughout their long sojourn in Minnesota.

The Youngers learned they were to be for-mally charged with robbery of the First National Bank of Northfield, Minnesota, with attacking the bookkeeper A. E. Bunker with the intent to do bodily harm, and as accessories to the murder of Joseph L. Heywood. In addition, Cole was charged as principal and his brothers as accesso-ries to the murder of Nicholas Gustavson, despite the findings of the coroner's jury in Northfield.

Sketch of the Rice County Courthouse as it appeared in 1876, when the Youngers were arraigned.

During the week of November 10, the Youngers met with Retta, Richard Hall, and attorney Rutledge to discuss what plea to enter. Rutledge advised them that Minnesota law mandated they be hanged if they were convicted by jury of the murder charges. On the other hand, if they entered guilty pleas, the sentence would probably be life imprisonment with the possibility of parole within ten years.

When brought before the judge for their formal hearing on November 18, the Youngers in turn quietly stated "Guilty" when each was directed to enter a plea. When asked if he had anything to say, each responded, "No." Judge Samuel Lord then ordered that Thomas Coleman Younger, James Younger, and Robert Younger were to be confined to the Minnesota State Penitentiary at Stillwater until the end of their natural lives.

On November 20, two and a half months after the Northfield robbery attempt, the Youngers were escorted to a train to St. Paul in the company of Sheriff Barton and guards John Passon, Thomas Lord, W. H. Dill, and Phineas Barton. Upon their ar-

Minnesota State Penitentiary at Stillwater as it appeared in 1876.

rival they were transferred to a wagon bound for the town of Stillwater. Cheers and words of encouragement were shouted to them by some people along the Stillwater streets. Others, though, jeered and applauded their forthcoming incarceration. Quietly, Cole, Bob, and Jim Younger passed through the gates of Stillwater Penitentiary to begin a new phase of their lives.

As residents of the state of Minnesota the Youngers were identified as convicts #699 (Cole), #700 (Jim), and #701 (Bob). The three were treated no differently from other prisoners: they were searched, registered, bathed, weighed, clothed, and read the rules. Their hair was clipped, they were fingerprinted, given complete physical examinations, and measured in detail as specified by the Bertillon system of individual identification in use in prisons at the time.

The morning after their arrival, they met with Warden J. A. Reed to be given work assignments. At first all three brothers were assigned to make tubs and buckets so that the guards could keep an eye on them together. Warden Reed, however, soon noted that they were different from other prisoners in intelligence and social behavior, and he allowed them to change their occupations. Cole and Jim took jobs in the thresher factory where Cole put sieves together and Jim made belts. Because Bob was unable to straighten his arm or use the fingers of his right hand, the prison doctor thought perhaps the physical therapy of painting walls would be good for him. Bob could not tolerate the pain of that job for more than a few weeks, however, and asked to be transferred. He then joined his brothers in the thresher factory where he made straw elevators.

At about this time, the three were promoted to second-grade prisoners. This status allowed them certain amenities: they could eat in the dining room with other inmates, grow their hair to a length that could be combed, draw a ration of tobacco, write two letters per month, and receive visitors once a month. The brothers were not allowed to converse with each other more often than once a month, a condition that made their incarceration difficult. The one activity the prisoners were allowed without restriction was reading. All three took constant advantage of that luxury. Cole read historical biographies and classics while Jim continued his habit of studying theology, metaphysics, and literature. Bob read periodicals and medical books.

The physical damage from the Northfield disaster remained with all three of them. The bullet Jim had received in his mouth remained lodged near his ear. He would never again eat a meal except through a straw, and he suffered excruciating headaches and bouts of melancholia. Bob's right arm was almost useless, and he began to feel the effects of his chest wound as he developed a series of lung problems due to the dampness of his cell. For his part Cole suffered chronic headaches and experienced all the soreness and vulnerability to infection associated with a body full of lead: he still had several slugs buried deep in his body. The Youngers were resigned to being in Stillwater Penitentiary for a long time, however, and by all accounts they accepted their fate with stoic reserve.

FAR FROM MINNESOTA: THE JAMES BOYS

The lives of the James boys had taken a different turn from that of the Youngers. On September 25, while the Youngers were in Faribault county jail being stared at by fascinated citizens, Dr. Sidney Mosher of Sioux City, driving his buggy toward the town of Kingsley, Iowa, to treat a patient, was accosted by two men on horseback waiting on a bridge. Mosher identified himself as a doctor, but the men accused him of being with the St. Paul police. Mosher insisted that he was a doctor and invited the pair to search him. They did so. All they found was a small box containing a scalpel. If they still doubted him, Dr. Mosher said, they should ask the people at the next farmhouse to describe Dr. Mosher of Sioux City. This appeased the two men, who decided to go on with the doctor as hostage. They proceeded on horseback alongside the buggy until a couple of hours later, when the group came upon a farmhouse. One of the two, later tentatively identified as Jesse James, approached and told the farmer that the buggy belonging to Dr. Mosher of Sioux City had broken down and the doctor needed to borrow a saddle. The saddle was freely given but was put to use on the other outlaw's horse. The trio then continued together until after dark.

Spotting a light from another farmhouse in the distance, the pair stopped and ordered Dr. Mosher to climb down from the buggy and remove his clothes. Dr. Mosher was then given the taller outlaw's ragged outfit to wear while the outlaw donned the good doctor's pants and coat. Dr. Mosher was then released unharmed to find his way to the shelter of the farmhouse. The description Dr. Mosher later gave of his captors, including their courteous treatment of him, closely fit what was known of Frank and Jesse James.

Dr. Mosher's encounter was probably the last sighting of the James brothers for quite some time. In a detailed, though suspicious, account published by G. W. Hunt of the *Sioux City Democrat*, Hunt described encountering the James brothers the next day. Hunt claimed that he reassured the outlaws that he had no desire to capture them but merely wanted to hear their story; with that, Frank and Jesse provided him with an in-depth account of the raid on Northfield. Why the outlaws, who never discussed their illegal activities with anyone other than close friends and relatives, would have stopped for a garrulous chat with a reporter, is not fully accounted for in Hunt's story.

It is possible that Frank and Jesse headed either to Kentucky or Texas after their escape from Minnesota. They had family in both states who would have willingly hidden them away. Their exact movements and locations across the next nine months, until the summer of 1877, are unclear.

During this time Chief James McDonough, rather than the Pinkerton agency, was leading the hunt for the outlaws. McDonough believed, no doubt reasonably, that at some point the James boys would return to Missouri and to their mother's home. Several newspaper editorials, however, expressed a belief that the Jameses would never be caught in Clay County; friends and neighbors there would always protect them. Although a number of people in that county were unhappy with the notoriety the James brothers had brought to their neighborhood, it remained true that the Jameses had many staunch friends who would shield them. Another media blitz debated this issue at length.

At one point in the manhunt, after a report was received that Frank and Jesse had returned to the Jackson-Clay County region, Chief McDonough arranged for Sergeant Morgan Boland and other policemen from St. Louis to make an unannounced visit at the home of Dr. William W. Noland of Independence. Dr. Noland was known to be treating a man for a bullet wound in the leg, and McDonough believed that either Frank or Jesse had been wounded in the leg during the Northfield escape. Neither Dr. Noland nor his patient, John Goodin, could convince the posse that arrived in Independence that Goodin was not Frank James. Goodin had to remain in custody until after he was taken to St. Louis, where doctors confirmed that Goodin's leg wound was indeed several months old.

In fact, the James boys did return briefly to Missouri, but by the summer of 1877 Frank and Jesse had bade a temporary goodbye to friends there and taken up residence in Humphreys County, Tennessee, where Jesse thought they had better lie low. He retrieved his wife, Zee, and infant son, Jesse E., from their rented rooms in Kansas City and then, under the alias of "John Davis Howard," leased a house and small farm from W. H. Link, near Box's Station. When Jesse had last been in the Tennessee area he had posed as a grain speculator. This time he posed as a farmer. To confuse those who might suspect him, Jesse played the role of "Dave Howard," a man who was timid and unwilling to fight, who would ask other men to help him one day when he was challenged by a group of rowdies near the town of Waverly. Jesse kept up this charade for a couple of years while attempting for the first time to live a life that did not include robbery.

Jesse and Zee experienced a profound sorrow after living on the Link farm for about eight months. Zee gave birth to twin boys, whom Jesse named Gould and Montgomery, in February 1878. Both boys died within days of their birth.

Frank James was also trying to put his past behind him. Frank probably decided that he and his brother were better off with a few miles between them. He took Annie to live on the Josiah Walton farm off the Clarkesville Pike near Nashville. There Frank went by the name of "Ben J. Woodson" and Annie was known as "Fannie." On the Walton farm their only child, Robert Franklin James, was born on February 6, 1878.

Back on the Link farm, Jesse's misfortunes continued. In the mosquito-ridden climate of Tennessee he contracted malaria and was extremely ill and weak for several months, during which time his inability to care for his family financially became a pressing problem. Sometime during this stressful period Jesse borrowed a thousand dollars from a man in Nashville, Steve Johnson. Eventually Johnson demanded repayment, "Dave Howard" was unable to come up with the money, and Johnson brought suit. Playing fast and loose, Jesse purchased a small herd of cattle from a farmer named Ennis Cooley and paid for the herd with a check that bounced. Cooley sought payment and eventually sued "Dave Howard" as well. Under the alias of "Mr.

Young," Jesse sold the cattle, and it is likely that he then paid off his debt to Steve Johnson, as Johnson's suit was dismissed on September 11, 1878. Farmer Cooley was never paid.

Jesse and Zee abandoned the Link farm and moved to Nashville in the winter of 1878. Jesse was plagued by debts and weakened by recurrent bouts of malaria. Frank James stepped in at this point. It was dangerous for the James brothers to live together since they might draw more attention, but they decided that for the time being Jesse, Zee, and little Jesse, now aged two-and-a-half, would move in with Frank, Annie, and baby Robert on the Felix Smith farm. The farm spread atop a knoll east of the Clarkesville Pike outside Nashville, where Frank had moved his family after Robert's birth. There, half a year later, Jesse's wife gave birth to a daughter, Mary, on July 17, 1879. Without Frank, Jesse headed back to Missouri shortly after his daughter's birth.

THE NEW JAMES GANG

Jesse needed money badly and knew only one easy way to get it. The problem, he had learned, was not planning a robbery so much as effective execution of the plan. Since the Youngers were not available, Jesse had to think carefully about accomplices. Frank was succeeding in his efforts to be law-abiding and was not willing to take up the outlaw life again now. Reviewing those he thought he could trust, Jesse first considered his and Frank's former comrades in Missouri. Jesse had not kept in close contact with such men over the past few years. He knew that many who might have been eager to participate years before had either moved out of the area or were now family men who would not want to be involved in such activities.

Jesse was desperate. He had a dependent wife and son and baby daughter, and no way he could see to make an immediate change in his financial circumstances. In the long run, outlawry, as he knew, did not offer an easier life. For Jesse, however, robbery was an activity that fulfilled two of his greatest personal needs: money and excitement.

Eventually Jesse recruited five men, among them his cousin Wood Hite, former Quantrillian Dick Liddil, and Clell Miller's younger brother Ed. Tucker Bassham was asked to join, not because Jesse knew him well, but because Tucker's brothers had served as guerrillas. Bill Ryan, a man whose reputation for drinking outshone any of his other less-than-admirable qualities, rounded out the group.

On October 8, 1879, it was evident that Jesse James was back in action. His new gang successfully robbed the express car and passengers aboard the Chicago & Alton Railroad as it stopped at the Glendale, Missouri, station. The take was approximately six thousand dollars.

The Gang split up after the Glendale heist. Jesse returned to Nashville along with Ed Miller. He did not resume the life of farming. Instead, he and Ed used their share of the robbery money to purchase a promising racehorse called Jim Malone. After winning several races, Jesse and Ed traveled with the horse to a track in Atlanta. Jim Malone was less successful in Georgia. Jesse's and Ed's losses were so deep they had to sell the horse to finance their trip home.

On November 4, 1879, as Jesse was touring the racetracks, an article appeared in a Kansas City newspaper declaring that Jesse had been murdered by his longtime friend, George Shepard, a man suspected of several robberies with the James-Younger Gang, including the Russellville holdup for which he had served a ten-year term in the Kentucky penitentiary. The rumor of Shepard's betrayal reached all the way to the Stillwater prison in Minnesota. Cole Younger was asked by prison officials and fellow convicts whether he believed that Jesse was dead at the hand of a friend. Cole's usual response was, "I believe it is true if George Shepard says it is true." Shepard's response was vague when he was questioned about the matter, and not many people believed they had heard the last of Jesse James.

Meanwhile, Frank James was thriving in Tennessee. He and his family were now living on the Jeff Hyde place near Nashville, and Frank had taken a job at the Indiana Lumber Company. While Jesse had posed as a coward to make himself uninteresting, Frank, still known as "Ben Woodson," boldly befriended various law enforcement officials in the area. Jesse returned to his family in Tennessee in the winter of 1879, then went back to Missouri, still with Ed Miller, early in the summer of 1880.

During this period, Tucker Bassham came to the attention of the law when he recklessly spent his proceeds from the Glendale robbery around Jackson County. Bassham broke down under questioning and admitted he had been one of the robbers of the Chicago & Alton Railroad. He was tried quickly and sentenced to ten years in the Missouri penitentiary.

Another member of the James Gang disappeared soon after: Ed Miller, who did not survive the journey back to Missouri with Jesse James. Some accounts claim that Jesse was suspicious that Miller, having learned of Bassham's confession, might expose Jesse as the leader of the Glendale robbery. This theory has Jesse shooting Miller before Miller could turn himself in to the law. In the account by Jesse's cousin Clarence Hite, however, it was during a violent argument with Jesse that Ed Miller died. Pulling his gun, Miller took a shot at Jesse that knocked off Jesse's hat. Jesse then fired on Miller and buried his body somewhere at the side of the road. No confirmation or additional details have come to light.

Jesse returned to his family in Nashville in July 1880, now in the company of Dick Liddil and Bill Ryan, both of whom were coarse and violent men. Frank James was irate that Jesse had brought his new associates to Nashville, where Frank and his family had been able to merge with some of the more successful citizens. Confronted by Frank, who was greatly concerned that Jesse and his low-life friends would destroy his careful cover, Jesse compromised. Bill Ryan was sent to stay for the rest of the summer with a cousin of the Jameses in Adairville, Kentucky.

Jesse retrieved Ryan in September and headed for Mammoth Cave, Kentucky. It is possible that Dick Liddil was also along for the ride, but he may have been asked to stay behind to keep an eye on Jesse's family. There Jesse and Bill Ryan robbed a tourist stagecoach halfway between Mammoth Cave and Cave City. With characteristic flair, Jesse performed the robbery as if he were an actor in a comic role. The stage passengers were told that he and Ryan were poor moonshiners who needed cash to escape revenue agents. They even jotted down the names of all the passengers and promised to return their money as soon as times were better. They then made off with watches, jewelry, and more than two thousand dollars in cash.

Despite a five-hundred-dollar reward offered for their capture by the governor of Kentucky, Jesse and Ryan successfully made their way back to Nashville. Attention was diverted from the two when law enforcement officials mistakenly arrested Dr. Thomas Hunt of Scottsdale, Kentucky, for the stagecoach robbery. Two weeks later Jesse James returned to Kentucky and, along with Bill Ryan and Dick Liddil, robbed the payroll of the Dovey Coal Mines at Mercer. The three outlaws had expected a large haul and were disappointed when they managed to net less than fifteen dollars.

In November 1880 Jesse and Dick Liddil returned briefly to Missouri to recruit more members. They were back in Tennessee by the end of the month, accompanied by former guerrilla Jim Cummins. Cummins had probably been a member of the group who committed the Roberts bank robbery in Independence in 1867. He was possibly a participant in the train robbery in Muncie, Kansas, in 1874, although it is unclear which group he was with at that time. Cummins had recently been implicated in the Glendale robbery of 1879, and although he was probably innocent of that particular felony he was anxious to get out of Missouri for a while. Cummins took up temporary residence with Frank and Annie in Nashville since Jesse and his family were now staying in a boarding house on Summer Street.

Cummins had been a good friend of Ed Miller and was suspicious that Jesse may have murdered his friend. Eventually Cummins became so ill at ease around Jesse that Jesse began to joke to Liddil that they ought to get rid of the man. When Dick Liddil privately shared this information with Cummins, Cummins left Tennessee immediately.

Jim Cummins.

Now Frank and Jesse James had to consider the possibility that Cummins might betray their presence in Nashville to the law. The two decided it would be a good idea to hide out in Alabama for a while and see what developed. Before leaving Tennessee, Jesse moved his family to another address in Nashville, 903 Woodland Street, where he left them in the care of Dick Liddil. During Jesse's absence there was an incident on Woodland Street during which Liddil took a shot at a man throwing rocks at the door of the house. Soon after that, Zee and her two children moved to 711 Fatherland Street.

Sometime shortly after Jesse and Frank's return to Tennessee, Jesse decided to put into action a scenario that he and Frank had apparently developed while they were in Alabama. Frank may have been kidding when he and Jesse spoke about robbing a Muscle Shoals paymaster, but Jesse evidently thought the idea a good one. On March 11, 1881, Jesse, Dick Liddil, and Bill Ryan robbed government paymaster Alex Smith near the small, riverside town of Muscle Shoals, Alabama. The take was more than five thousand dollars. Frank was no doubt furious to learn that Jesse had pulled a robbery so close to where Frank and his family were living. He often told his younger brother that Jesse's impulsiveness was going to cause them both a lot of grief. The grief would turn out to be Frank's when he had to stand trial for that robbery a few years later.

Two weeks after the robbery an incident occurred in Davidson County, Tennessee, which proved Frank right. Bill Ryan, on a drunken spree, bragged that he was outlaw Tom Hill; he then got into an argument and pulled a gun on a man. The disreputable Ryan was arrested and immediately fell under suspicion as a Muscle Shoals bandit because he had so much money on him.

Dick Liddil read about this in the *Nashville Banner* the day after Ryan's arrest. He immediately brought the paper to Jesse. Since Frank and Jesse could not be sure of what Ryan might do under the pressure of interrogation, they made plans to leave Nashville immediately. Wives and children were put on a train for Nelson County, Kentucky, to stay with friends, while Frank and Jesse took off on stolen horses to Adairville, Kentucky, to visit their Uncle George Hite. They also stayed with another longtime friend, Donny Pence in Nelson County, Kentucky, through whom they sent messages to their families.

Bill Ryan was extradited to Missouri and convicted there of participating in the Glendale train robbery. Tucker Bassham, serving time for the same crime, was pardoned after he agreed to testify against Ryan. In Bassham's incriminating statement, he declared that Jesse James, Ed Miller, Dick Liddil, Bill Ryan, and Wood Hite had been his accomplices during the Glendale job. Soon after volunteering this testimony, Bassham found his home in Jackson County, Missouri, burned to the ground. He quickly left the state in fear for his life.

Meanwhile, putting distance between themselves and Alabama, Frank and Jesse took separate routes back to Clay County, Missouri. Zee and her two children arrived in Kansas City on May 1, 1881, escorted by Jesse's cousin Clarence Hite, and stayed with Zee's sister, Mrs. Charles McBride. Annie and little Robert were the guests of General J. O. Shelby for a few days before traveling on to Annie's father's home in Independence. Shelby had returned from his adventures in Mexico and was attempting to live out his life quietly with his family.

The James brothers met up with their wives again about a month later, in Kansas City. For safety the men kept a separate address from their families. Jesse rented some rooms at the Doggett House on Sixth and Walnut, and on June 1, he rented a house for his family on Woodland Avenue from former newspaperman D. R. Abeel. Jesse, now going by the name of "J. T. Jackson," furnished the house using his share of the money from Muscle Shoals. As was his practice, he wore no physical disguise; instead, he posed as a sour eccentric who wanted nothing to do with his neighbors. Some who encountered him thought "Jackson" might be a gambler, as it was known he did not have a job. Zee was well-liked by the women of Woodland Avenue and would help them out in times of trouble. Little Jesse E. was not allowed to play with children of the neighborhood. His father had bestowed the name of "Tim" upon him, but for more protection Jesse and Zee decided the boy was not to venture beyond his own fenced lawn. Zee would later say that it broke her heart to watch Jesse E. standing by the window watching other children play outside.

It was only a short time before Jesse needed more money and began to plan another robbery. This time Frank decided to join him. It is anyone's guess why Frank returned to a life that caused his wife and child so much discomfort. Thanks to Jesse, though, Frank's life of respectability was a thing of the past. Perhaps Frank needed money, perhaps he simply missed the excitement of living outside the law. Frank was never one to explain his actions; he simply did what he wanted to do. As usual, Frank put his needs ahead of his family's, just as his brother Jesse did.

In any event, the James boys together laid plans to rob the Chicago, Rock Island & Pacific Railroad near Chillicothe, Missouri, on June 8. Their accomplices would be Dick Liddil and their cousin Wood Hite. This plan had to be canceled, though, after heavy rains flooded the roads. The group then rode their horses back to the area of Gallatin, Missouri—the town where the Daviess County Savings Association had been robbed and cashier John Sheets killed back in 1869. Near Gallatin they attempted to put together another robbery, but that plan too was put aside when Jesse had to board a train for Kansas City to get treatment for an abscessed tooth. A third robbery was aborted near Gallatin on July 4 when the train passed by before the Gang could stop it.

There were other possibilities for robbery in Missouri, though, and one included a possibility of revenge. The Confederate guerrilla network of information was still functioning, and Frank and Jesse may have heard through that grapevine that William Westfall—the man believed to have been in charge of the train involved in the bombing of the James-Samuel house—was now a conductor for the Chicago, Rock Island & Pacific Railroad. On July 15, 1881, a train belonging to that company was stopped by outlaws outside the small town of Winston, Missouri. It was reported later that at least five men participated.

Some of the robbers boarded the express car while others climbed aboard the passenger cars. Westfall, the conductor, was found in the smoking car and shot in the back after he was told to raise his hands and after he complied with the demand. The man who fired that bullet then walked up to Westfall as he lay on the floor of the car and shot him again. Passenger Frank McMillan, watching in horror, became the next victim; he was fatally shot after he somehow became involved in the drama. Later, Dick Liddil would testify that he was part of the group, along with Frank and Jesse and Clarence and Wood Hite. Liddil swore to an officer of the court that it was Jesse who deliberately murdered Westfall, but that it was Frank who shot McMillan.

Etching of the Blue Cut robbery.

The men rode south all night and finally stopped when they reached the Crooked River. They divided their booty only to find they received a mere $130 each. Leaving Liddil behind, Jesse, Wood, and Frank rode into the town of Lawson, Missouri, where they ate dinner at a farmhouse. They then proceeded to the James-Samuel farm where they camped in a grove of trees behind the house; there they enjoyed a large meal brought to them by Zerelda, their half-brother John, and Will Nicholson, their half-sister Sallie's husband. Jesse was on his way back to his wife the following morning while Frank stayed to have a short visit with his mother.

Soon after the Winston robbery, on advertisements throughout the state, Missouri Governor Thomas Crittenden, a man who would loom large in the James boys' future, offered rewards of five thousand dollars each for delivery of Jesse and Frank James to the sheriff of Daviess County. An additional five thousand each would be awarded upon conviction for the Winston or Glendale robberies or the murders of cashier Sheets, conductor Westfall, or passenger Frank McMillan. Five thousand dollars was also offered for any of their accomplices during these crimes. Such an intervention by a state governor was unusual. Crittenden was under a great deal of pressure to ensure that Missouri did not become again the outlaw state it had been during the reign of the James-Younger Gang. His humor still intact, Jesse liked to tell his family of how his neighbor John Murphy, Marshal Con Murphy's father, asked him once if he would like to join a posse to look for the James boys. "Mr. Jackson" politely declined. Jesse thought it was probably once again time to move on to another city.

PAROLE FOR THE YOUNGER BOYS?

Life in the summer of 1881 was quieter among the Younger brothers. By that time they had served five years and felt it was time that a formal parole drive be organized. Their uncle Littleton Younger had traveled from St. Clair County to St. Paul earlier in the year for a private meeting with Minnesota Governor John S. Pillsbury. Littleton suggested at that meeting that the governor grant pardons to all the Youngers on the grounds that they had been driven to their crimes by circumstances beyond their control. Governor Pillsbury cordially refused to comply.

In July 1881 a pamphlet was published and distributed in Minnesota. Entitled "A Brief History of the Younger Brothers and the Reasons Why They Should Be Pardoned," the pamphlet's contents resembled John Newman Edwards's essay, "A Terrible Quintet." Late in the fall Littleton Younger returned to Minnesota to appeal once again to Governor Pillsbury. This time he brought letters solicited from several influential people in Missouri. Again his request was denied. For the time being, and in fact for many years to come, the Youngers would stay put.

NO TURNING BACK

On August 30, 1881, Jesse and Frank rented a large house on East Ninth Street in Kansas City. Frank had sent Annie and little Robert to visit family in California, but now he wanted them back. He sent for them and waited. The rental house was spacious enough to house both families if Frank decided to remain with Jesse after his family returned.

Meanwhile, four men had robbed the Davis and Sexton Bank in Riverton, Iowa, on July 11. The new James Gang was immediately suspected, but authorities soon concluded instead that members of a gang led by Poke Wells were the culprits.

The James Gang did strike again on the night of September 7, five years to the day since the Northfield robbery. The St. Louis Express was stopped near Blue Cut, Missouri. A new recruit named Charlie Ford probably had participated in the Winston robbery. Ford had become acquainted with Jesse through Wood Hite. Hite had met Charlie and his younger brother Bob while visiting their sister Martha Bolton, who was a paramour of Dick Liddil's. The youthful Ford brothers were from Ray County, Missouri, adjacent to Clay County. From his later actions, Jesse seemed to view them as possible protégés. He decided to try out the older brother Charlie first.

With Charlie Ford in tow, Jesse, Frank, and their boys broke open the express car at Blue Cut. Demanding that messenger H. A. Fox open the safe, they beat him with the butt of one of their guns when the money turned out to be less than they expected. Passengers were accosted with ugly threats. The leader of the Gang wore no mask and boldly announced himself as Jesse James. Engineer "Choppey" Foote refused to cooperate further with the robbers and found himself threatened by a man who claimed that the gun aimed at the engineer's head was the same gun that had killed Westfall. Then brakeman Frank Burton, hearing the advance of a freight train, broke away to warn the approaching freight of another train stopped on the tracks. The outlaws shot at Burton as Burton ran down the tracks, and it was some moments before Burton was able to make his intent clear to the robbers. This new Gang obviously lacked the finesse and the compassion of the James-Younger organization.

Some of the old theatricality was still there, though. In his deposition later, Foote stated that after the men had taken all the money they could get their hands on, the leader of the band escorted the engineer to the front of the train and there presented him with two silver dollars. The robber expressed his opinion that the engineer was a brave man and advised Foote to use the two dollars "to drink the health of Jesse James [with] tomorrow morning." The same outlaw then offered to have his men remove the stones they had placed on the track to stop the train. Engineer Foote declined the help. As he declared later, "I was so tickled to get out of the scrap so smoothly that I told him not to mind the stones, we could take them off ourselves if he would only take himself and party off." With that the engineer was wished a good night and the outlaws disappeared into the darkness. Foote also claimed that he heard one of them yell, "Goodbye, old fellows, this is the last time you will ever see or hear of the James Boys."

When the Gang split up with their shares, Jesse, Frank, and Clarence Hite returned to Jesse's house on Ninth Street. Frank's wife and son had returned from California, and Frank now decided to take them to his mother's farm to recuperate from their trip and to prepare for another trip east. After he put his family on the train, Frank returned to the farm. Jesse had become unhappy with the Ninth Street house. On October 1, he rented another place at 1017 Troost Avenue. By November 5, something bothered Jesse enough for him to move yet again. With Charlie Ford along for the ride, Jesse departed Missouri with his family and headed to Atcheson, Kansas. The family did not stay there long before returning to Missouri. This time they took up residence in a lovely cottage on a hill overlooking the bustling town of St. Joseph.

At this time Jesse was using the alias of "Tom Howard," under which he rented the cottage at 1318 Lafayette Street from a St. Joseph city councilman for fourteen dollars a month. For her part Zee continued to use the name of "Josie" while little Jesse was known as "Tim." Evidently the baby's name posed no threat as it appears she continued to be called by her given name, Mary. Family members later claimed that Zee, who must have been exhausted from frequent moves and incessant worry, pleaded with her husband to give up outlawry and settle down with her and the children in the comfortable little town. Jesse, tired of the life himself, agreed to consider it.

There were other reasons to consider returning to lawful employment. With the reemergence of the James Gang, offered rewards grew larger for the capture of Jesse, dead or alive. The press continued its habit of giving the Gang a lot of publicity, but for the first time the majority of public sentiment was turning against the outlaws. Robberies committed by the James-Younger band had been performed in an almost gentlemanly manner, but this new Gang was ruthless and brutal. Robbery motives that had once been thought of as retaliation against a dominating Northern force now looked like nothing so much as greed.

Jesse was growing increasingly suspicious and uneasy. He had enjoyed the loyalty and trust of the Youngers, but while he naturally trusted Frank he knew that some of his associates—Tucker Bassham and Bill Ryan, and now Charlie Ford and Dick Liddil—were just small-time thieves glad of a chance to make some easy money and glad of the notoriety of riding with Jesse James. Jesse was constantly nervous, on guard day and night against one of his own men betraying him. He told his family that he wanted to give up outlawry and settle on a farm, but by now he did not know how to live differently. Robbery had become his way of life, and he must have realized there was no turning back now. Having committed so many felonies, even if Jesse reformed at this point he would still have to live on the run or serve the rest of his life in prison. The likelihood of his getting what he would consider a fair trial was small.

UNARMED AND BETRAYED: THE DEATH OF JESSE JAMES

In February 1882 Clarence Hite was arrested in Kentucky and extradited to Missouri for arraignment for his participation in the Winston robbery. Hite pled guilty and was sentenced to twenty-five years in prison.

In the meantime, a group of farm boys had been arrested and indicted for the September train robbery at Blue Cut. Their leaders' overblown claims of having been part of the robbery with the great Jesse James led law enforcement officials to be suspicious when the group came to trial. The case, in fact, was subsequently dropped, and the search for the James Gang continued.

Jesse's fears about his comrades grew stronger after Clarence Hite's arrest. Dick Liddil was well aware that Ed Miller had disappeared mysteriously when Jesse became suspicious. Liddil later claimed that he believed it only a matter of time before Jesse considered him a liability that would have to be eliminated.

Dick Liddil, born September 16, 1852. During his stint as a guerrilla he was present at the slaughter in Centralia, Missouri. Liddil is buried at Woodlawn Cemetery in Independence.

In March 1882 Liddil left Jesse and returned to Missouri, where he stayed at the Ray County farmhouse of Martha Bolton, a widow who was the sister of Charlie and Bob Ford. Wood Hite, the James brothers' cousin, was also there. The attractive Martha had a reputation as a rather loose woman who encouraged men to vie for her attentions. She was known to enjoy the company of the carefree and somewhat dangerous buddies her twenty-year-old brother Bob brought to her house. Bob Ford had not yet participated in a significant robbery, but he had stolen a couple of horses. He made it known to Liddil and Hite that he would be an effective and valuable member of a gang if they would just give him the opportunity.

One morning during Hite and Liddil's visit a violent argument began in the parlor. The result was Wood Hite's death at the hands of Dick Liddil and Bob Ford. Hite's fatally shot body was taken upstairs and stashed. That night it was wrapped in a horse blanket, taken some distance from the house, and buried.

Liddil knew there would be hell to pay when Jesse learned of his cousin's death. Rather than risk a confrontation with Jesse, Liddil decided to turn state's witness. He enlisted the help of his mistress, Mattie Collins, another woman with a reputation for associating with outlaw men. Liddil sent her to Jackson County prosecuting attorney William H. Wallace to arrange a deal. Mattie reported to Liddil that Wallace told her he would not prosecute Liddil if he provided information that would help him indict other Gang members. Hearing this, Martha Bolton visited Missouri governor Thomas T. Crittenden to seek pardons for members of the James Gang other than Jesse and Frank. Crittenden would not guarantee pardons in advance but did promise to use his influence to see that any Gang members who surrendered would not be severely punished.

Dick Liddil turned himself in to Sheriff James Timberlake of Clay County, Missouri, on January 24, 1882. Law enforcement representatives recorded Liddil's confession and then began to implement a plan to eliminate Jesse James. By common agreement, Liddil's surrender was not announced to the press for more than two months, until March 31, 1882.

Meanwhile, Jesse was living a quiet life with his family in St. Joseph. He spent a great deal of his time thinking of ways to give up the outlaw business. Jesse had read of a 160-acre farm with ninety acres of fine bottomland for sale near the town of Franklin, Nebraska, and he began to consider relocating there. The owner advertised it "As good educational, religious, railroad and other facilities as any point in western Nebraska." Nebraska was much like western Missouri in its social mores and Jesse had many friends and relatives there. Using his "J. D. Howard" alias, Jesse corresponded with J. D. Calhoun, the farmer offering the land, and began yet another plan to start life anew. After hearing from Calhoun, Jesse took Charlie Ford with him to look over the property. While Jesse was interested, he made no commitment.

Charles Wilson Ford, born July 9, 1857. Ford served in the Confederate cavalry under Col. Upton Hays. Distraught over the role he played in the assassination of Jesse James, he shot himself in a field near his home in Richmond, Missouri, on May 6, 1884.

Returning home from Nebraska, Jesse decided to visit his mother. He and Charlie stopped in Ray County to pick up Charlie's brother Bob. The three arrived in Clay County near the end of March. It is not clear where Frank was at this time, but he evidently had left the James-Samuel farm. He would later say that he was in Lynchburg, Virginia, with his family.

Jesse spent time with his sister Sallie Samuel Nicholson during his brief visit. When Jesse told Sallie that Jesse E. desperately wanted a puppy, Sallie encouraged him to bring one home for the boy. Sallie was surprised when Jesse told her that he felt that efforts by his mother and others to appeal to Governor Crittenden to let him surrender and stand trial might be successful. In reference to Jesse's visit to his sister that day, Jesse E.'s wife Stella later wrote, "He said if he were convicted he would go ahead and serve his time. At least then his family would be free to live at home in Missouri. And if he were acquitted, he'd build a home on his land and live as a human being should." Jesse spent the night at Sallie's while the Ford boys probably passed the night nearby at the schoolhouse.

To Jesse's surprise, his mother disliked the handsome and gregarious Bob Ford. Zerelda told Jesse she did not trust either of the Ford brothers, and she warned him to be careful around them. Zerelda later said that Jesse laughed as he mounted his horse to return to St. Joseph. With a puppy for Jesse E. tucked under his coat, Jesse off-handedly told his mother, "Ma, if we don't meet again, we'll meet in heaven."

Thomas H. Crittenden.

Before he could buy the Nebraska farm Jesse needed the financial benefits from one more robbery. He began plans to raid a bank in Platte City, Missouri, on April 4. He would use only the Ford brothers as accomplices as he was not sure where Dick Liddil and Wood Hite were. Suspecting that Wood Hite may have met with foul play since none of his family had seen him in a while, Jesse had gone to Kentucky in February. He turned up no clues and returned home. Bob and Charlie stayed with Jesse and his family in St. Joseph for several days while Jesse developed his plans for Platte City.

What Jesse did not know was that he had already been betrayed. Bob Ford had secretly negotiated with Kansas City police commissioner Henry Craig to arrange the assassination of Jesse James. Craig had arranged a meeting between Ford and Governor Crittenden on February 22 in Kansas City so that the governor could give his blessing to the plan. The deal involved a reward of ten thousand dollars and immunity if Bob and Charlie would deliver Jesse James, dead or alive. It is unclear where and when these negotiations began. There seems to be credence to the theory that Ford was first approached by Clay County Sheriff J. R. Timberlake after Timberlake's talks with Martha Bolton and Mattie Collins indicated the Fords might be willing to betray Jesse. Timberlake seems to have been a part of the conspiracy.

It was on the morning of April 3, 1882, in St. Joseph that Jesse and the Ford brothers finished a breakfast prepared by Zee and then removed to the living room to talk:

Jesse did not like discussing business in the presence of his wife and children; he made every effort to keep his outlawry separate from family life. When Charlie and Bob had joined him at the breakfast table, Jesse had angrily shushed Bob when Bob brought up the topic of the upcoming robbery at Platte City. The news of Dick Liddil's surrender had appeared in the newspaper that morning. Jesse read it at breakfast. Though he was quite agitated, Jesse simply folded the paper; its contents would be discussed later.

After breakfast the men moved to the living room. Jesse reopened the newspaper and asked the Fords what they knew about Liddil's surrender. They both claimed to be as surprised as Jesse. Bob Ford later said that Jesse dropped the subject of Liddil's surrender and the brothers' knowledge of it so quickly that Bob was sure he was a dead man. He was confident, though, that Jesse would not kill him or his brother in front of the family; more likely Jesse would wait until he had them alone out on the trail to Platte City.

Jesse stretched and then did something unusual. He removed his guns. By this time it had become a rule in life that Jesse was always armed, always on the alert for potential trouble, even inside his own home. That Jesse would remove his weapons when alone with the men his mother distrusted, especially when he had been reminded of Dick Liddil's betrayal just moments before, has been the source of considerable conjecture. It is almost as if the man had become tired of the long effort of defending himself.

Robert "Bob" Newton Ford, born near Hume, Virginia, on January 31, 1862, the youngest of the eight children of James and Mary Ann Ford. His family moved to Missouri in 1871. Bob Ford and his brother later toured the west as part of a revue in which they reenacted the murder of Jesse James, much to the distaste of their audiences. Bob Ford eventually established a saloon in Creede, Colorado. He was shot and killed in Creede by Ed O'Kelley on June 8, 1892. Ford is buried in Richmond, Missouri.

Noticing that a framed sampler on the wall stating "God Bless Our Home" was dusty, Jesse got a feather duster, moved a chair, and stood on the chair seat to dust and straighten the sampler. His back was to his two guests. The Fords later said that the unarmed Jesse turned only slightly at the sound of a trigger being cocked. Jesse's head jerked forward and hit the wall as it was struck with a bullet from Bob Ford's Smith & Wesson .45 Model 3. Collapsing to the floor, Jesse James was dead at the age of thirty-four, murdered from behind by one of his own men.

Charlie and Bob Ford stood motionless as Zee rushed into the living room and knelt to hold her dead husband in her arms and looked at her two houseguests in horror. The Ford boys quickly dashed out of the house, ran into town, and sent wires to Governor Crittenden, Commissioner Craig, and Sheriff Timberlake, announcing that their deed was accomplished. They then surrendered to Marshal Enos Craig and were placed in the St. Joseph jail.

A crowd in St. Joseph gathered at the James home at 1318 Lafayette Street on April 3, 1882, to view the slain outlaw.

Some neighbors on Lafayette Street rushed to the house when they heard the gunshot. At first Zee, known to her neighbors as "Josie Howard," told them that her husband "Tom" had been murdered. Zee's grief, however, was such that under questioning she soon admitted that her husband had been none other than Jesse James. Citizens of St. Joseph soon crowded to the house on the hill to see the body of the slain outlaw. Jesse's body was removed to the Sidenfaden Funeral Parlor as soon as assistant coroner James W. Heddens was made aware of the killing. Efforts were made to positively identify the body. There was so much at stake, and the authorities wanted to be sure that the slain man was indeed Jesse James.

Jesse's mother, notified by wire, arrived by train the next morning. When asked at the coroner's inquest if the dead man was her son Jesse, Zerelda replied, "Would to God that it were not!" Several other persons from Clay County were called to identify the corpse. Sheriff Timberlake of Clay County had, of course, known Jesse for years. Harrison Trow and James Wilkerson, who had served in the guerrillas with the James brothers, also positively identified the body as that of Jesse James.

In addition to these witnesses, a Clay County farmer by the name of William Clay accompanied Sheriff Timberlake to view the body, and Dick Liddil's former paramour, Mattie Collins, also showed up. As everyone close to Jesse knew, he had blown the tip off the middle finger of his left hand when he was seventeen, earning himself the nickname "Dingus." The body of the slain man displayed this injury as well as scars from the two serious chest wounds Jesse had suffered in the war. Before the body was buried there was no doubt among those in authority that the man on the slab before them was the infamous Jesse Woodson James.

BURIAL IN MISSOURI

Now the St. Joseph authorities descended on the Zee James household to confiscate any and all articles that might have been acquired through Jesse's thefts. An engraved gold watch was found and determined to belong to John Burbank of Indiana; Burbank claimed to have lost the watch eight years earlier, during the Hot Springs, Arkansas, robbery in 1874. Among the several horses and saddles in the James stable were some horses put up there shortly before Jesse's murder. It was later determined that those horses had been stolen by the Ford brothers.

Following Governor Crittenden's request that the St. Joseph police release Jesse's body to his widow, Jesse's body was placed in the baggage car of a Hannibal & St. Joseph Railroad train to begin the first leg of the removal to his mother's homestead at Kearney, Missouri. It was later reported in the newspapers that Zerelda James Samuel could not restrain herself when the train reached Kearney. As she left the company of Sheriff Timberlake, Zerelda called to him, "Oh, Mr. Timberlake! My son has gone to

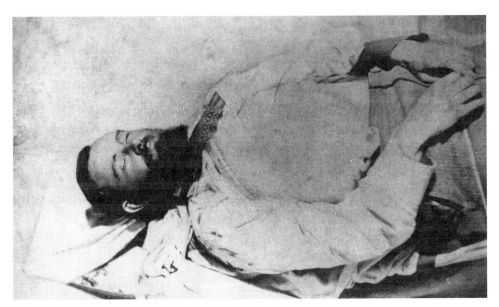

Jesse Woodson James in death.

God, but his friends still live and will have revenge on those who murdered him for money!" Jesse's body was taken to the Kearney Hotel where it was viewed by hundreds of people he had known throughout his life. Jesse's friends and family, as well as spectators only interested in looking into the casket of a famous outlaw, arrived from all over the state. No doubt some of the mourners came out of curiosity as well. Whether Jesse's brother would attend the funeral and possibly turn himself in was a much discussed question. There were law enforcement officials from several towns, cities, and the state of Missouri who would have been delighted to have had a personal encounter with Frank James. They would be disappointed, as no one saw Frank that day and he sent no official message.

On April 6, 1882, the casket was placed in a wagon and driven to Mt. Olivet Baptist Church. The funeral service was attended by hundreds of people. Reverends R. H. Jones of Lanthrop, Missouri, and J. M. Martin of Kearney preached the sermons.

Zerelda James Samuel on her Clay County farm, at the grave of Jesse.

After the funeral, Jesse's body was removed to the James-Samuel farm. His half-brother John Samuel was ill in bed; Jesse's casket was carried to the young man's bedside so that he could say goodbye. Jesse was then buried near the coffee tree in Zerelda's yard. The grave itself was simple, topped with small stones, with the following dignified legend and protest engraved on the tombstone: "Devoted Husband and Father, Jesse Woodson James. Sept. 5, 1847, murdered Apr. 3, 1882 by a traitor and coward whose name is not worthy to appear here." After the death of Zerelda Samuel and Zee James, Jesse E. supervised the removal of his father's body so that Jesse could be buried beside his wife and other family members at the Mt. Olivet Cemetery in Kearney.

One hundred thirteen years later, in 1995, the body of Jesse James was exhumed from Mt. Olivet Cemetery by a forensic team from George Washington University led by Professor James Starrs. In addition to DNA testing that resolved claims by various imposters as to whether the body buried there had really been Jesse's, Professor Starrs's findings showed that Jesse James was between five feet eight and five feet ten inches tall; that he had been buried in a pine box with ash handles; and that two bullet wounds were still evident: one on the lower right side of the back of his head and another in the right ribs.

On October 28, 1995, the remains of Jesse James were laid to rest again at Mt. Olivet Cemetery, following a funeral service at the Knights of Columbus Community Center.

PARDONS FOR THE FORDS, POVERTY FOR ZEE

The grieving Zee James, suffering in poverty after Jesse's death, was forced to sell most of his belongings at auction in order to support herself and her two small children. That auction netted her the paltry sum of approximately one hundred and seventeen dollars. Jesse's family was taken in by Zee's brother, Tom Mimms of Kansas City.

The Ford brothers fared better, though not in press coverage and public estimation. What with the outrage and disgust felt toward the man who had shot his unarmed friend from behind, everyone involved in arranging the assassination of Jesse James denied all knowledge of having struck a deal with Bob Ford. Even Bob Ford himself later claimed, "I am the one who removed the lamented Jess & am freed of it but I was not hired by Gov. Crittenden or any one else or did I act under anybody's instruction."

Judicial action against Bob and Charlie Ford certainly proceeded as if a prior agreement with the highest state authorities had been arranged. Both brothers were indicted on April 17, 1882, charged in a warrant sworn out by Zee James. Bob was charged with first-degree murder and Charlie with aiding and abetting. The two men pled guilty and were sentenced to be hanged. The very afternoon of the sentencing, however, Governor Crittenden granted the Ford brothers complete amnesty. Soon Bob and Charlie Ford were touring the country reenacting the murder of the notorious Jesse James in a theatrical presentation.

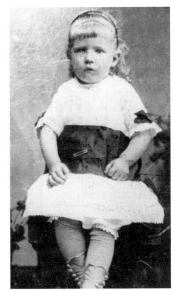

(Top) *Mary Susan James, born to Jesse and Zee in Nashville on June 17, 1879. She married Henry Lafayette Barr on March 6, 1901. The couple had four children: Lawrence, Forster, Chester, and Henrietta.* (Bottom) *Jesse Edwards James, born August 31, 1875, in Nashville, and named for newspaper editor John Newman Edwards. Both Jesse and his sister Mary were at home the morning their father was murdered.*

The pardon issued for Bob and Charlie Ford.

It is doubtful that the Fords received much of the reward they had been promised. Distribution of the ten thousand dollars—a fortune at that time—remains unclear. The reward might have been divided among several of those who played a role in bringing down the James Gang. In *The Crittenden Memoirs* published in 1936, Governor Crittenden claimed that "the proclamation of a reward accomplished its purpose in less than one year at a cost not exceeding twenty thousand dollars, not one cent of which was drawn from the state." Crittenden offered no explanations or apology for any of his actions, presumed or otherwise, in regard to Jesse James. He freely expressed the opinion that the Ford brothers should not be condemned but praised for their role in ridding the state of a dangerous criminal.

The media continued to play up the lurid murder and all its ramifications. Newspapers in many states debated the propriety of the governor of the state of Missouri being so directly involved in the assassination of a citizen. John Newman Edwards, who had left the Kansas City *Times* and was now the editor of the *Daily Democrat* in Sedalia, Missouri, wrote several outraged articles. His most embittered essay was published on April 13, 1882. Summarizing Jesse's betrayal by Bob Ford, Mattie Collins, and Martha Bolton, Edwards declared, "Tear the bears from the flag of Missouri. Put thereon in place of them as more appropriate, a thief blowing out the brains of an unarmed victim, and a brazen harlot, naked to the waist and splashed to the brows in blood."

Edwards went so far as to use his paper to organize a charity drive for the benefit of Zee James. Several hundred dollars were contributed for Jesse's widow. In response, the editor of the competing paper, the Sedalia *Bazoo*, organized a drive for the benefit of conductor William Westfall's widow.

After thirteen traumatic years as an outlaw's lady, Zee James gradually withdrew into deep despondency. Taking her two children to live with her brother in Kansas

City, she encountered there all the daunting difficulties of a woman without a husband in the late nineteenth century. She had little money, two small children to care for—Jesse E. and Mary were six and three years old at the time—and little prospect for earning an income. In the year following Jesse's death, Zee James signed a contract with a publisher to tell the story of her life, but gave only one interview before deciding she could not continue. For a brief period she made stage appearances as the widow of Jesse James, but the two shows she appeared in were poorly staged and poorly received. There would be no others.

Aged thirty-six at Jesse's death, Zee evidently did not feel that she had many familial options. She did not return to her mother's house. Her mother, after all, had never approved of Jesse's activities and had only reluctantly agreed to Zee's marriage. Zee Mimms James, in fact, never saw her mother again after her marriage to Jesse. Rather than move in with Zerelda James Samuel, her strong-willed mother-in-law, Zee stayed in Kansas City.

THE LATER LIVES OF JESSE'S CHILDREN

Zee struggled in poverty in Kansas City until her son, Jesse E., was old enough to work. At the age of eleven, Jesse worked part-time as a stockboy at the Bee Hive Department Store in downtown Kansas City. When he was twelve, he applied for and won a position as office boy during his school vacations for the Crittenden and Phister Real Estate Company in Kansas City. His employer, ironically, was the son of former governor Thomas Crittenden, the man in part responsible for his father's death. Jesse E. got along well with Tom Jr. and enjoyed his part-time job with the firm for the next six years. By the age of fifteen he was also a clerk at the Armour Packing Plant in Kansas City. He owned a jewelry and pawn shop while attending the Kansas City School of Law. He and his sister, Mary, were able to attend school in Kansas City thanks to his hard work. In addition, a loan from Tom Crittenden enabled the family to build a modest home on a piece of Kansas City property that Crittenden sold to Zee.

In 1898 Jesse E., aged twenty-one, was accused of being involved in a train robbery of his own, a crime of which he was acquitted by jury on the first ballot. In 1900 he wrote *Jesse James My Father*. He married Stella McGown in 1900 and pursued a career as a businessman, owning and operating a cigar and tobacco store in Kansas City. The couple had four daughters: Lucille, Jo Frances, Jessie Estelle, and Ethelrose.

Jesse graduated from the Kansas City School of Law in 1907, placing first in his class of thirty-seven. He began practice as a corporate attorney shortly after. Retiring from the law in 1926 and moving to California with his family, he portrayed his father in an unsuccessful film entitled *Under the Black Flag* that was partially funded by Jesse E. and his friends. He declined into a chronic depression that did not lift for the last decades of his life. Jesse Edwards James died on March 26, 1951, at the age of seventy-five. Jesse Edwards is buried in Los Angeles, at Forest Lawn Cemetery.

After the death of her mother in 1900, Mary James decided to live with her grandmother Zerelda Samuel on the family farm in Kearney. While living there she met neighboring farmer Henry L. Barr. Mary married Barr in 1901. The couple had three healthy boys: Lawrence, Forster, and Chester. A daughter named Henrietta died at the age of seven months. The family lived in a beautiful, large house called Claybrook, which stood across the road from the James-Samuel farm. Mary died on October 11, 1935, at the age of fifty-six.

FRANK JAMES SURRENDERS

In the wake of his brother's death, Frank James, who was probably in Lynchburg, Virginia, at the time, considered a radical change of course. Jesse had been much on his mind even though he had not attended Jesse's funeral and burial. Frank had watched helplessly as Jesse had found himself unable to move away from the life of outlawry. Frank had been drawn back into that life for a while, but now, at the age of thirty-nine, he could see nothing appealing about organizing robberies on his own and remaining on the run. Even if he remained law-abiding, though, a great deal of attention was going to focus on him now as the sole member of the James-Younger Gang still at large.

Frank felt that the time had come for him to surrender. He approached the sympathetic John Newman Edwards in Sedalia for advice. Edwards offered to approach Governor Crittenden on Frank's behalf. Together, the outlaw and the newspaperman composed a letter to Governor Crittenden asking that Frank be granted amnesty. Crittenden replied that although he could not grant a pardon in this case, he was willing to ensure that Frank receive a fair trial. Crittenden further promised that he would consider additional action in Frank's favor if the jury turned in a verdict of guilty.

It is likely that this correspondence between Frank James and Governor

Crittenden was only the initial part of negotiations for Frank James's surrender. Later events seem to indicate that much more had been agreed to by Crittenden.

Frank James and John Newman Edwards arrived by train in Jefferson City, Missouri, on the night of October 4, 1882. They registered at the McCarty House, where Frank went by the name of "B. F. Winfrey" of Marshall, Missouri. Next morning they strolled about the city, then returned to the hotel in the afternoon. Earlier the same day, Governor Crittenden announced to a group of officials and newspapermen he had called together that he would have something important to show them at five o'clock.

At five, as the Governor displayed the letter from Frank James, Frank and Edwards entered Crittenden's office. It was no doubt a moment of pride for Edwards when he announced, "Governor Crittenden, I want to introduce you to my friend Frank James." Still with a sense of theatrical timing and dash, Frank removed his pistol and cartridge belt from his waist and handed them to Crittenden, saying, "Governor Crittenden, I want to hand over to you that which no living man except myself has been permitted to touch since 1861, and to say that I am your prisoner."

The governor then directed his secretary to make arrangements for Frank James to be delivered to the sheriff of Jackson County. Frank was not immediately incarcerated; instead, he and John Edwards returned to the McCarty House to await their departure. Within the next few hours, several hundred people visited the outlaw there. It was a big day in Jefferson City—people were excited about being near such a notorious individual.

The following morning, Frank and his entourage left for Independence by train. Again, as in the case of the Youngers, hundreds of people lined the tracks along the way to catch a glimpse of this last representative of the most famous outlaw band in American history.

Frank's mother, Zerelda; his wife, Annie; and his four-year-old son, Robert, were among the crowd of onlookers who met him at the Independence station. Frank and his family were allowed to spend some time together at a hotel in Independence before Frank was removed to the Independence jail. Because one of the charges leveled against Frank James by Jackson County was the murder of Pinkerton detective James W. Whicher in 1874, the outlaw's request for bail was denied.

Frank O'Neill, a reporter from the St. Louis *Missouri Republican*, was on hand during the entire process of Frank's surrender to the governor. O'Neill saw to it that a lengthy article on Frank and his surrender subsequently appeared in his paper. Frank was portrayed as a man driven to participate in the war as a guerrilla, a man who now wanted to start over and live a good and productive life.

Frank stayed in the Independence jail for several weeks. There he greeted friends who came to see him and lived with an unusual amount of comfort in his cell. He was allowed books, a comfortable chair, and many of the other amenities of home. After all, he was unlikely to try a jailbreak and unlikely to be convicted on any charges, due to the passage of time and unavailability of witnesses. Sentiment in favor of a pardon for Frank was running high, possibly because there were a number of people in the state who saw him as sharing their own longing to finally put behind themselves the unsavory events of the war and subsequent conflicts.

William H. Wallace, Jackson County prosecuting attorney in the trials of Dick Liddil and Frank James.

Initial charges against Frank James included the robbery of the Roberts bank in Independence in 1867—fifteen years earlier—and the more recent train robbery at Blue Cut, Missouri, in 1881. Prosecutor William Wallace dismissed the first charge, however, when no evidence could be produced. Several other entities then stepped forward to have their day with Frank James. The governor of Minnesota put in the request that Frank James be extradited to be tried for the Northfield robbery, but Governor Crittenden refused, saying Frank James would first have to answer all charges against him in Missouri.

Indictments were then brought against Frank James for other felonies in Missouri: the robbery of the Daviess County Savings Association in Gallatin in 1869; the murder of cashier John Sheets during that episode; the Winston train robbery in 1881; and the murders of conductor William Westfall and passenger Frank McMillan during the Winston holdup. Frank was transported to Daviess County to stand trial.

To develop its case, the prosecution needed a substantial witness, someone from within the outlaw group. Bill Ryan was currently serving time in the Missouri penitentiary and would not have made an impressive witness. As for Clarence Hite, rumor had it that he was providing information to Prosecutor William Wallace as part of an exchange for Hite's pardon; however, Hite died of tuberculosis shortly after Frank's surrender, and whatever information he had confided was unusable.

Dick Liddil was the remaining option. Liddil had already confessed to being a member of the James Gang and had turned state's witness. During his 1882 trial Liddil swore that he himself had remained behind in Kentucky during the Muscle Shoals robbery, but that Jesse James, Frank James, and Bill Ryan had committed that Alabama crime. The jury was instructed to bring in a conviction if Liddil had been a member of the Gang, regardless of whether he had made the trip to Muscle Shoals. Liddil of course was found guilty, but the jury recommended executive clemency. Liddil's actual sentencing was postponed until the court's next term.

Now a movement was begun by prosecutor Wallace and others to obtain a pardon for Dick Liddil from President Chester A. Arthur to ensure that Liddil could be put on the stand against Frank James. Arguing that Liddil was a necessary prosecution witness, Wallace reminded the president that Liddil had been partially responsible for the breakup of the James Gang. Federal District Attorney William A. Smith protested this move, declaring it was not right that one murderer be pardoned in order to testify against another. Ultimately, the presidential pardon request was rejected. In the meantime, however, Liddil was released on bail in April 1883 and was free to make arrangements to testify against Frank James.

Exactly two years after the Winston holdup, on August 21, 1883, Frank James went to trial for the murder of Frank McMillan during that robbery. Serving as primary council for Frank James was former Lieutenant Governor and prominent attorney Charles P. Johnson. John Newman Edwards had asked his friend Johnson to assist Frank; although Frank had no money for legal fees, Edwards said, Frank's multitude of friends would no doubt be grateful and would certainly remember Johnson in his future endeavors. Assisting Johnson were Commissioner of the Supreme Court of Missouri and former Congressman John F. Phillips, as well as John M. Glover, William M. Rush, C. T. Garner, James H. Slover, and Joshua W. Alexander, all noted citizens and attorneys, all Democrats, and all volunteers. The prosecution, equally illustrious, was made up of William Wallace, Daviess County Prosecuting Attorney William D. Hamilton, Joshua F. Hicklin, Marcus A. Low, Henry C. McDougall, and John Shanklin. The case was heard by Daviess County Judge Charles Goodman. Because the number of people wishing to attend the proceedings far outnumbered seats available in the local courthouse, the trial was conducted in the Gallatin Opera House. Public tickets to the event were issued by Sheriff George Crozier.

Accusations of unfairness and rumors of conspiracy surfaced quickly during jury selection. Every man on the jury who would examine Frank James's behavior was a

Democrat; moreover, most of the jury members were young farmers. Two of them were Civil War veterans of the Confederacy. Attorneys Phillips and Johhson would later speak of their service in the Union Army in an effort to demonstrate their impartiality in regard to Frank James.

It was clear, however, which side the prosecution's star witness Dick Liddil was on. Liddil was called as a material witness shortly after the trial began and swore that he had been a member of the Gang who committed the Winston train robbery and that others with him included Frank James, Jesse James, Wood Hite, and Clarence Hite. Liddil declared that he himself had not gone into the smoking car where Frank McMillan was a passenger, but that Frank James had told him after the robbery that Frank had killed one man and Jesse another.

Some passengers aboard the Winston train were also called as witnesses. Although these witnesses could swear that the murderer of Frank McMillan resembled Frank James, the robbery had taken place two years before and no one could make a positive identification. Other witnesses for the prosecution gave supporting testimony that Frank James had been in the Winston area in the late summer of 1881 and in the company of the other robbers at that time. These later witnesses included Sarah Hite (stepmother of Frank's cousins Wood and Clarence); Sarah's father, Silas Norris;

The jury in the trial of Frank James. Front row (l to r): W. F. Richardson, L. W. Gilreath, R. E. Hale, J. W. Boggs. Standing (l to r): J. Snyder, B. F. Feurt, C. R. Nance, Joseph B. Smith, B. H. Shellman, William R. Merritt, Jason Winburn, Oscar Chamberlain.

Martha Bolton; Reverend Jamin Machette; blacksmith Jonas Potts; and J. T. Ford, the father of Bob and Charlie Ford.

In Frank's defense, other witnesses claimed that Frank was not the man believed to have been present in the Winston area at the time of the holdup. When Frank himself took the stand, he denied participating in the Winston robbery and swore he had been living a peaceful life in Tennessee until the arrest of Bill Ryan. At that point, he told the jury, he felt it necessary to leave the Tennessee area so that he would not be arrested on some trumped-up charge. He admitted that he did travel to Kentucky with the others named, but swore that he did not go on with them to Missouri but instead went south, to Texas, to visit his sister, Susie Parmer. Frank further testified that at this time he had sent his wife and son on to Missouri so that Annie could contact General J. O. Shelby with the request that the general appeal to the state governor to support fair trial proceedings if Frank should surrender. According to Frank's testimony, Annie did contact General Shelby and sent word to Frank that the general did not believe such a guarantee could be promised by the governor. Annie then rejoined Frank in Kentucky and the couple and their son traveled on to Lynchburg, Virginia. It was while they were in Lynchburg, Frank stated, that they learned of Jesse's death.

Susan Parmer and her husband, Allen, corroborated Frank's story that he had visited them in Texas. Frank's mother, Zerelda James Samuel, took the stand to say that Frank had not been with the group of men who visited her farm. An inebriated J. O. Shelby confirmed Annie's testimony about visiting him. Shelby went on to assert that although he had seen others of the Gang in Missouri, he had not seen Frank James anywhere in the state since 1872. Prior to taking the stand, Shelby had looked at Frank and then had turned to ask the judge if he could approach Frank James and "shake hands with an old soldier." His request was denied.

Governor Thomas Crittenden was also called as a witness for the defense. He proved to be the prosecution's undoing. Crittenden testified that initially Dick Liddil had told him that Jesse was the one who had murdered passenger McMillan. That stunning testimony was the climax of the case. Now the only witness to link Frank James directly with the Winston holdup was Dick Liddil, and no one believed that Liddil was anything more than a traitor to his friends, a man whose word could not be trusted. Summation oratory lasted three days, with the main thrust of the closing arguments centering around events of the war.

The jury deliberated three-and-a-half hours before finding Frank James not guilty of the murder of Frank McMillan. Once again the newspapers gave the James family front-page coverage. The fairness of the trial was debated fiercely, including what repercussions the not-guilty verdict might have on the good people of the state of Missouri.

There was little that prosecuting attorney Hamilton could do now with the other charges. He entered a plea of *nolle prosequi* in regard to the murder of conductor Westfall and a continuance was granted in the matter of the murder of cashier Sheets during the Gallatin holdup. Frank James was transported back to Jackson County, Missouri, and released on bond on December 13, 1883. He was quickly rearrested and sent back to Gallatin, as the continuance still called for the accused to remain in someone's custody. Holding Frank James was difficult, though, and he was released on bond again a few days later.

Around this time word reached Governor Crittenden that the state of Alabama was preparing to press for Frank's extradition to stand trial for the Muscle Shoals robbery. Crittenden attempted to block the move. Finally an agreement was reached whereby Frank James would appear to answer charges in Alabama only after the Missouri courts were through with him. It was agreed that Alabama would be given precedence over any further requests from Minnesota.

At this time Frank still faced charges in Jackson County for his involvement in the Blue Cut train robbery in 1881. Governor Crittenden, again behaving like a member of the defense attorney's team, had recently upheld a ruling of the Missouri Supreme Court which stipulated that the testimony of a convicted felon could not be admissible against another person in court. As a result Dick Liddil could not be called to testify against Frank James again for any crimes committed in Missouri. Moreover, Crittenden would not grant an executive pardon to Dick Liddil in order to change Liddil's status as a witness. Few people in the judicial system were surprised on February 11, 1884, when Crittenden dismissed all pending charges against Frank James. Again the press went wild: papers across the country ran stories and editorials about the events, and again the question was raised as to whether the governor had made a deal in advance with Frank James.

A couple of months later, on April 17, 1884, Frank was arraigned in Huntsville, Alabama, for the Muscle Shoals robbery in 1881. Frank's attorney in Alabama was former Confederate Gen. Leroy Pope Walker. Dick Liddil was once again removed from his Missouri jail cell to testify, but his assertions failed to persuade the jury. The defense attorney also produced witnesses from Nashville who stated that on the day of the robbery—March 11, 1881—Frank had been in Nashville, where he was known as "B. J. Woodson." Jonas Taylor, a blacksmith in Nashville, even produced a receipt book showing that "Woodson" was having his horse shod at the time the robbery was being committed. With no clear identification of the defendant and so strong an alibi, it did not take the Alabama jury long to find Frank James not guilty.

A peculiar maneuver took place at the conclusion of the trial. As soon as Frank James was declared innocent, he was immediately rearrested by Sheriff John F. Rogers of Cooper County, Missouri—to face indictment, it was announced, for the Rocky Cut robbery in Missouri in 1876. Evidently a rumor had reached the Missouri capital that authorities from Minnesota might be present at the Alabama trial and might try to get their hands on Frank to bring him to trial for the Northfield robbery. It seems that whatever deal Frank's friend Edwards had made long ago with Crittenden extended to the governor's doing everything possible to protect Frank from the Minnesota authorities. Governor Crittenden may have found it politically expedient to assist Frank James at this time, in view of the public criticism the governor had received in regard to Jesse's assassination. In any event, it was Sheriff John Rogers to the rescue in Alabama; Frank was never apprehended by the Minnesotans.

As it happened, Governor Crittenden had already dropped all Missouri charges against Frank James before the Alabama trial began. Once Frank was safely within the Missouri border the charge of the Rocky Cut robbery, another event that would have been futile to prosecute, was dropped again. By mid-1884, then, at the age of forty-one, Frank James was a free man.

MORE YEARS IN PRISON: THE YOUNGERS

Having declared repeatedly that they were not friendly with the James brothers at the time of the Northfield robbery, the Youngers continued to keep their promise of silence even after news of Jesse's death arrived at the Stillwater prison. Since the last report of Jesse's death had been a hoax, Cole wondered whether this latest story might be untrue as well. He made no public comment, but through friends he quickly contacted his sister Retta, then living in St. Joseph, Missouri, and asked her to view Jesse's body herself and let Cole know whether the reports were true. Retta did as her older brother asked and then sent him a confirmation. Cole probably worried at times about the fate of his boyhood friend, but he was familiar with Frank James's resiliency and could be confident Frank would be a survivor.

Another event affected the Youngers in the winter after Frank's surrender. The prison at Stillwater erupted in flames on January 25, 1884. The fire, which broke out at eleven-thirty at night, caused widespread panic among the prisoners locked in their cells. The Stillwater volunteer fire department responded to the fire alarm at the prison, and every piece of fire-fighting equipment within a thirty-mile radius was deployed to put out the flames. During the evacuation more than 350 prisoners had to stand chained together in sub-zero weather while the prison burned.

The Deputy Warden's house at the Minnesota State Penitentiary at Stillwater.

Head guard George Dodd was in charge of removing the crowds of men to safety. When the Youngers were moved out of their cells to join the others, Cole asked Dodd if there was any way he or his brothers might help. He later said he was surprised when Dodd decided that Cole, Jim, and Bob could come with him to help relocate Dodd's wife and the female inmates. Dodd even went so far as to hand a gun to Cole Younger, an ax to Bob, and an iron bar to Jim. Quickly, the Youngers led the women's group to the Deputy Warden's house, then surrendered their various weapons. Later there was some speculation by the press that the Youngers may have used the fire as a decoy to draw attention while they attempted a prison breakout, but Dodd and Warden Reed then shared the details about the men's cooperation during the crisis and the Younger names were cleared.

While the prison was under repair, the Youngers were transferred to Washington County jail in Minnesota. They remained there for more than a month. Returning to Stillwater Penitentiary, they found themselves with new job assignments. Cole was sent to work in the prison library while Jim was put in charge of the mail. Bob Younger was assigned the job of binding medical books.

Because of ill health Bob was unable to keep the job for long. He was soon sent instead to the prison steward, with whom he worked as an accounting clerk. Bob had developed a chronic cough that was gradually worsening, a condition he believed to be the result of the gunshot wound to his chest during his surrender at Hanska Slough.

Cole, Jim, and Bob were now aged forty, thirty-six, and thirty-one, respectively. It was 1884, eight years since their capture. Their mother's sister, Frances Fristoe Twyman, began to explore ways to mount a parole drive that might bring the boys home to Missouri. The distinguished Fristoe family continued to be influential in Independence; Mrs. Twyman set about gathering letters of support from prominent individuals throughout her state.

At about this same time an unusual coincidence occurred. A Missourian by the name of Warren "Wal" Carter Bronaugh visited the Youngers at Stillwater Penitentiary in the autumn of 1885. A fellow Confederate, Bronaugh told them he had long wanted to meet the Youngers and was pleased that the opportunity presented itself when he happened to be in Minnesota on his honeymoon. Bronaugh later declared that it was only after he obtained a letter of introduction to Warden Reed and then met Cole Younger that Bronaugh recognized Cole as the man who had saved Bronaugh's life in 1862, during the war. It had been just after the bloody battle at Lone Jack, in August of that year. When Bronaugh and another soldier attempted to enter the town, Cole had stopped the two young men and advised them not to proceed in the direction they were headed or they would encounter the enemy face to face in its camp.

A letter Bronaugh later wrote to Frank James suggests another scenario. In this letter Bronaugh described his visit to the Youngers but, oddly, made no mention of being surprised to recognize Cole. Bronaugh went on to say that he had a great deal more to tell Frank about his visit to Stillwater, but would wait until he and Frank met in Clinton. It is possible, then, that Frank James was responsible for Bronaugh's visit in the first place and that Frank and Bronaugh conspired

(Top) *Frances Fristoe Twyman, born April 20, 1829, the youngest of seven children of Judge Richard and Mary Fristoe. She and her husband, Dr. Lydall Twyman, were active in community and social affairs of Independence, Missouri. Mrs. Twyman died in April 1909 and is buried in Independence.* (Bottom) *Warren "Wal" Carter Bronaugh, born in Buffalo, West Virginia, in 1841. His grandfather had been a member of Washington's council during the Revolutionary War; his father had fought in the War of 1812. Bronaugh fought under General Price in Company B of the Confederate Army and later served on the Board of Directors of the Confederate Home in Higginsville, Missouri.*

to hide this fact from anyone but the Youngers. This may have been Frank James's effort to repay his debt to the Youngers for keeping silent about the James boys' participation at Northfield.

Bronaugh's visit to Stillwater would come to mean a great deal to the Youngers.

Having met the three, Bronaugh pledged to do everything in his power to secure their paroles. Across the next several years he worked tirelessly on their behalf, whether solely on his own or in conjunction with Frank James.

The Youngers continued to bide their time as model prisoners. Cole later gave a lengthy interview to the Cincinnati *Enquirer* on April 17, 1889, which did not directly mention Frank James, but which did include the pointed remark that everyone who had attempted to rob the bank at Northfield was now dead. It was left to the readers to conclude that Jesse James may have been one of the robbers, but Frank James could not have been, as Frank was still alive.

To pass the time, Cole and Jim had taken up the hobby of woodworking. They became expert at creating beautiful wooden boxes, chests, canes, and picture frames. Bob was unable to participate in such a craft due to the immobility of his right arm. His brothers claimed that the young man was growing increasingly despondent as his guilt for involving his brothers in the ill-fated robbery began to overwhelm him.

Their aunt Mrs. Twyman eventually gathered many letters of support from prominent Missourians willing to lend their names in support of the Youngers' parole. She even managed to enlist the aid of former Minnesota governor William R. Marshall. Before the war Marshall had moved his family out of Missouri and north to Minnesota, but the families of Marshall and Judge Richard Fristoe had been well-acquainted.

(Top) *Minnesota Gov. William R. Marshall.* (Bottom) *Minnesota Gov. Andrew Ryan McGill.*

Wal Bronaugh met with Mrs. Twyman to discuss leading a parole drive. Mrs. Twyman provided Bronaugh with a letter of introduction to Governor Marshall, and Marshall in turn introduced Bronaugh to Missouri Governor Thomas Crittenden. Crittenden, who ironically had lost his bid for reelection after the trial of Frank James, pledged his support for the parole drive and stated that he did not believe the Younger brothers posed any threat now to the state of Missouri. Former governor Marshall composed several letters on behalf of the Youngers that appeared in the St. Paul *Pioneer Press*. After Marshall's first letter appeared, Cole himself wrote a letter to the editor of that paper in which he described his exploits as a war hero.

A new governor of Minnesota, Andrew McGill, took office in 1887. McGill took a personal interest in the Youngers and went so far as to visit them in Stillwater. He listened to their requests for parole and told them he would think about what might be done. In the following year, editor John Newman Edwards sought to help the Youngers as he had previously helped Frank James. Edwards drafted and published an eloquent petition requesting the parole of Cole, Jim, and Bob Younger, claiming that since the Youngers had already served twice the length of time usually allotted to life prisoners and since they had been decent, honorable men driven to their crime by the mitigating circumstances of the war, the matter of parole should be given immediate consideration. Edwards pointed out that all three were exemplary prisoners and were now "old men" by outlaw standards who posed no threat to the states of Minnesota or Missouri.

Time passed, with no change in the Youngers' status. Edwards then enlisted the help of Wal Bronaugh and of Missouri State Representative Waller Young to circulate an official petition for parole. The petition was signed by the majority of the membership of the Missouri legislature and was then presented to William R. Merriam, the new governor of Minnesota who took office in 1888. Like his predecessor, Merriam took a personal interest in the plight of the Youngers, but for a different reason. Governor Merriam happened to be the son of John L. Merriam, the bank official who, in 1874, had been aboard the train robbed at Gad's Hill and who may have been put out of the train in a state of embarrassing undress. Although

(Top) *Minnesota Gov. William R. Merriam.* (Bottom) *Minnesota Gov. Henry H. Sibley.*

his father experienced a moment of satisfaction in the Faribault jail when he revealed his identity to Cole Younger, Governor Merriam would exact his own revenge and absolutely refuse to consider a parole for the Youngers.

Governor Merriam never cited this particular reason for preferring to keep the Youngers behind bars, although he did admit to feeling prejudiced against the three.

Merriam simply informed Wal Bronaugh, "I cannot pardon these men. My duty to the state and my personal prejudice against them make it impossible." Henry H. Sibley, Minnesota's first governor, put in a plea to Merriam: "Minnesota has shown her power to punish malefactors, let her now manifest her magnanimity, by opening the prison doors to the men who have so long suffered for a violation of her laws, and bid them 'go and sin no more.'" Governor Merriam was not to be swayed.

THE DEATH OF BOB YOUNGER

Bob Younger had been plagued by respiratory infections and other ailments since the beginning of his imprisonment in the Minnesota penitentiary. His health took a severe turn for the worse in 1889, after thirteen years of incarceration. He was constantly fatigued and pale. Then aged thirty-five, Bob Younger pretended to his older brothers that nothing was out of the ordinary. With his nagging guilt about the Northfield fiasco, the youngest brother kept pretty much to himself. He did become friendly with Deputy Warden Jacob Westby, but did not confide in the officer. Only after Westby repeatedly expressed concern about his health did Bob finally agree to see the prison physician.

The diagnosis was not good. Bob had contracted a fatal case of phthisis, commonly known as consumption or pulmonary tuberculosis. Bob told his brothers about his condition, but asked them not to mention his illness in his presence. According to Jim, what was in Bob's mind was the hope that all of them might be paroled in time for him to return to Missouri to die. The heartbroken Cole and Jim Younger agreed to Bob's request and then found themselves having to ask the prison officials how their brother was doing. It was their only source of information.

Some time earlier, Bob had tried to cut his ties with Maggie, the New England woman he had met in Missouri and set up a farm with in Jackson County. He had written Maggie years before that he did not want to see her again until he was back in Missouri as a free man. Although Maggie found she could not stay on their farm alone because she missed Bob too much, she was ready to make a home for him as soon as he returned to Missouri. Maggie would not see her wish fulfilled.

Friends in Missouri now learned that Bob Younger was not expected to live much longer. Another letter-writing campaign was mounted in the spring of 1889. Former Union Army officer E. F. Rogers, along with former Confederate officer Stephen C.

Reagan and Wal Bronaugh, gathered more than 163 letters from prominent citizens in the states of Minnesota and Missouri, requesting that all the Youngers be allowed to return to Missouri. There were letters from former governors, legislators, Union and Confederate officers, United States senators, judges, and secretaries, as well as the current governor of Missouri and even members of the posse to whom the Youngers had surrendered. Bronaugh then arranged for an impressive group to present the letters to Governor Merriam: ex-Governor Marshall, ex-Warden Reed, Sheriff Ara Barton of Faribault, Colonel Rogers, Colonel Reagan, Mrs. Twyman, and Retta Younger. Merriam astonished the group by again refusing to consider the request.

Wal Bronaugh, Mrs. Twyman, and Retta Younger did not give up the fight, however. Now they focused their efforts on finding a way for Bob Younger to be released to go home to die. Bob consented to an examination by another physician, sent by former Northfield bank president G. M. Phillips, to confirm whether Bob's condition was indeed terminal consumption. Phillips's doctor concurred with the earlier diagnosis, and Phillips recommended that Bob be pardoned to live out his last months at home.

Nevertheless, Governor Merriam held fast to his position. Bob Younger had pled guilty as an accessory to the murder of Northfield bank cashier Joseph Heywood; Merriam obviously had that in mind when, referring to the recent death of Heywood's widow, Merriam told Bronaugh and Marshall in July, "I would not pardon the Youngers even if Mrs. Heywood should come to life again and make the request." When Bronaugh and Marshall pushed the issue, offering to take Bob's place in prison if only Bob could be allowed to go home, Merriam asked the two men to leave his office.

By the end of the summer, Bob Younger had to be transferred to the prison hospital, where he remained on a full-time basis. Cole had been working as a hospital trustee and so was able to visit his brother more often than was usually allowed. In September 1889 Retta arrived to look after her brother's last needs. When it was clear to the authori-

The hospital in Minnesota State Penitentiary at Stillwater at the time Bob Younger was a patient.

Retta Younger with her brothers Bob, Jim, and Cole, in the prison at Stillwater, six days before Bob Younger's death, 1889.

ties that Bob's days were almost over, Cole and Jim were relieved of their duties and allowed to remain at their brother's bedside. Retta and Bronaugh arranged for a photographer to come to the prison hospital and photograph the Younger group: Bob, his brothers, and sister.

On the evening of September 16, 1889, Bob Younger summoned his close friend Deputy Warden Westby to his side to join Cole, Jim, and Retta. According to Jim, Bob listened to a bird chirping outside his window and spoke of the birds back home in Missouri. He asked Cole to raise him up so that he might see the sky again. Bob quietly remarked that he believed his soul might rest on the hill outside his cell window after he died. When Retta began to weep, he admonished her not to cry for him. Evidently his last thoughts, though, were of Maggie. Asking Cole to bend near, Bob whispered to him, "Tell her I died thinking of her."

Bob Younger died at the age of thirty-five, a year older than Jesse James had been. After a small funeral service at the prison, his body was returned to Lee's Summit, Missouri, for burial beside his mother. Hundreds of people—family, childhood friends, and those who had served alongside his brothers in the war—attended the funeral in the little town. Delivering the eulogy, Pastor A. B. Francisco offered this summary: "This is an ordinary and yet extraordinary occasion; ordinary inasmuch as we have the living before the dead; extraordinary because the life which he has lived has been so entirely different from the lives of most of us." Serving as pallbearers were Buford Lewis, Frank Gattrell, A. Flannery, J. S. Whitsett, J. W. McBride, and William Anderson. More than a hundred carriages followed Bob Younger's casket as he was driven slowly to the Lee's Summit Cemetery to be laid to rest.

Bob Younger, six days before his death.

THE 1897 PAROLE BOARD

Earlier in the 1880s, when it was clear to Jim Younger that he was likely to remain behind bars for years to come, he began to write short essays on topics he thought might be of interest to other prisoners. When he shared his writings with his brothers, they encouraged him to publish his ideas and viewpoints in a newspaper format, something that could be enjoyed by all the occupants of Stillwater. At first Jim was

From Jim Younger's Prison Hash *newspaper.*

reluctant and said that he had really only written the articles to amuse himself. When Bob and Cole added the contributions of fifteen other inmates to their own donations for start-up money, Jim reconsidered. The masthead of his first newspaper, published in 1889, said *The Prison Hash.* Fellow inmate Lew Schoonmaker served as the first editor. Now Jim had a direct outlet for his quick mind and his pent-up frustrations. The newspaper was such a success that *The Prison Hash* continues to be published to this day.

Jim had grown depressed during Bob's decline and more despondent after his brother's death. Cole continued to believe that the two of them would be paroled eventually, but Jim was doubtful. In the late 1880s Jim remained at work in the mailroom while Cole continued as a trustee at the prison hospital. Cole later expressed disgust when he learned that three of their paternal cousins, the Dalton brothers, attempted to outdo the daring of the James-Younger Gang by robbing two banks at the same time, in Coffeyville, Kansas. The Daltons' attempt, on October 5, 1892, had dire consequences for the young outlaws. Bob and Grat Dalton died in the ensuing shootout; their youngest brother, Emmett, was arrested and sent to prison for life although he was released in 1907 after serving fifteen years.

In 1895, after David Clough had been elected to replace William Merriam as governor of Minnesota, Wal Bronaugh once again petitioned to have the Younger brothers paroled. Cole and Jim had been behind bars for nineteen years. Bronaugh welcomed the help of the Youngers' sister Anne's son Harry Jones, who was now an attorney practicing in Pleasant Hill, Missouri. Governor Clough was sympathetic to their presented case, but felt that his office alone should not decide the fate of such long-term prisoners. Clough suggested Bronaugh and Jones appeal to the newly formed Board of Pardons.

Meanwhile, Jim's former sweetheart Cora McNeill decided to do what she could to help. Although her romance with Jim appeared to be long over, Cora had remained his friend and had corresponded with him throughout his incarceration. The novel she drafted at this time, *Mizzoura*, was a fictionalized account of the Younger brothers and the women they loved. It was Cora's hope that this book would show a softer, more human side of the Youngers and win more sympathy for them. Cora wrote to Jim that she would go on doing everything in her power to help him. During her work with Bronaugh and Aunt Frances Twyman over the years to help obtain the boys' parole, Cora met Minnesota legislator C. P. Deming. Cora informed Jim she had decided to marry Deming and live in Minnesota.

On July 8, 1897, Wal Bronaugh appealed to the Board of Pardons with yet another batch of supportive letters from influential citizens. The Board was made up of Governor Clough, Attorney General Childs, and Chief Justice Charles M. Start, who was known to be unsympathetic to the Youngers' case. Several prominent men from Northfield and Faribault attended the first public meeting, held on July 12. Faribault Mayor A. D. Keyes proposed that the Youngers answer three questions before they be considered for parole: was Frank James a participant in the Northfield robbery; who was the last of the robbers to leave the bank; and who was the rider of the dun horse? Governor Clough responded by saying that Frank James was not the person under consideration by the Board. Mayor Keyes insisted, making a speech in which he declared, "It is not an element of good citizenship to conceal a murderer. . . . If the Youngers are now the good citizens they claim to be, they would go on the stand and by telling the truth would assist the authorities of this state in bringing the Northfield murderer to justice." After Keyes's oration, affidavits were presented from several men who claimed to be eyewitnesses to the shooting of the immigrant Nicholas Gustavson, even though no one had come forward with such affidavits at the time of the trial.

(Top) *Minnesota Gov. David Clough.* (Bottom) *Chief Justice Charles M. Start, whose vote in 1897 denied the Youngers' parole.*

Wal Bronaugh presented the Youngers' case. It proved to be another wasted effort. Chief Justice Start had decided against paroling the Youngers before the hearing began. Since a unanimous decision of the Board was required to grant parole, his negative vote was decisive. This appeals process was of great interest to the press, and public debate on the matter continued for some time.

Cole Younger in prison, ca. 1900.

Cole claimed that while Jim was discouraged, he himself had every intention to continue the fight. Jim had little hope that he would ever leave prison. He decided to concentrate on his reading and writing ventures rather than waste time dreaming of freedom. By this time Jim's range of learning had become extensive. The resident physician at Stillwater, Doctor Morrill Withrow, with whom Cole worked for a long time, once described Jim Younger as having "the most astounding fund of knowledge that I ever knew in one person."

MORE DRIFTING: FRANK JAMES

Meanwhile, Frank James had been trying to adjust to life as a free man. With Annie and his small son Robert, Frank drifted to various parts of the country and took an assortment of jobs. For a while he was a shoe salesclerk at a store in Nevada, Missouri. In 1886 he was working for the Mittenthal Clothing Company in Dallas, Texas. He did not return to Nashville, where he had enjoyed life as "Ben J. Woodson," a respected gentleman farmer. His reasons for drifting about are not entirely clear, but he may have been uneasy about confronting the many people he had deceived, especially in Nashville, people who had thought of him as a trustworthy friend.

Frank James moved on to become a wrangler for livestock dealer Shep Williams in Paris, Texas. He worked the dusty, difficult life of a cowboy for two years, then drifted to other parts of Texas as well as to New Orleans and then Guttenberg, New Jersey. In 1894, in St. Louis, at the age of fifty-one, he settled into what was steady employment for him, a seven-year stint as the doorman at Ed Butler's Standard Theatre. He supplemented this with work at the fairground during the racing season, where his job was to drop the timer's flag.

Meanwhile, Jesse and Frank's mother was holding court out at her farm. Visitors came by the dozens, and Zerelda greeted them and told her story. One of her prized possessions was a carved stick she called her "memory cane." Some visitors to the farm later sent her colorful ribbons which she tied around the cane in remembrance of their visit. "Aunt Charlotte," Ambrose, and Perry, three of the Samuels' former slaves who had remained at the farm, helped Zerelda and Reuben tend to household chores. Over 3,500 people visited the James-Samuel farm between 1895 and 1898, according to the Kansas City *Star*.

As for Jesse's wife, Zee, she never fully recovered from the anguish caused by the assassination of her husband and her subsequent life. Her health gradually deteriorated to the point that she became housebound. She was confined to her bed the last eleven months of her life and eventually slipped into a coma. She was lovingly nursed by her daughter Mary. Zerelda Amanda Mimms James finally died of sciatic rheumatism and nervous prostration at her home in Kansas City on November 13, 1900.

Jesse E. arranged for a double burial of his parents. Zee was interred at the Mt. Olivet Cemetery and Jesse's body was removed from his James-Samuel farm resting place under the supervision of his son. Zerelda Samuel did not take part in this event as Frank James had returned home to help Jesse E. but had become extremely ill with influenza; Zerelda nursed Frank in his hotel at Kearney. Later, Frank was well enough to host a small country dinner for the pallbearers, who were guerrilla friends of both James brothers.

In 1901 some Missouri state legislators, Democrats all, approached Frank James and asked if he would like for them to grant him the position of doorkeeper for the state legislature. Frank readily agreed, probably thinking that such a position would vindicate him from past accusations once and for all. Within the Democratic caucus this proposal won fifteen votes, but then a small political crisis developed. The very legislators who had initially approached Frank James ended up withdrawing their support as fear of reprisals for championing an outlaw made them reconsider their position. Frank was greatly disappointed.

Still a lover of Shakespeare and the classics, Frank James moved from being a theater doorman to being a minor stage actor after he was turned down for House doorkeeper. He joined a traveling theatrical company and periodically appeared as an actor in such melodramas as *Across the Desert* and *The Fatal Scar*.

COLE AND JIM ARE FREED

Cora McNeill, Jim's old sweetheart, stayed true to her vow to help him however she could. Later in 1901, a bill introduced in the Minnesota legislature by her husband, C. P. Deming, was passed by both houses. The bill allowed a prisoner serving a life sentence to be paroled after serving at least twenty-four years, provided consent

(Top) *Minnesota State Sen. George P. Wilson, co-author of a bill to procure the release of the Youngers.* (Middle) *Minnesota State Auditor R. C. Dunn.* (Bottom) *Minnesota Gov. Samuel Van Sant, who pardoned the Youngers in 1901.*

was obtained from the Board of Pardons. Minnesota State Senator George P. Wilson, who had introduced a similar bill the previous year, advised Wal Bronaugh to gather letters from the highest officials in Missouri and address them to the highest officials in Minnesota.

The persistent and loyal Wal Bronaugh readily followed Wilson's suggestion. The Board of Paroles, conducting individual meetings to discuss eligible parolees, found the Youngers' names on their agenda for July 10, 1901. It was possible, though, that Chief Justice Start would again sabotage the appeal. Wal Bronaugh, saying he could not stand the suspense, did not attend the meeting but sat in the lobby of St. Paul's Merchants Hotel and was given a minute-by-minute account by Minnesota State Auditor R. C. Dunn, who kept running in with updates. At the last minute another obstacle arose, this time having to do with the new governor, Samuel Van Sant, whose signature was required to authorize any parole and who expressed some reluctance about signing the Board's recommendation that the Youngers be allowed to leave prison. Van Sant acquiesced, however, when he was assured by Warden Henry Wolfer that press coverage of the event would be kept to a minimum.

It was while Bronaugh was eating his supper that R. C. Dunn approached the man who had worked so steadily through the years on behalf of the Youngers to inform him that Cole and Jim Younger, now aged fifty-seven and fifty-three, were to be free men at last.

Stillwater Warden Wolfer had quickly become friends with the Youngers following his appointment in 1889. Wolfer now asked that the two men be brought to Deputy Warden Jack Glennon's office to receive the official news. Bronaugh later wrote that Cole was overcome with emotion. After shaking Wal Bronaugh's hand, Cole told the reporters present, "I feel like shaking hands with the whole world. As I stand here today, I ain't got a grudge against any human being alive or dead. Men, I'm happy."

Jim too was shaken when he got the news and asked if he could stay in his cell rather than meet with reporters.

Immediately upon leaving Glennon's office, Cole asked Bronaugh to send a wire to Lizzie Brown Daniel in Kansas City, his adolescent love with whom he had begun corresponding several months before. It was to Lizzie that Cole sent the first announcement of his freedom; he was eager to visit her upon his return home to Missouri. Cole was aware, though, that Lizzie had married a prosperous lawyer many years before and was happy and content in her marriage. The Youngers were released the following morning. On July 11, 1901, they walked out the prison doors to a world they had not seen for twenty-five years. Cole and Jim strolled around the town of Stillwater and were astounded by the changes the past two decades had brought. The small group of reporters who accompanied them noticed how they marveled at such things as electric street cars, elaborate window displays, and the architecture of some of the newer buildings.

Warden Wolfer along with the Parole Board had arranged for Jim and Cole to take local jobs in Stillwater. They joined the world of the structured work force as tombstone salesmen for the P. N. Peterson Granite Company of Stillwater and St. Paul. Jim's job was in the company's Stillwater office, while Cole traveled the area selling tombstones. After a few months, Jim realized he was not well suited to his position. He liked the paperwork of the job but was extremely uncomfortable in his sales duties. Cole, however, enjoyed moving around freely and meeting new people.

(Top) *Elizabeth "Lizzie" Brown Daniel, daughter of Mary Jane and Robert Brown. Cole Younger first visited her home in the company of her brother Tom. Throughout his incarceration Cole recalled with great fondness Lizzie's piano concerts at "Wayside Rest." While a student at the Christian College in Columbia Lizzie met her future husband Henry Clay Daniel. (Bottom) Judge Henry Clay Daniel, a prominent attorney who served as mayor of Harrisonville.*

BACK IN MISSOURI: FRANK JAMES

About the time that the Youngers were adjusting to their new lives in the town of Stillwater, Frank James decided to stop working in the theatrical world and to move with Annie and Robert back to western Missouri. Zerelda and Reuben Samuel, now in their seventies, were unable to work the James-Samuel farm. Reuben's mind had grown progressively weaker, and he had been placed in a home in the State Insane

(Left) *Frank James.* (Right) *The James-Samuel family on their farm.*

Asylum in St. Joseph. Despite her age Zerelda James Samuel remained feisty, but she was in need of someone to keep her company and help with her daily affairs. Perry Samuel was the half-black son of one of Reuben Samuel's slaves, born in 1862. It is possible that Reuben was his father, but the family has never said. Perry was treated as one of the family, as were a couple of other former slaves the family had owned. Perry lived on the James-Samuel farm his entire life and looked after Zerelda's needs with the loyalty of both a family member and a friend.

Frank's plan was to return to his Missouri roots and work the James-Samuel farm even though the farm now required more than just attention to agriculture—ever since Jesse's murder, Zerelda had been giving tours of Jesse's gravesite. She sold pebbles from the grave, twenty-five cents apiece, to curiosity seekers who came to view the outlaw's final resting place. The supply of pebbles was replenished from time to time by her grandchildren, who restocked Uncle Jesse's plot from the farm's creek bed.

Frank was uncomfortable with the gawking tourists and would remove himself as often as he could. Occasionally he would chat with some visitors but would never address any subject having to do with outlawry.

COLE, JIM, AND ALIX

Missouri remained a distant hope for the Youngers. Their paroles specifically forbade them to return to their home state. Both brothers were constrained to report their every movement to their parole officer, F. A. Whittier. Cole, still gregarious, enjoyed watching stage productions, attending meetings and conventions of various organizations, and making new friends. Jim Younger's life was the opposite. At the end of his workday he returned to his rented room to read before retiring at eight o'clock.

There was a special aspect to Jim's isolation at this time. While in prison he had consented to only a few interviews, but one day there he had been intrigued by an interview request from a young reporter named Alix Mueller. He agreed to speak to this woman and found he enjoyed their interview. The feeling was mutual. Jim and Alix began a correspondence, and Jim grew increasingly fond of her. After his release from Stillwater, Jim was able to spend some time with Alix in Minnesota, and in a short time the couple fell in love. Unfortunately, though, Alix was soon forced by a mild case of tuberculosis to leave Minnesota for the dryer climate of her family home in Boise, Idaho. Jim continued to write to her there. Alix replied with promises that she would soon return to him.

(Top) *Jim Younger.* (Right) *Alix J. Mueller, born in St. Paul, Minnesota. Because of her childhood tuberculosis, her father moved her to Grand Rapids, Michigan. Alix returned to St. Paul after college. She compiled a history of the St. Paul police and fire departments and by 1900 was working as a freelance reporter for several newspapers. Alix later referred to herself as Jim Younger's "widow in spirit." In 1902 she moved to Oklahoma City to keep house for her brother. She began* Lives of Great Men and Women, *but her book was unfinished at the time of her death in April 1904.*

Jim remained preoccupied and morose. He was still working at his job with the tombstone company, but he seemed unable to separate himself from prison life and establish a new home. His frequent letters to parole officer Whittier and to Warden Wolfer complain of being hounded, that his and Cole's every action seemed to attract attention: "It's hard to have people write things about you that are not true and put words in your mouth that you never uttered."

In September 1901 Jim was thrown from his buggy onto a Stillwater street after his horse gave a sudden start while he was climbing down from the seat. The bullet near his spine that he had caught in Hanska Slough had never been removed and continued to cause him periodic back pain. Jim made use of this problem to convince his parole officer that he would be better suited to some other employment. He was allowed to relocate to the nearby city of St. Paul and take a job as a cigar counter clerk

Part of a 1901 letter from Jim Younger to Warden Wolfer. "I have hoped for just a few years of married life, with wife, and children to love, and to make me happy—and to make them happy in return."

Part of Alix Mueller's 1902 letter to Minnesota Governor Van Sant. "(Jim) stands as the noblest man I have ever met. To be so strong to endure, for the sake of others whom he must protect, a life of ignominy and shame, requires a character of almost superhuman strength and power, and I long for the time when the world will appreciate, and honor, this man as I do."

with Andrew Schoch. He became offended, however, when Schoch encouraged potential customers to visit the store to meet the famous Jim Younger. As Dr. Morrill Withrow, the physician at Stillwater who so admired Jim's intellectual abilities, observed, "Jim . . . never could accustom himself to the thought that he was an object of curiosity."

Jim retreated even further from the world as he awaited Alix's return. His depression lifted when Alix came back in November 1901. Soon after, in a letter to his parole officer Jim mentioned that he was "gaining health and flesh and full of good cheer." Jim even mentioned in a letter to Warden Wolfer that he would like to get married.

The addition of Alix to Cole and Jim's relationship created a sad divisiveness. Cole had been so busy with his social life in 1901, and Jim so deep in depression without Alix, that the brothers gradually had gone their separate ways. Cole found he missed his family during the holiday season and attempted to restore the relationship, but Jim rebuffed his advances in favor of spending time with Alix. Cole's resentment of Alix and her influence over his younger brother grew to the point that he later indicated to Lizzie Daniel that he wished the two had never become involved.

In January 1902, Alix Mueller appealed directly to Governor Van Sant with a request that she and Jim Younger be allowed to marry. The governor never sent a reply.

THE DEATH OF JIM YOUNGER

Alix Mueller's family had been disturbed to learn of her relationship with the notorious Jim Younger. The subsequent publicity was embarrassing and made them more uneasy. They pleaded with Alix to return to Boise. Reluctantly, Alix finally agreed.

Jim took to his bed for several weeks after she left. In an effort to lift his spirits he requested a change in employment from his parole officer. At another cigar store, this one in Minneapolis, he went to work for James Elwin.

The new job and new city were not enough to restore his spirits. Jim turned more inward and remained in his room reading every night. As Cole wrote later, "Instead of putting in his free afternoons among men or enjoying the sunshine and air which had so long been out of his reach, he would go to his room and revel in scholastic literature, which only overloaded a mind already surcharged with troubles."

In July 1902 Jim lost his job when Elwin sold his store. Jim tried briefly to sell office supplies as an independent contractor, but he remained short of money and without good prospects for other employment. He wrote parole officer Whittier in September to say he had taken a job with the Samuel Johnston Insurance Company and was now waiting to be granted a sales license. That license was subsequently denied on the grounds that, as an ex-convict, James Younger was not empowered to sign a legal contract.

Wal Bronaugh visited Minnesota in September and Jim visited him at Bronaugh's hotel. Jim told his old friend, "I reckon a fellow might as well cut his throat and be done with it." The reality of Jim's future overwhelmed him when a position with another insurance agency fell through within a few months. Insurance agent John Whitaker, who met Jim when Jim applied for work for Samuel Johnson, liked him and wanted to help him find employment if he could. Whitaker later reported that when he spoke with Jim on October 17, Jim told him, "The fact is that I believe there is nothing left of me but the soul I started with. I should like to win at something, but all the rest, Quantrill and the old game of fight and war, are just as remote as if they had been another man's experiences. If they would let me be Jim Younger, I'd start under the handicap and beat it before I quit. . . . Walkin' around here people might suppose I'm alive, and if it was on the square I could write insurance with the best of them, but I'm as dead as Caesar."

The following night Jim sent a telegram to Alix Mueller in Boise. It read simply, "Don't write." From the telegraph office Jim returned to his rented room at the Reardon Hotel where he spent the night alone. Around eight o'clock the following morning, on October 19, 1902, he put a bullet through his head. In a long last letter to Alix Jim wrote, "Forgive me, for this is my only chance."

Jim Younger's body was returned home to Missouri a few days after his death. There he was given a proper funeral. Although she did not attend Jim's funeral, Alix was included in the prayers Presbyterian minister S. F. Shiffler offered when he said, "We evoke thy tender mercies upon her who gave this one comfort by imparting unto him the affections of a human tender heart." Pallbearers George Wiggenton, J. S. Whitsett, Frank and William Gregg, O. H. Lewis, and Dr. M. C. Miller laid Jim's body to rest in Lee's Summit Cemetery beside his mother and his brother Bob.

(Top) *The Reardon Hotel, next to the Merchants Hotel in St. Paul.* (Bottom) *Jim Younger's death certificate.*

STAY OUT OF MINNESOTA: COLE'S PARDON

Around 1901 Cole Younger had begun to be overcome by poor health. His body had aged remarkably well for a man with so many pieces of lead in him, but traveling salesman work for a tombstone company was tiring. He had given up that job by January 1902. As he later wrote, "The change from the regularity of prison hours to the irregular hours, meals and various changes to which the drummer is subject was too much for me." With his background of prison-hospital work, he was able to secure a job as a clerk in the office of the Interstate Institute of St. Paul, a hospital for those with liquor and morphine addictions.

Cole worked at that hospital only briefly, however, before accepting a job offered by St. Paul Police Chief John J. O'Connor. Cole served as personal assistant to O'Connor, taking on whatever household or delivery jobs the police chief needed done. His daily tasks for the most part were inconsequential gofer work, and Cole enjoyed spending time at O'Connor's house or down at the police headquarters, where he could chat with a variety of people. Cole felt comfortable as a celebrity and took the attention he received with good humor.

After Jim's death a niece of Cole's, Jeanette Duncan Hull, moved with her husband and family to Minnesota. Cole was asked to move in with her family there, which he was happy to do. Cole later said that the presence of a young family around him only made Cole long increasingly for his former home. Cole's rheumatism flared up and he developed a case of grippe during the months after Jim's death. These led him to submit another request for a pardon, in January 1903. In this appeal he claimed that the severe climate of Minnesota was detrimental to his health and was making it difficult for him to earn a living.

With uncharacteristic speed the parole board awarded Cole Younger a conditional pardon on February 4, 1903. Two stipulations of the parole were specified: Cole Younger was not to place himself on exhibition, and Cole Younger was to leave Minnesota immediately, never to enter the state again. Cole had won many friends in Minnesota but was only too happy to comply. He made immediate plans to return to Missouri.

On February 16, Cole arrived by train at Kansas City, where he was met at the Union Station by his niece Nora Hall and her brother Harry Younger Hall. The little group boarded another train and arrived at the Missouri Pacific Depot in Lee's Summit later that afternoon. Meeting him at the station was an

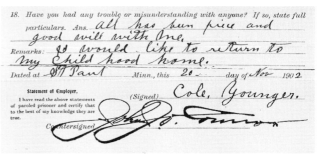

(Top) *Cole Younger with two of his Hull nieces, in Minnesota.* (Middle) *St. Paul Police Chief John J. O'Connor.* (Bottom) *Part of Cole Younger's November 1902 Parole Report. "I would like to return to my child hood home."*

Cole Younger, ca. 1903.

enormous cheering crowd. Cole Younger, fifty-nine years old, was home at last.

For a few months, Cole visited friends and family and refamiliarized himself with the area he had not seen for twenty-six years. Cole often held court informally at the insurance office of his new friend Todd George. Cole accompanied George on George's business rounds, during which Cole came across old acquaintances and made new friends. He was briefly associated with a business venture to install an electric trolley line between Lee's Summit and Kansas City, but soon discovered that his proposed business partners were interested only in the use of his name.

TOGETHER AGAIN: COLE YOUNGER AND FRANK JAMES

Cole got in touch with Frank James only after an appropriate period of time. Cole had never admitted that Frank James had been involved in the Northfield robbery, and he admitted nothing now. There were no uncomfortable questions about how they knew each other, though, since the two had served in the war together. Cole was fifty-nine, Frank sixty when the two resumed a friendship that had begun four decades before.

Soon after their reunion they discussed how they might take advantage of their continuing notoriety for financial gain. Wild west shows were extremely popular at the turn of the century, and it was not long before Cole and Frank were approached to participate in such a venture. The one drawback was that Cole's pardon forbade him from appearing in public shows. Cole thought he might get around that provision by only lending his name to a production but not participating in any of the acts.

Some of Cole's former associates in the North were deeply annoyed when news reached the Minnesota papers in 1903 that Cole Younger and Frank James were involving themselves in plans for a public spectacle. R. C. Dunn, the state auditor, had remained friendly with Cole and wrote to him saying that he hoped Cole would not violate the conditions of his pardon since that would alienate many of his Minnesota supporters. Cole wrote back, assuring Dunn that he would not do so: "It is distinctly stipulated in my contract that I shall do nothing to break the conditions of my parole, and the people with whom I have connected myself would be the last ones in the world to ask me to break any agreement which I have made. I shall not in any way be paraded or exhibited in public and shall have nothing to do with the giving of entertainment."

While Cole waited for plans to be finalized with a company formed by Val Huffman and H. E. Allot, he decided to publish an autobiography that he had written while living with the Hulls in Minnesota. The book had been put together with the help of a ghostwriter and had little connection with the reality of Cole Younger's history. In the pages of *Cole Younger by Himself*, Cole recounted his glory days, emphasizing his brave war experiences, but saying little about his postwar activities other than to provide detailed explanations of how it was impossible for him to have been present at the various robberies of which he had been accused over the years. The Northfield robbery, he claimed, was his one and only indiscretion. Not many copies of the book were printed, and the book did not become a sought-after item until the 1950s.

Flyer for the Nashville appearance of "The Great Cole Younger and Frank James Historical Wild West Show."

Finally, plans were in place for "The Great Cole Younger and Frank James Historical Wild West Show." Frank would step forward as master of ceremonies. Cole's title was that of manager, and he was to work behind the scenes. Of course, it was only to be expected that the manager would appear often at the gate to check on various matters, so the public did get to see the notorious Cole Younger as well. Advertised in the show, which went on the road in the spring of 1903, were "Russian Cassocks, American Cowboys, Rough Riders, Indians, Mexicans and broncos."

The first stop was Chicago in the spring of 1903. The show was fairly well received, but as the troupe moved on to other Midwest cities, Cole and Frank found the venture was not all they had hoped. It was typical of such a show to employ a cast and crew who were not always the most upstanding or sober citizens. On May 24, in Memphis, two of the "Rough Riders," Eugene Scully and Charles Burrows, got into a brawl that ended when Scully pulled a gun and nicked Burrows in the leg. Scully was arrested on charges of carrying a loaded pistol and assault with intent to kill. A few days later in Nashville, ten of the show's employees were arrested for involvement in an illegal gambling operation.

Cole and Frank both explained their joining the production as a means to earn money for their retirement. Their paychecks were not always prompt, however, and several times they were not paid at all. Rather than hailing their arrival, local papers often accused the two of selling out by allowing their names and persons to be used in a shoddy enterprise. Warden Wolfer in Minnesota was outraged to receive a letter asking whether he knew the whereabouts of Cole Younger and Frank James; the letter

was from a company that was owed money by the production. Wolfer, who had worked hard to ensure the release of the Youngers, was offended that Cole would behave in a manner that clearly violated the terms of his parole.

The show was barely holding together, but it eventually arrived in Cole's family area of St. Clair County. There Cole, Frank, and a third man got into a scuffle in Osceola that resulted in the arrest of the third brawler. It was later admitted that the fight had been a hoax, staged only to draw people to that evening's performance. This irritated the local police and did not win the production much good will.

The business situation become steadily worse. On September 21, Frank and Cole demanded that their names be withdrawn from the show's advertising. They had not been paid in some time. When that move did not produce a paycheck, the two withdrew from the production altogether. The owners threatened to bring suit, but Frank and Cole threatened similar action in return. Nothing came from either threat, and the production continued with Frank and Cole resuming their roles for another couple of months.

By the time the wild west show returned to Illinois in November, the two old outlaws had made up their minds to quit. During a dispute between Cole and one of the owners

(Top) *Cole Younger with his sister Laura Kelley.* (Bottom) *Frank James.*

about some funds left in Cole's custody, Cole, who was still a man unwilling to be threatened or intimated, drew a gun on the man and informed him that Cole Younger and Frank James would no longer be a part of the production.

It had not been uncommon for Cole and Frank to grant interviews during their tour of the country with the wild west show. Cole would go on at length about the prestigious background of his family and his deeds during the war, but Frank did not contribute much. He would not discuss Jesse or anything having to do with life outside the law. To the astonishment of those who knew him well, Frank even claimed during one interview, "I have no bitterness against anyone who wore the blue. . . . I am willing to forgive and forget. My son wore the blue in the Spanish-American War, and when he put it on it looked beautiful and brave. I hated it no longer. For years I wanted to feel for my pistol when I saw it, but I love everybody." Cole too at this time claimed to feel affection for his former enemies. It may be that the two old robbers had put the war behind them at last, but there were those who wondered whether the old outlaws were offering magnanimous

Robert Franklin James, born February 6, 1878, the only child of Frank and Annie James. Robert married twice, first to May Sullivan, later to Mae Sanboth. He had no children.

words in order to bring Union sympathizers to the shows or perhaps to disassociate themselves from their previous deeds and present themselves now as differing little from people in the mainstream of American life.

COLE REFORMS

By 1904 both men returned to their families in Missouri. Cole looked into other business ventures, while Frank oversaw the various work needed to maintain the James-Samuel homestead. Cole briefly became president of the Hydro-Carbon Oil Burner Company, but nothing ever came from his association with that company. By August 1905 he was involved with another electric railroad venture being put together by the newly created Kansas City, Lee's Summit and Eastern Railroad. Cole was named president of the construction company for this venture but again dropped out of the organization after a short while. He went back to show business by the end of the year, this time making nightly appearances as a "guest" with the Lew Nichols Carnival Company.

This second venture into public entertainment infuriated the already irate Warden Wolfer, who wrote in a letter to Cole, "You have not only violated the spirit of your pardon but you have, by your conduct, outraged every principal of manhood."

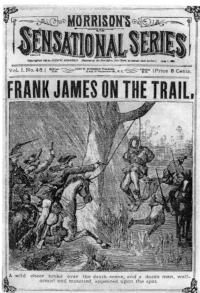

(Top) *Flyer from Cole Younger's 1910 lecture tour, "What My Life Has Taught Me."* (Bottom) *Cover of a typical dime novel, ca. 1882.*

The letter was even released to the press. Nevertheless, Cole continued with the Nichols show for several months of each year until 1908.

Frank James preferred a quieter life. In 1907 he and Annie bought a small ranch in Fletcher, Oklahoma. The ranch afforded him serenity after having to deal with the many sightseers who still made daily pilgrimages to the James-Samuel farm. He and Annie remained on the ranch for four years.

Cole, meanwhile, decided to take to the road with a lecture he had written many years before. In 1909, at age sixty-five, he began delivering "What My Life Has Taught Me" to audiences throughout the Midwest, South, and Southwest. Cole's manager for the tour was L. A. Von Erickson. Cole's grandniece's husband, Rolland Marquette, served as Cole's assistant. It was Cole's expressed intent that his talk "might have impressed a valuable lesson on those who took it to heart." In addition to describing the unpleasant, strenuous aspects of his life on the run and his consequent imprisonment, Cole admonished the crowds for supporting the market for dime novels so popular at the time. Many of those novels were based on imaginary exploits of the James-Younger Gang, and Cole denounced them as sensational and misleading. The outlaw life, he told his listeners, might be depicted in those novels as "easy and heroic to the impressionistic young fellow." As his speech pointed out, however, "No mention is made of the hunted, hounded existence, when every man's hand is turned against you; the nights filled with dread and the days of suffering. No mention is made of the end of it all, a violent death or a prison cell." The talk, based so openly on firsthand observations, was well received. It even overwhelmed some of those who heard it.

With the money he earned on the lecture circuit Cole was able to purchase a house on Market Street in Lee's Summit. There he lived with his maiden niece Nora Hall, who looked after her uncle's household needs. On his front porch the affable Cole Younger spent long talkative afternoons telling war stories to adoring youngsters and chatting with his friends.

One of his visitors in 1913 was a young evangelist by the name of Charlie Stewart. Cole found Reverend Stewart congenial, and they had a number of talks. Cole later told the press that he shared some personal thoughts with Reverend Stewart. Cole revealed, "As a young man I had three goals in my life: to become a Mason, to marry a good woman and to become a Christian." Cole confided his desire now to fulfill the one goal still available to him. On August 21 of that year, during a revival meeting that convened, ironically, on the fiftieth anniversary of the bloody massacre at Lawrence, Kansas, Cole Younger walked up the aisle and acknowledged himself a sinner seeking Christian redemption. He was baptized the following week in the Christian Church of Lee's Summit and for the rest of his life regularly attended services there.

(Top) *Cole Younger in Texas during his lecture tour.* (Bottom) *Cole Younger's niece, Nora Lee Hall.*

At the time of Cole Younger's conversion, though, there was some speculation as to his actual motives for such a public and controversial act. Several national newspapers carried editorials questioning Cole's sincerity. The old outlaw was not phased and continued to contend that his desire to renounce in public his checkered past had been inspired by only the best intentions.

THE DEATH OF FRANK JAMES

By the beginning of 1910 Frank's mother, the eighty-six year-old Zerelda James Samuel, had grown restless. Perry Samuel, her longtime helper, had married and was no longer living with her. It was increasingly difficult for Zerelda's family to find anyone who would care for the old woman in the manner to which she had become accustomed. Zerelda lived in two successive hotels in Kearney during the winter months, then moved in with a couple who had invited her into their home. That did not prove entirely comfortable, either, and the redoubtable old woman moved on to Kansas City, where she lived for some months with her grandson Jesse E., then thirty-five, and his wife Stella.

Frank James with half-brother John Samuel.

With all the restlessness of her two famous sons, Zerelda visited Oklahoma in the winter of 1910. Zerelda had been given a lifetime pass on the railroads, evidently as some sort of apology for the cooperation of railroad officials in the Pinkerton's attack on her home. She stayed with Frank and Annie on their ranch until February. Then Zerelda decided to return home to Clay County. Annie James insisted on accompanying her spunky but frail mother-in-law. During the trip home on the train, Zerelda became overheated and fell ill. On February 10, 1911, Zerelda Cole James Samuel, certainly one of the most colorful women of her time, suffered a heart attack and died. She was taken home to Kearney to be buried in the Mount Olivet Cemetery beside Dr. Reuben Samuel, who had died on March 1, 1908, at the State Insane Asylum in St. Joseph. Also at Zerelda's side were her little son Archie, her daughter-in-law Zee, and her beloved son Jesse.

Following Zerelda's death Frank James decided to leave his ranch and return to the family homestead in Missouri. Amidst the fields and cottonwood trees of his youth, Frank lived out the remainder of his days. His nephew Jesse often visited Frank at the farm and asked questions about the famous father he had barely known. When asked about this or that particular robbery or event, however, Frank still avoided the issue, speaking only in the third person about "the Frank James I knew."

Fairly often in those days Frank would leave the farm to visit Cole in Lee's Summit. On Cole's porch the two old men would have quiet, private conversations about the old days, but did not share the details of those intimate talks with other visitors.

As for Cole's conversion, Frank made no public comment. Back on the farm, which was now identified by a sign proclaiming the "Home of the James', Jesse and Frank James," Frank escorted visitors on periodic tours. Admission was fifty cents. As always, though, Frank had little to say to his wide-eyed visitors. He lived quietly until February 18, 1915, when at the age of seventy-two he died suddenly of heart failure. Cole Younger said nothing when he was told of the death of his closest and oldest friend. He sat alone in his room in Lee's Summit for the rest of the day.

A private funeral was held for Frank, with a eulogy delivered by one of Frank's attorneys, former congressman Judge John Phillips. Phillips offered his opinion of the deceased: "In important respects, Frank James was a man of admirable qualities. Without the adventitious aid of academic education, or very inspiring associations, his wonderful mentality, keen acumen, and thirst for knowledge, enabled him to absorb such information about men, books and nature as demonstrated that had opportunity and dame fortune seconded his gifts, he would have achieved a brilliant career and honorable fame."

Frank's body was taken to St. Louis. Annie saw to it that the body was cremated in accordance with her husband's wishes. His ashes were then stored in a bank

(Top) *Frank James at the James farm.* (Bottom) *Jesse Edwards James at the grave of his father.*

One of the last photographs of Frank James.

vault at the Kearney Trust Company for twenty-nine years. In one of the final ironies of Frank James's history, his remains were protected by bank officials, the kind of men whom he had counted among his worst enemies. In 1944 his ashes were interred beside Annie's buried ashes at Hill Cemetery in Independence. True to form, Frank's simple headstone designates the burial plot of "Alexander F. James."

The quiet Annie James never talked about her life as Frank James's wife during his outlaw career, even to her son. She never allowed herself to be interviewed or photographed for public view. After Frank's death, their son Robert moved back to the Kearney farm with his wife, May Sullivan. Annie lived with the childless couple until her death there on July 6, 1944. Robert's wife died and he married again, to Mae Sanboth. He remained a gentleman farmer on the James-Samuel farm until his death on November 18, 1959.

THE LAST: COLE YOUNGER

Cole had been in ill health for several years by the time the new year of 1916 arrived. He suffered from uremia and other illnesses and was seen regularly by his attending physician Dr. Thomas Ragsdale. Throughout the winter of 1915–16 he remained confined to his room. Two of his frequent visitors were Jesse E. and Cole's closest new friend, Jackson County Marshal Harry Hoffman. Hoffman and Jesse E. had lived next to each other as boys during the time when Jesse E. was with his parents and sister in Kansas City. Hoffman liked to remind Jesse jokingly that when Hoffman first knew him he had been known as "Tim Howard." Hoffman had been introduced to Cole Younger shortly after Cole's return to Jackson County. Through Jesse, Hoffman met Frank James.

It was on March 19, 1916, that Cole asked his niece Nora to bring Jesse and Harry Hoffman to his bedside. On their arrival Cole told the two that he was soon going to die and there were some things he wanted to tell them. Cole wanted his confession to

Last known photograph of Cole Younger.

The Market Street house in Lee's Summit where Cole lived with his niece Nora Hall. Cole died in his bedroom, marked by an X on the right upper floor.

A ca. 1918 gathering of Quantrill veterans at Independence, including guests Harry Hoffman (l, bottom row) and Jesse Edwards James (r, bottom row).

Harvey "Harry" Hoffman, born December 31, 1873, near Smithfield, Illinois. His family moved to Kansas City in the early 1880s. It was not until after Jesse's death that Hoffman and his family realized that their neighbors had not been the "Howards" after all. Hoffman worked many years for the Central Union Telephone Company before serving as deputy marshal for Jackson County. Hoffman was soon appointed chief deputy. In 1917 he served as marshal of Jackson County.

remain a secret, however, and he swore the two men to secrecy. His private talk with them went on for several hours. Cole spoke in detail about his outlaw days and eventually about the disastrous events at Northfield.

For the first and only time Cole Younger revealed the identity of the rider of the dun horse and confirmed that the rider of the dun horse was the one who shot cashier Joseph Heywood. Listening to Cole, it was clear to Jesse E. that the killer of Heywood had been in fact his uncle, Frank James.

After Cole's death Jesse kept this revelation to himself, eventually confirming the fact only to his family. The James family today accepts that Frank killed Heywood, though some claim the shooting was in self-defense. Hoffman concealed for a long time what Cole had told him, but later he was able to circumvent his oath by not denying that it had been Frank James who purchased the dun horse for use in the Minnesota robbery. Hoffman also composed a valuable account of Cole Younger's life as related to him by the outlaw.

At his home on Market Street, seventy-two-year-old Cole Younger, the same age Frank James had been at his death, breathed his last. It was March 21, 1916.

The funeral was attended by hundreds of people from the area and beyond. Cole's pastor, Reverend J. T. Webb, officiated. The church was so full that the doors were kept open in order to allow those who could not find places to sit or stand inside to hear the service as they stood on the lawn of the church. In his eulogy Pastor Webb spoke of Cole's efforts to lead a "consistent Christian life" after his confession of faith.

Cole's pallbearers included some of the most prominent men in the community: Marshal Harry Hoffman, Dr. T. J. Ragsdale, banker Lee Garvin, druggist Charles N. Spencer, and shop owner O. C. Browning. A sixth man was present but his identity has been muddled over the years; while the newspapers reported his name as George Crisp of Kansas City, Cole's family believes it was Harris Shawhan of Lone Jack.

After the funeral, the last member of the James-Younger Gang was laid to rest beside his brothers and mother at Lee's Summit Cemetery.

SOURCES AND BIBLIOGRAPHY

The contents of this book were researched over a period of sixteen years. Several hundred sources were examined and used. The majority of the data presented was cross-checked several times. The fact finding involved in this story was difficult due to several factors. The personal accounts of the various people involved often differed. Just as family members many times see the same event in a different way, those present at a historical incident often relate information employing their personal perspectives. The newspapers of the 1800s wrote their narratives of the events seeking to entertain rather than to inform through the use of hard facts. Names are often misspelled and previous folklore is reiterated. The tales of the James-Younger Gang have become more complex with every decade as the incidents have been complicated and people have sought to have their family members included in the adventure or discovered that they indeed were. The legend has grown and developed a life of its own, independent of fact and reason.

The accounts of those who actually participated were used extensively, although it is freely acknowledged that these versions often benefited the objective of the person relating them. These voices served as a starting point by which the story presented could be checked against other accounts and existing documentation. Access to many of the letters and personal accounts by the Gang members themselves was certainly a benefit to the study. These stories were checked against other information as well. Each specific robbery was researched and examined as best as time and available information would allow.

The files of the State Historical Society of Missouri, the Minnesota Historical Society, the James Farm, the papers and files of Dr. William A. Settle, Jr., the personal scrapbooks and records of the James and Younger families, and the letters of Jim Younger were tremendously helpful in the preparation of this study.

Most of the people who were interviewed provided additional information and/or clues either to specific incidents or to the picture as a whole. More than one hundred people were interviewed and/or exchanged letters with me over a period of several years. I'd like to take this opportunity to thank and acknowledge their contributions. They include the following descendants of members of the James-Younger Gang, descendants of those involved with the Gang, and James and Younger historians: Betty Barr, Thelma Barr, Lawrence Barr, Patrick Brophy, Gary Chilcote, Naohm

Hoffman Coop, Mary Withrow Davidson, Nancy Ehrlich, Ruth Coder Fitzgerald, Carolyn Hall, Donald R. Hale, John Mills, C. E. Miller, John Nicholson, Ethelrose James Owens, Chuck Parsons, Milton F. Perry, James R. Ross, William Settle, Jr., N. David Smith, Lee Smith, June Spicer, Nancy Samuelson, Phillip Steele, George Warfel, Ruth Whipple, Florence Wiley, Jack Wymore, Ted P. Yeatman, Dreat Younger, and Wilbur A. Zink.

All sources marked by + are contained in the files of the Joint Collection, University of Missouri Western Historical Manuscript Collection—Columbia & State Historical Society of Missouri Manuscripts. Sources marked by * are contained in the files of the Minnesota Historical Society.

The following is an abbreviated list of the sources used:

BOOKS

Appler, Augustus C., *The Life, Character and Daring Exploits of the Younger Brothers*. St. Louis, Eureka Publishing, 1876.

Beamis, Joan M. and William E. Pullen, *Background of a Bandit: The Ancestry of Jesse James*. 1970

Brant, Marley, *The Families of Charles Lee and Henry Washington Younger: A Genealogical Sketch*. Burbank, California, The Friends of the Youngers, 1991.

Brant, Marley, *The Outlaw Youngers: A Confederate Brotherhood*. Lanham, Maryland, Madison Books, 1992.

Breihan, Carl W., *Quantrill and His Civil War Guerrillas*. Denver, Sage Books, 1959.

Bronaugh, W. C., *The Youngers Fight for Freedom*. Columbia, E. E. Stephens, 1906.

Brownlee, Richard, *Gray Ghosts of the Confederacy*. Baton Rouge, Louisiana State University Press, 1958.

Buel, J. W., *The Border Outlaws*. St. Louis, Dan. Linahan Publisher, 1881.

Cantrell, Dallas, *Youngers' Fatal Blunder*. San Antonio, Texas, The Naylor Company, 1973.

Castel, Albert, *William Clarke Quantrill: His Life and Times*. Reprint, Marietta, Ohio, The General's Books, 1992.

Connelly, William E., *Quantrill and the Border Wars*. Cedar Rapids, Torch Press, 1910.

Crittenden, Henry Houston, *The Crittenden Memoirs*. New York, G. P. Putnam's Sons, 1936.

Cummins, Jim, *Jim Cummins, The Guerrilla*. Denver, Colorado, The Reed Publishing Company, 1903.

Eakin, Joanne C. and Donald R. Hale, *Branded As Rebels*. 1993.

Edwards, John Newman, *Noted Guerrillas*. St. Louis, Bryan, Brand and Co., 1877.

George, Todd M., *Twelve Years with Cole Younger*. Kansas City, n/d.

Hale, Donald, *We Rode with Quantrill*. 1975.

Helbron, W.C., *Convict Life at the Minnesota State Prison*. 1909.

History of Cass and Bates Counties. Harrisonville, Missouri, 1883.

History of Jackson County. Independence, Missouri, 1888.

History of Independence. Independence, Missouri.

History of Lee's Summit. Lee's Summit, Missouri.

Huntington, George, *Robber and Hero*. Northfield, Minnesota, Christian Way, 1895.

James, Jesse Edwards, *Jesse James, My Father*. Cleveland, The Arthur Westbrook Company, 1906.

James, Stella Frances, *In the Shadow of Jesse James*. Thousand Oaks, California, Revolver Press, 1989.

Love, Robertus, *The Rise and Fall of Jesse James*. New York, G.P. Putnam's Sons, 1926.

McCorkle, John, with O.S. Barton, *Three Years With Quantrill*. Reprint, Norman, University of Oklahoma Press, 1992.

McNeill, Cora, *Mizzoura*. Minneapolis, Mizzoura Publishing, 1898.

Miller, George, *The Trial of Frank James for Murder*. Columbia, Missouri, W. W. Stephens, 1898.

Morris, Richard B., *Encyclopedia of American History*. New York, Harper & Row, 1982.

O'Flaherty, Daniel, *General JO Shelby: Undefeated Rebel*. Chapel Hill Publishing, 1954.

Pinkerton, William A., *"Train Robberies, Train Robbers and The 'Holdup' Men."* Pinkerton's address to the annual convention of the International Association Chiefs of Police, Jamestown, VA, 1907. Reprinted by Arno Press, Inc., 1974.

Ross, James R., *I, Jesse James*. Thousand Oaks, California, Dragon Publishing, 1988.

Settle, William A. Jr., *Cole Younger Writes to Lizzie Daniel*. Liberty, Missouri, James-Younger Gang, 1994.

Settle, William A. Jr., *Jesse James Was His Name*. Lincoln, University of Nebraska Press, 1977.

Steele, Phillip W., *Jesse and Frank James: The Family History*. Gretna, Louisiana, Pelican Publishing, 1987.

Steele, Phillip W. with George Warfel, *The Many Faces of Jesse James*. Gretna, Louisiana, Pelican Publishing, 1995.

Triplett, Frank, *The Life, Times and Treacherous Death of Jesse James*. St. Louis, J. H. Chambers & Co., 1882.

Wybrow, Robert J., *Ravenous Monsters of Society: The Early Exploits of the James Gang*. London, The Brand Book, The English Westerners' Society, Vol. 27, No. 2, Summer 1990.

Wybrow, Robert J., *From the Pen of A Noble Robber: The Letters of Jesse Woodson James, 1847-1882*. The English Westerners' Society, Vol. 24, No.2, Summer 1987.

Yeatman, Ted P., *Jesse James and Bill Ryan at Nashville*. Nashville, Depot Press, 1981.

Younger, T. C. and D. McCarthy, *The Story of Cole Younger by Himself*. Chicago, The Henneberry Company, 1903.

Zink, Wilbur A., *The Roscoe Gun Battle*. Appleton City, Missouri, Democrat Publishing Co. Inc., 1982.

ARTICLES

"The Borderland," *Colliers*, September 26, 1914.

Bowman, Don R., "Quantrill, James, Younger, et al.: Leadership in a Guerrilla Movement. Missouri 1861–865," *Military Affairs*, Vol. XLI, No. 1, February 1977.

English Westerners Society, "The James Gang in West Virginia," date unknown.

Mankato *Spotlight*, "Edward Noonan Interviewed," date unknown.

Mink, Charles R. "General Order No. 11: The Forced Evacuation of Civilians During the Civil War," *Military Affairs*, December 1970.

Southern Minnesotan, "The Gettysburg of the James-Younger Gang," date unknown.

Yeatman, Ted. P., "Jesse James in Tennessee." *True West*, July 1985, pp. 10-15.

Yeatman, Ted P., "Allan Pinkerton and the Raid on 'Castle James'." *True West*, October 1992, pp. 16-27.

Yeatman, Ted P., "Jesse James' Surrender." *Old West*, Fall 1994, pp. 14-19.

Zink, Wilbur, "From Bandit King to Christian," 1971.

NEWSPAPERS

Dozens of newspaper articles were read and examined for cross-checking purposes.

Cincinnati *Enquirer*, April 17, 1889.

"Cole Younger Calls Lurid Tales Vicious," June 15, 1909, newspaper unknown.

Columbia *Daily Herald*, June 9, 1903.

Daily Missouri Democrat, September 1, 1863.

Faribault *Democrat*, September 14, 1876, September 22, 1876, October 6, 1876.

Huntington *Advertiser*, September 21, 1875.

Independence *News*, 1868.

Kansas City *Star*, "Account of Eliza Harris Deal," November 19, 1911.

Kansas City *Times*, "Interview with Cora McNeill Deming," 1897, "Doctor Recalls Younger Brothers as Men Above Outlaw Class," October 24, 1958.

Lee's Summit *Ledger*, March 25, 1874.

Lexington *Union*, September 5, 1863.

Liberty *Tribune*, December 1879, February 27, 1880.

Louisville *Daily Journal*, March 21, 1868.

Memphis *Commercial Appeal*, May 26, 1903.

Missouri Democrat, Cass County, Missouri, August 1863.

Omaha *Daily Bee*, August 2, 1887.

St. Louis *Republican*, February 2, 1874.

Wheeling *Intelligencer*, September 17, 1875.

White Cloud Kansas *Chief*, September 3, 1863.

PUBLIC RECORDS

Adjutant General's Report, State of Kansas, Seventh Regiment.

Affidavit of Frank J. Wilcox, G. E. Hobbs, and J. S. Allen, September 1876.

Campaigns and Battles of the Civil War, Government Printing Office.

Clelland Miller Trial Transcript, Iowa, 1871.

Cole Younger Parole Reports, August 1901 to January 1903.

Coroner's Inquest: "Heywood and Others," September 1876.

Indictment against T. C., James and Robert Younger for the Northfield Robbery and Murders, 1876.

Indictment for Otterville, Missouri robbery, 1876.

Jim Younger Parole Reports, August 1901 to September 1902.

Missouri Confederate Veterans Record.

Missouri State Assembly, Record, 185.

National Archives Military Record of John Jarrette, Cole Younger, Frank James, Jesse James, and Irvin Walley.

St. Clair County Coroner's Inquest into the deaths of John Younger and Edwin Daniels, Testimony of Theodrick Snuffer, W. J. Allen and G. W. McDonald.

"The War of the Rebellion: A Compilation of the Official Records of the Union and Confederate Armies," 1888.

Warrant for the arrest of Frank and Jesse James in regard to the Glendale robbery, 1879.

Warrant for the arrest of Frank James, 1882.

CORRESPONDENCE

Thelma Barr to author, 1981–1995.

Patrick Brophy to author, July 9, 1983.

W. C. Bronaugh to Frank James, June 13, 1884.

B. J. George to Bob James, undated.+

B. J. George to Homer Croy, miscellaneous.+

Harry Hoffman to B. J. George, June 3, June 25, 1958.+

Frank James to W. C. Bronaugh, February 19, 1903.

Frank James to John Trotwood Moore, June 21, 1903.

Jesse James to Governor McClurg, June, 1870.

Jesse James to Governor McClurg, July, 1870.

Jesse James to (Editor?), date unknown.

Jesse James to Gentleman, July 5, 1875.

Jesse James to Kansas City *Times*, date unknown.

Jesse James to St. Louis *Dispatch*, December 20, 1873.

Jesse James to Editor of the Nashville *Banner*, date unknown.

Jesse James to the Nashville *Banner*, August 4, 1875.

Jesse James to Jim, June 10, year unknown.

Jesse James to My Dear Friend, date unknown.

Jesse James to the Nashville *American*, September 21, 1875.

Jesse James to the Kansas City *Times*, August 14, 1876.

Jesse James to Dear Sir (Kansas City *Times*), August 18, 1876.

Stella James to B.J. George, February 11, 1959.

Alix J. Mueller to Governor Van Sant, January 8, 1902.*

Milton F. Perry to author, 1979–1991.

Donna Rose to author, May 25, 1993.

James R. Ross to author, 1989–1995.

William A. Settle, Jr. to author, 1982–1988.

Jack Wymore to author, 1983–1994.

Ted Yeatman to author, May 14, 1987.

Ted Yeatman to author, August 1992.

Ted Yeatman to author, September 1992.

Ted Yeatman to author, October 1995.

Bob Younger to "Aunt," 1877–1888.

Cole Younger to J.W. Buel, October 31, 1880.

Cole Younger to Lizzie Daniel, 1901.

Cole Younger to W. C. Bronaugh, March 19, 1891.*

Cole Younger to Harry Hoffman, April 4, 1907.

Correspondence of Jim Younger, 1899–1901.

Jim Younger to Henry Wolfer, miscellaneous.*

Jim Younger to Lizzie Daniel, 1901.

PERSONAL ACCOUNTS

Statement of Cole Younger to Harry Hoffman, 1914.

Statement of Greenup Bird.

"Cole Younger" Harry Younger Hall, undated.

"The Youngers Last Stand" by Harry Hoffman, undated.+

"What My Life Has Taught Me" by Cole Younger, 1903.

"Interview with Bob Younger" by George Craig, 1889.

"A Jackson County Citizen Writes of the Time of Quantrells and the Jayhawkers," Jacob Teaford Palmer, undated.

Charles Pomeroy, 1877.

George Bradford, 1877.

Hiram George.+

Kitty Traverse, St. Paul, 1878.

L. M. Demaray, 1876.

Perry Samuel to Harry Hoffman, undated.+

Robert Younger, 1885.

Sophia Braden, undated.

T. L. Voight, 1876.

"The Life of Mrs. Frances Fristoe Twyman by Herself," 1901.

The scrapbook of Hardin Hall.

William Henry Ogden Jr.

"Withrow Family" (sent to author by Mary Withrow Davidson).

PICTURE SOURCES

Photographs and illustrations are courtesy of the following:

p.10: George L. Warfel. p.11 (top): Phillip W. Steele. p.11 (bottom): Marley Brant. p.12 (top): State Historical Society of Missouri, Columbia. p.12 (bottom): Younger/Hall Families. p.13: Jackson County Historical Society. p.14: ibid. p.15: Margarette Hutchins/Marley Brant Collection. p.17: Photography by Vern. p.18: State Historical Society of Missouri, Columbia/Younger Family. p.20: State Historical Society of Missouri, Columbia. p.22 (top): The Armand De Gregoris Collection. p.22 (middle): Kansas State Historical Society. p.22 (bottom): Buffalo Bill Historical Center, Cody, Wyoming. p.23: The Armand De Gregoris Collection. p.24 (both): State Historical Society of Missouri, Columbia. p.25: Marley Brant. p.27 (both): State Historical Society of Missouri, Columbia. p.28: Cass County Historical Society. p.29 (top, left): State Historical Society of Missouri, Columbia. p.29 (top, right; bottom, right): Marley Brant. p.29 (bottom): Marley Brant Collection. p.31: Harriet Baird Wickstrom. p.32: Jesse James Farm, Kearney, Missouri. p.33: State Historical Society of Missouri, Columbia/Donald Hale/Forrest Miles. p.34 (both): State Historical Society of Missouri, Columbia. p.35: Watkins Community Museum, Lawrence, Kansas, and Roger Fitch. p.36: State Historical Society of Missouri, Columbia. p.37: Frank H. Graves. p.38: Jesse James Home, St. Joseph, Missouri. p.39: State Historical Society of Missouri, Columbia. p.40 (top): California State Library, Sacramento, California. p.40 (middle): James Chase. p.40 (bottom): Dave

hnson. p.41 (top): State Historical
ciety of Missouri, Columbia. p.41
ottom): State Historical Society of
issouri, Columbia/Donald Hale. p.44
op): Jackson County Historical Society.
44 (bottom): State Historical Society of
issouri, Columbia. p.45 (top): Ethelrose
mes Owens/James R. Ross. p.45
ottom): Photography by Vern. p.46:
ckson County Historical Society. p.47:
illiam A. Settle, Jr./Marley Brant
ollection. p.48: The Armand De
regoris Collection. p.49 (top): Jack
ymore, Liberty Bank Museum, Liberty,
issouri. p.49 (bottom): Marley Brant.
51: ibid. 52: ibid. p.53: JoAnn Byland
d Sandra Reynolds Ogg. p.55: The
mand De Gregoris Collection. p.57:
ate Historical Society of Missouri,
lumbia. p.58: ibid. p.59 (top): Jesse
mes Farm, Kearney, Missouri. p.59
ottom): Ethelrose James Owens/James
Ross. p.60 (top): Ted P. Yeatman. p.60
ottom): Marley Brant. p.61: The
mand De Gregoris Collection. p.62
oth): Donald R. Hale. p.64: State
istorical Society of Missouri, Columbia.
65: Jackson County Historical Society.
66 (top, left; top right: bottom, left):
ate Historical Society of Missouri,
lumbia. p.66 (bottom, right): Ruth
hipple. p.68 (top; bottom, right): The
mand De Gregoris Collection. p.68
ottom, left): Phillip W. Steele. p.69:
helrose James Owens/James R. Ross.
72: State Historical Society of Missouri,
lumbia. p.74 (both): ibid. p.75:
rayson County Historical Society. p.76
op): State Historical Society of Missouri,
lumbia. p.76 (bottom): From *Mizzoura*
Cora McNeill. p.77: Dallas Historical
ciety. p.79 (top): C. E. Miller. p.79
ottom): State Historical Society of
issouri, Columbia. p.80: Wayne County
istorical Society, Corydon, Iowa. p.81:
arolyn Hall. p.82: The Historic New
rleans Collection. p.83: State Historical
ciety of Missouri, Columbia. p.84: ibid.
85: Historical Society of Southern
alifornia. p.86: Donald R. Hale/Betty S.
ouse. p.87: Jackson County Historical
ciety. p.88: Donald R. Hale. p.90: Jesse
mes Museum, Adair, Iowa. p.91 (top):
id. p.91 (bottom): Marley Brant. p.92:
ckson County Historical Society. p.94:
arley Brant. p.95: Minnesota Historical
ciety. p.97: State Historical Society of
issouri, Columbia. p.98 (top): ibid.
98 (bottom): Wilbur A. Zink. p.99
op): State Historical Society of Missouri,
lumbia. p.99 (bottom): Marley Brant.

p.100 (top): Younger Family. p.100
(bottom): Marley Brant. p.101 (top):
Dreat Younger. p.101 (bottom): Gene
Younger. p.102: Wilbur A. Zink. p.103
(top): Fred Egloff. p.103 (bottom):
Marley Brant. p.104: Jesse James Farm,
Kearney, Missouri. p.105: ibid. p.106:
The Armand De Gregoris Collection.
p.107 (top): Dabmira Still MacLean.
p.107 (bottom): Marley Brant. p.108:
Carolyn Hall. p.109: Kansas State
Historical Society. p.111 (top): Jesse
James Farm, Kearney, Missouri. p.111
(bottom): Marley Brant/Jesse James Farm,
Kearney, Missouri. p.112: The Nashville
Banner Publishing Company, copyright,
1994. p.115: Carolyn Hall. p.116:
Northfield Historical Society. p.117:
Marley Brant. p.118: The Armand De
Gregoris Collection. p.119: Phillip W.
Steele. p.121: Minnesota Historical
Society. p.122: Goodhue County
Historical Society. p.123: Goodhue
County Historical Society. p.124 (both):
The Collection of the Blue Earth County
Historical Society. p.125 (top): Northfield
Historical Society. p.125 (bottom):
Minnesota Historical Society. p.126:
Northfield Historical Society. p.127: ibid.
p.128 (both): ibid. p.129 (top): ibid.
p.129 (bottom): Marley Brant. p.130:
Northfield Historical Society. p.131 (all):
ibid. p.132: ibid. p.139: Watawon
County Historical Society. p.140:
Watawon County Historical Society.
p.141: Robert G. McCubbin Collection.
p.142 (top, right): Northfield Historical
Society. p.142 (bottom, right; left): Robert
G. McCubbin Collection. p.143:
Watawon County Historical Society.
p.145: Western History Collections,
University of Oklahoma. p.147: ibid.
p.148: State Historical Society of Missouri,
Columbia. p.149: Rice County
Courthouse. p.150: Washington County
Historical Society. p.157: Donald R. Hale.
p.160: State Historical Society of Missouri,
Columbia. p.164: The Armand De
Gregoris Collection. p.165: State
Historical Society of Missouri, Columbia.
p.166: ibid. p.167: The Armand De
Gregoris Collection. p.168: Jesse James
Home, St. Joseph, Missouri. p.169: State
Historical Society of Missouri, Columbia.
p.170: Jesse James Farm, Kearney,
Missouri. p.171 (both): The Armand De
Gregoris Collection. p.172: Missouri State
Archives. p.176: State Historical Society
of Missouri, Columbia. p.178: Marjorie
Settle. p.182: Minnesota Historical
Society. p.183 (both): From *The Youngers*

Fight for Freedom by W. C. Bronaugh.
p.184 (both): Minnesota Historical
Society. p.185 (both): ibid. p.187: The
Washington County Historical Society.
p.188: Younger/Duncan/Hall Families.
p.189: The State Historical Society of
Missouri, Columbia. p.190: Wilbur A.
Zink. p.191 (both): Minnesota Historical
Society. p.192: State Historical Society of
Missouri, Columbia. p.194 (all):
Minnesota Historical Society. p.195
(both): Marjorie Settle/Mary Daniel
Whitney. p.196 (left): State Historical
Society of Missouri, Columbia. p.196
(right): Ethelrose James Owens/James R.
Ross. p.197 (top): Younger/Duncan/Hall
Families. p.197 (bottom): Brookings
Public Library. p.198 (top): Younger
brothers case files, Stillwater State Prison
Records, Minnesota State Archives,
Minnesota Historical Society. p.198
(bottom): Governor Van Sant Records,
Minnesota State Archives, Minnesota
Historical Society. p.200 (top): Minnesota
Historical Society. p.200 (bottom): The
City of St. Paul. p.201 (top): Jackson
County Historical Society. p.201
(middle): Minnesota Historical Society.
p.201 (bottom): Younger brothers case
files, Stillwater State Prison Records,
Minnesota State Archives, Minnesota
Historical Society. p.202: Jackson County
Historical Society. p.203: Ted P. Yeatman.
p.204 (top): Jackson County Historical
Society. p.204 (bottom): Collection of
Robert G. McCubbin. p.205: Jesse James
Farm, Kearney, Missouri. p.206 (top):
Carolyn Hall. p.206 (bottom): Ted P.
Yeatman. p.207 (top): Western History
Collections, University of Oklahoma
Library. p.207 (bottom): Jack Hall.
p.208: The Armand De Gregoris
Collection. p.209 (top): Jesse James Farm,
Kearney, Missouri. p.209 (bottom):
Ethelrose James Owens/James R. Ross.
p.210: Collection of Robert G. McCubbin.
p.211 (top, left): Marjorie Settle/Mary
Daniel Whitney. p.211 (top, right):
Jackson County Historical Society. p.211
(bottom, right): Naohm Hoffman Coop.
p.211 (bottom, left): Ethelrose James
Owens/James R. Ross.

INDEX